T0069756

RENEGADE AMISH

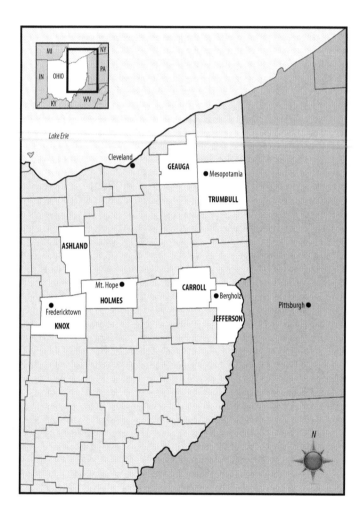

Lake Erie

Cleveland

GEAUGA

Mesopotamia

TRUMBULL

ASHLAND

Mt. Hope

CARROLL

HOLMES

Bergholz

Pittsburgh

Fredericktown

JEFFERSON

KNOX

MI

NY

IN

OHIO

PA

KY

WV

N

RENEGADE AMISH

Beard Cutting, Hate Crimes,
and the Trial of the Bergholz Barbers

DONALD B. KRAYBILL

JOHNS HOPKINS UNIVERSITY PRESS   *Baltimore*

© 2014 Johns Hopkins University Press
All rights reserved. Published 2014
Printed in the United States of America on acid-free paper

Johns Hopkins Paperback edition, 2018
2 4 6 8 9 7 5 3 1

Johns Hopkins University Press
2715 North Charles Street
Baltimore, Maryland 21218-4363
www.press.jhu.edu

*The Library of Congress has cataloged
the hardcover edition of this book as follows:*
Kraybill, Donald B.
Renegade Amish : beard cutting, hate crimes, and the
trial of the Bergholz barbers / Donald B. Kraybill.
pages cm
Includes bibliographical references and index.
ISBN 978-1-4214-1567-3 (hardcover : alk. paper)—
ISBN 978-1-4214-1568-0 (electronic) —
ISBN 1-4214-1567-4 (hardcover : alk. paper) —
ISBN 1-4214-1568-2 (electronic)
1. Hate crimes—Ohio—Case studies.   2. Amish—
Crimes against—Ohio—Case studies.   3. Amish—
Customs and practices.   4. Amish—Doctrines.
5. Beards—Religious aspects.   6. Hair—Religious
aspects.   7. Offenses against religion—Ohio—Case
studies.   I. Title.
HV6773.53.O3K73 2014
364.15'55—dc23   2014013198

A catalog record for this book is available from the British
Library.

ISBN-13: 978-1-4214-2512-2
ISBN-10: 1-4214-2512-2

Frontispiece is by Linda Eberly.

*Special discounts are available for bulk purchases of this
book. For more information, please contact Special Sales
at 410-516-6936 or specialsales@press.jhu.edu.*

Johns Hopkins University Press uses environmentally
friendly book materials, including recycled text paper that
is composed of at least 30 percent post-consumer waste,
whenever possible.

For the women who had the courage to say no,
the children who were trapped in a tragedy,
and all those who suffered in any way

Contents

PREFACE IX   CHRONOLOGY XV

1: The Attacks   3

2: The Clan   23

3: The Bishop   43

4: The Cult?   63

5: The FBI   83

6: The Trial   101

7: The Sentencing   123

8: The Aftermath   135

Epilogue   154

APPENDIX I. MULLET FAMILY TREE   163

APPENDIX II. WHO ARE THE AMISH?   166

NOTES   173

BIBLIOGRAPHY   197

INDEX   201

Preface

Amish. Hate. Crimes. These three words suddenly linked arms in the fall of 2011 when a string of beard-cutting attacks startled the Amish community in eastern Ohio. The fact that the perpetrators were Amish generated an avalanche of news stories about Amish-on-Amish violence as the bizarre story played out until the defendants were sentenced in February 2013. Pundits and late-night talk shows alike poked fun at the Amish—these supposed saints who now had streaks of sin on their faces. Even a cartoonist joined in the humor by depicting a distraught Santa Claus with only stubbles on his chin, waiting in vain for children to sit on his lap. Apart from beards, bonnets, and buggies, nonviolence is a cardinal signature of Amish identity. That a band of supposedly pacifist Amish had assaulted their own people shattered all the Amish stereotypes in the popular imagination.

When this cultural brawl finally ended, ten men and six women from a maverick Amish community near Bergholz, Ohio, were behind bars. A federal jury found them guilty of multiple charges involving conspiracy, hate crimes, kidnapping, lying, and obstructing justice. Most shocking of all, the three Bergholz clergymen—Bishop Samuel Mullet and his two ministers—were among those charged and convicted. The jurors found evidence that the assailants had attacked the Amish victims because of their religion.

Apart from etching violence into the annals of Amish history, the case set a new legal precedent—under the 2009 Matthew Shepard and James Byrd, Jr., Hate Crimes Prevention Act—for its first-time conviction of assailants for religion-driven hate crimes. Moreover, it was also the first one within the *same* faith community. In addition, because a hate crime conviction requires evidence of "bodily injury," the jury had to judge whether cutting a beard qualified as disfigurement, which is one type of bodily injury. The verdicts stretched the definition of bodily injury for hate crimes and the nature of acceptable evidence for interstate commerce—one requirement for federal jurisdiction and prosecution of hate crimes. Some legal experts considered the interstate commerce evidence tenuous in the Bergholz case, and others have even raised questions about some aspects of the constitutionality of the Shepard-Byrd Act.

The Bergholz defendants filed an appeal to the United States Court of Appeals for the Sixth Circuit, which will likely announce its decision in late 2014. The national import of the Bergholz verdict was underscored in March 2014 when forty prominent civil rights, human rights, religious, and law enforcement organizations, led by the Anti-Defamation League, urged the appeals court to uphold the constitutionality of the Shepard-Byrd Act and to affirm its application to violence within the same faith. The wide range of organizations included the American Association of People with Disabilities, Hindu American Foundation, Interfaith Alliance Foundation, National Center for Transgender Equality, National Urban League, Women of Reform Judaism, Police Executive Research Forum, and many others.

It is a sad irony that ostensibly peace-loving Amish people became the first to be convicted—under the Shepard-Byrd Act—of religiously motivated violence. The legal issues of the case include not only bedrock constitutional ones but also the future application of the hate crimes statute in the United States. Indeed, several constitutional law scholars and the trial judge Daniel Aaron Polster have speculated that the case might eventually wind its way to the United States Supreme Court.

In 2006, the Amish were in the media spotlight for their quick and astonishing forgiveness after a non-Amish gunman shot ten girls in a one-room Amish school in Nickel Mines,

Pennsylvania. That story, overflowing with Amish acts of goodness, kindness, and compassion, touched the lives of thousands, if not millions, of people around the globe—but not the Bergholz story. This tragedy had few if any signs of goodness—only sadness, revenge, and violence. While the "good Amish" in Nickel Mines readily forgave the shooter and his family, the "bad Amish" of Bergholz showered vengeance on their own people. How forced beard cuttings could ever cohere with Amish values was the perplexing riddle in hundreds of media stories.

The media coverage of the beard attacks was the most prominent Amish-themed reporting since the shooting at Nickel Mines. Journalists tracked the beard-cutting saga over eighteen months (September 2011 to February 2013), riveting it into the pages of Amish history and the public record. The story of the Bergholz barbers appeared in some 150 television programs and in more than seven hundred print and web stories worldwide. The *New York Times*, for example, reported four major stories in 2012—two in September and two in December—in addition to its initial coverage of the attacks.

Although the three-week federal trial in Cleveland unpacked evidence about the assaults and presented witnesses—who did what to whom, when, and where—it did not probe the cultural fabric or social history of the Bergholz clan, nor did it address the questions of why and how some gentle, pacifist folks had turned violent against members of their own tribe.

This book tackles those questions by exploring the sociocultural factors that transformed a small clan of Amish—nurtured in a religious tradition of nonviolence and forgiveness—into a culture of revenge and retaliation. What socioreligious conditions propelled this remarkable conversion within a few short years? What prompted the group to create cultlike practices and an ideology of malice aimed at its own people? This story is significant not only for its legal ramifications but also because it clarifies the factors that led to the moral collapse at Bergholz and the lessons it offers for all of us, Amish and non-Amish alike.

I was contracted by the US Department of Justice to assist the federal prosecutors in understanding Amish culture as they developed the case against the defendants. I also served as an expert witness at the three-week federal trial in September 2012, explaining Amish traditions and religious beliefs. The views and analysis expressed in this book, however, do not in any way reflect the opinions of the US Department of Justice or the prosecutors involved in this case.

My involvement with the prosecution and the trial offered insights into the case and provided valuable resources for my research. In addition, I conducted interviews with thirty Amish people (twenty-two men and eight women), several law enforcement officers, and a few non-Amish people, most of whom were involved with the Bergholz community in some way. I also relied on court testimonies, legal documents, instructions to the jury, notes of a juror, Amish-written documents, police reports, and media reports.

The voices that speak in this book emerged from my interviews, trial and hearing transcripts, and the other written sources noted above. These voices include fifteen members of Bishop Mullet's immediate family—siblings, children, children's spouses, nieces, and grandchildren—some of whom lived in Bergholz at the time of the trial. Eighteen of my sources had lived in Bergholz for an extended period at some point in their lives. I also present the voices of law enforcement officers, non-Amish people who were involved in the case, and Amish people living outside of Bergholz. A multitude of credible eyewitnesses, many of whom testified under oath in court, provided accounts of behavior in Bergholz in their testimonies and interviews.

In telling this story, I use the names of those victims, defendants, and other Amish people whose names have previously appeared in trial and hearing transcripts, media stories, and signed correspondence published in Amish periodicals. However, I do not use the names of the Amish people I interviewed or of Mullet family members who did not testify at the federal trial, given the nature of the crimes and to protect their requested privacy.

Citations for all of the sources appear in the endnotes. That an individual, organization, or group is a source of information for this book does not mean that the publisher or I endorse the information.

I sincerely thank all of those who generously shared their time, ideas, and opinions in the interviews. I benefited immensely from the suggestions of several colleagues and others who read a draft of the manuscript and for the advice of an anonymous peer reviewer. Finally, I could not have hoped for a better and more professional editorial team than the one at Johns Hopkins University Press. They were a delight and pleasure to work with through every step of the project.

Chronology

Bergholz Timeline

1995	The settlement is founded
1997	Sam Mullet is ordained minister
2000	Johnny Mullet is ordained minister
	Levi F. Miller is ordained minister
2001	Sam Mullet is ordained bishop
	Laverne Troyer is ordained deacon
2006	The Purge: nine families (including the Troyers) leave
	Three hundred ministers meet at Ulysses, Pennsylvania (Sept.)
2007	Custody dispute begins over two children
2008	Sam Mullet et al. file $35 million suit against Jefferson County
	Eli Hostetler is ordained deacon (spring)
	Eli Mullet and family leave (fall)
2009	Eli Hostetler and family leave (fall)
2009–10	The community experiences Winter of Lament (remorse and renewal)
2010	Appellate court upholds Aden Troyer's custody of children
2011	Beard-cutting attacks begin on Sept. 6

Legal Timeline

Sept. 6–Nov. 9, 2011	Five beard-cutting attacks
Oct. 5, 2011	First arrests in Holmes County
Nov. 23, 2011	FBI arrests in Bergholz
Nov. 30, 2011	Preliminary examination and detention hearing
Dec. 2011–Mar. 2012	Grand jury investigates
Dec. 20, 2011	Grand jury returns initial indictment
Mar. 28, 2012	Grand jury returns superseding indictment
May 31, 2012	Judge Polster denies defendants' motions to dismiss charges
July 30, 2012	Plea agreements rejected by defendants
Aug. 28–Sept. 20, 2012	Trial and verdicts
Dec. 6, 2012	Judge Polster denies defendants' motion for new trial
Feb. 8, 2013	Sentencing
Feb. 18–25, 2013	Defendants file appeals to United States Court of Appeals for the Sixth Circuit

RENEGADE AMISH

Preacher Johnny Mullet attacking Bishop Raymond Hershberger.

ONE

THE ATTACKS

September 6: "Terror Walked In"

Marty and Barb Miller were preparing to go to bed on Tuesday, September 6, 2011, the day after Labor Day. Marty was under the covers by 10:00 p.m. that night, but Barb decided to linger and read awhile by a small gas lamp in the living room. A soft night-light glowed in the bathroom, but the rest of the house was completely dark.[1]

The Millers' modest Amish home on their tiny farm in Trumbull County in northeastern Ohio is about an hour east of Cleveland and two hours north of Bergholz, a village in Jefferson County. Barb's brother Sam Mullet had established the Bergholz Amish settlement about two miles east of the village in 1995. The Millers, who were both fifty-nine, had lived in Trumbull County all of their lives. Marty worked in a sawmill and Barb, a homemaker, had raised their seven children.

All of the Millers' children were married, except for their youngest son, Billy, who still lived at home. In recent years, their other five sons and their daughter, Nancy, had moved to the Bergholz community where their uncle Sam was the bishop. By the end of 2006, the Millers had grown quite anxious after hearing about some turmoil in Bergholz. Their children rarely wrote or visited anymore. Yearning to be with their children and grandchildren, and worried about conditions in Bergholz, the Millers decided to move there in April 2007. What they found was so appalling that they abruptly left sixteen weeks later, giving

3

only an hour's notice of their plans to avoid being harassed and badgered to stay.

Nevertheless, within that hour, their children told them several times that they would go straight to hell if they left the community, and one son called Barb a whore. With all their possessions stuffed into black garbage bags, the Millers returned to Trumbull County with pain-filled hearts, leaving their offspring behind. After fleeing Bergholz, they had no visits from their children and only a few contacts with them through intermediaries.

■ ■ ■

Three sharp raps on the door shattered the silence as Barb, clad in her nightgown, was reading in the dark house. "It scared me. I jumped up and I looked at the clock. It was 10:30. . . . Before I could collect my thoughts, it happened again. Three hard raps on the door. It was strange." She walked through the dark kitchen, grabbed a flashlight, and pointed it through the window of the door. To the side, she saw a man with an Amish hat tilted over his face. "He was dressed Amish so I opened the door." As he walked in, she realized it was her son Lester. Her other sons soon followed, along with their wives and her daughter, Nancy, accompanied by her husband, Freeman Burkholder. Altogether, twelve adults and two small children entered the house. The Millers' children had finally come home but not for a friendly visit.

Wearing miner-style headlamps, the six men were prepared to work in the darkness. They pulled their frightened father out of bed and held him in a chair. Then they grabbed his beard until his face became distorted. Trying to calm Barb, they said, "We're not going to kill him." She saw "all the boys standing above him, holding him down, screaming into his face and . . . com[ing] up with the shears. . . . Cutting his hair. . . . He was crying and begging." Twice, Alan screamed, "God is not with you." When they were done with Marty, there was "nothing, nothing left of his beard and hair. All he had left was skin and blood pouring from one side of his head and a big razor burn on his neck."

Then the intruders turned on Barb. This time the women took charge. One grabbed her prayer cap, smashed it, and cut it into shreds. Next, they took off her glasses, removed her hairpins, and cut off her waist-long hair. "It was cut up just beneath my ears. There was nothing I could do." At some moment during the ordeal, both of the Millers started repeating, "Forgive them, God," to which one of the attackers responded sarcastically, "Oh, we have another Christian over there." Within about twenty minutes, the barbers were done. They gathered up the hair as a trophy to show the rest of the Bergholz clan, and left the house.

The non-Amish van driver, hired by the group to take them to the Millers' home, napped during the attack and was oblivious to the scuffle in the house. The whole evening had seemed odd to him, however. Although Amish people often employ outsiders to drive them to places they cannot reach by horse and buggy, they rarely request a ride in the late evening. Moreover, the driver thought, it was strange for a dozen people to leave Bergholz after 8:00 p.m. for a two-hour drive north, visit for a brief twenty minutes, and then turn around and endure the two-hour trek back to Bergholz, arriving at 1:00 a.m.

The Millers did not file a formal complaint with the police. "We wanted to show our children Christ's love. . . . It [filing a complaint] never crossed my mind," said Barb. Several days later they agreed to speak with a sheriff's deputy who came to their house. At nearly the same time, one of the attackers sent a message to his father, Marty, via an intermediary: Shut up about the attack or we will castrate you.[2]

In a letter in *Die Botschaft*, an Amish newspaper, nearly two weeks after the attack, Barb sounded merciful despite the excruciating trauma she had endured at the hands of her own children: "Tuesday night I opened the door unsuspectingly and terror walked in. In half an hour their wicked deed was done leaving us with hearts shattered, but our faith in God is stronger than it's ever been. 'Fear not those who harm the body, but cannot kill the soul.' Praise God! Though he slay me, yet will I trust. We forgive all involved and love you all just that much more."[3]

September 24: "Scared and Brokenhearted"

David and Sara Wengerd run a sheep farm near Fredericktown, Ohio, some two hours west of Bergholz.[4] Sara's brother, Levi F. Miller (no relation to Marty and Barb Miller), was one of the preachers in the Bergholz community. Levi and his wife, Mary, had lived in Ashland, Ohio, about forty miles north of Fredericktown, but relocated to Bergholz in 1999, a move that worried Levi's mother, Saloma, who had known of Bishop Sam Mullet long before he founded Bergholz in 1995.[5]

For about five years after Levi and Mary moved to Bergholz, David and Sara visited them annually, attending church services and even hearing Levi preach on one occasion. The Wengerds had last seen Levi and Mary in December 2006 when the Millers' extended family celebrated Christmas in Bergholz, with the explicit stipulation that they not discuss the turbulence that had erupted in the community earlier that year.

The friendly family ties became frayed after 2006. During the next five years, they only communicated with one another three times. On behalf of his wife and her two sisters, who wanted to express the wishes of their deceased mother, David wrote to Levi in 2009 and urged him to consider leaving Bergholz. Levi responded with a terse letter saying, "Sweep in your own house." In other words, mind your own business!

Later that year, family members heard that Levi was missing from Bergholz. Out of concern for Levi's safety, David called Sheriff Fred Abdalla of Jefferson County. After investigating, Abdalla reported that Levi was still in Bergholz but living apart from his family. Once again, in early September 2011, Abdalla reported that Levi was okay and provided a phone number where David could contact him. Levi did not answer, so David left a message giving a time when he would call back. Several days later the two had a pleasant conversation and, to David's surprise, Levi invited David and Sara to come for a visit the following Saturday, September 24. Levi assured David that they would be safe and that no one would spoil their visit.

At about 10:00 a.m. that day, David and Sara arrived at the home of Emanuel Shrock, where Levi and his family were living. During their pleasant visit that morning, they were served coffee. Unbeknownst to David, his was laced with a laxative. Following a cordial lunch, David, Levi, Eli Miller, Emanuel Shrock, and two of Emanuel's sons went for a stroll around the barn and into the nearby pasture—a typical Amish activity during a visit. Meanwhile, Linda Shrock (a daughter of Bishop Mullet) enjoyed friendly chitchat in the house with Sara.

As the six men walked in the pasture about five hundred feet from the barn, Preacher Miller suddenly turned and grabbed his brother-in-law. The other four men took off David's hat and glasses and held him. "I totally froze because I was scared. I mean I was scared. I didn't know what next was gonna happen," David recalled. During the attack, the men, whose demeanor had suddenly bristled, accused David of spreading rumors about Bergholz, of calling the sheriff, and of sexual improprieties. They quickly snipped off his beard, leaving only "little stubbles" on his chin, and cut his hair so short that his head was "bare, not shaved, but bare." One of the attackers snapped before-and-after shots with a disposable camera.

David did not resist or fight back because, in his words, he was "scared and brokenhearted." The loss of beard and hair "drove me batty. . . . I didn't want to see people," David confessed. "I was depressed . . . it's not the Amish way to walk around without hair and beard."

October 4: "Don't Shear Me, Don't Shear Me"

The earliest streaks of dawn had yet to scratch the darkness in Dillonvale, Ohio, when Michael Kanoski fired up his red Dodge 3500 truck at 4:00 a.m.[6] He was headed to Bergholz to pick up some Amish people who wanted to make the two-hour trip to the weekly Mount Hope Auction in Holmes County, which served as a festival as much as a sale for the Amish of eastern Ohio. Little did he know that this fateful trip would eventually take him to the witness stand in the federal courthouse in Cleveland.

Mike's oversized four-door pickup, with its dual rear wheels and hefty diesel engine, could tow a livestock trailer. With the truck and trailer, Mike generated side income from "hauling Amish," as many locals called the taxi service they provided for Amish people traveling long distances from home. Five passengers could sit in the cab, and the twenty-four-foot aluminum trailer was handy for transporting horses, hay, and on occasion an overflow of passengers on white plastic chairs. Although Mike could not speak Pennsylvania Dutch, the Amish dialect, he could easily converse with the Bergholz folks in English.

Bishop Mullet did not join the group that day, which to Mike's surprise and consternation was large: Twenty-seven people clamored to go to the auction. Five of them climbed into the cab and the rest—twenty-two men and women—rode in the livestock trailer, which was covered with a blue tarp for protection from the wind. The five riders in the cab included the two preachers at Bergholz: Levi F. Miller and Sam Mullet's son Johnny, who provided Mike with directions and instructions for the trip.

The party chattered away in Dutch until they arrived in Mount Hope at about 7:00 a.m. Shortly after 9:00 p.m.—some fourteen hours later—they left the auction and headed home. Johnny asked Mike to stop at an Amish farm about five miles down the road. The place was pitch black with no streetlights and no interior or exterior lights around the two houses on the property. Unfamiliar with the area, Mike passed the site, then turned around, came back, and parked his truck and trailer alongside the small country road in front of the houses. The five men climbed out of the cab and dissolved into the darkness as they headed toward the larger house. Returning about twenty minutes later, Johnny announced, "Let's go." Because the men were speaking among themselves in Dutch, Mike had no idea why they had stopped—and there were no barking dogs, no lights, no people, no noise, just an eerie silence. Back in the trailer, however, one young man heard screaming.[7]

■ ■ ■

A gentle man with a humble demeanor, seventy-six-year-old Raymond Hershberger was a retired farmer and longtime bishop in a cluster of Amish congregations in Holmes County known as the Andy Weaver churches.[8] He and his wife, Sara, lived five miles from the auction site in a small *Dawdyhaus* (grandfather house) ten feet from the large farmhouse where their preacher son, Andy Hershberger, and his family lived. Raymond and Sara's fifty-four-year-old bachelor son, Levi, lived with them. Like many Amish, who do not have electric lighting in their homes, Raymond and Sara had retired to their first-floor bedroom at about 8:30 that evening.[9]

Their son Andy was asleep in the farmhouse, but several of his daughters were awake and reading in their upstairs bedrooms. At about 9:30 p.m., the girls heard a knock on the door and ran downstairs to alert their father. Andy grabbed some clothes and a small light and opened the front door. There he saw five plain-dressed, straw-hatted Amish men, none of whom he recognized in the darkness. The leader (Johnny Mullet) simply said, "We want to talk with you and your dad. Is he here?"[10] Andy led the men over to the Dawdyhaus, where they waited in the small kitchen while Andy called his father out of bed. As Raymond staggered out to the kitchen and sat down in his rocking chair, Andy lit a gaslight. For the first time, he was able to see the strangers better, although he still did not recognize them.

Suddenly, Johnny Mullet tensed up and exploded into action with a high-pitched voice: "We're from Bergholz. We're here because of what you did with our shunned people." Looking at Bishop Hershberger, he asked, "Wasn't your name on that committee" that met in Ulysses, Pennsylvania, five years ago? "Oh, yes," replied Raymond. Immediately, the other four men jumped to their feet.[11] Three of them held Raymond in his rocking chair and began cutting his beard and his hair with a shears and clippers. He tried to cover his hair and begged, "Don't shear me, don't shear me."[12]

Meanwhile, Andy yelled for his brother Levi to come down from his upstairs bedroom. One of the intruders, holding Andy in an armlock, asked, "Are you a preacher?" As Andy recalled, "When I said yes, he really went for me. . . . I pushed him back with my foot. He came at me again. . . . He grabbed me by my beard . . . he was very angry."[13] The battery-powered clippers stopped working so he "just chopped at my hair and beard." By that time, Levi, who had come down the steps and was opening the stair door into the kitchen, was tackled by one of the barbers and thrown onto a couch, bruising his ribs and causing pain that persisted for three weeks.[14] Andy's seventy-nine-year-old mother, Sara, came out of the bedroom, grabbed for the shears, and then ran to the other house. Andy's wife and three daughters burst into the kitchen, the thirteen-year-old screaming, "You may not shear him!"[15]

According to Andy, "The act was very short. Suddenly it was over. Johnny said, 'Let's go.' And everybody released. Teamwork." The barbers left abruptly, with Bishop Hershberger still shaking, hair scattered everywhere, and "everyone crying."[16]

Levi wanted to report the attack to the police. His father grudgingly said, "I guess so." They did not have a phone on their property, so Levi ran up the road about a quarter of a mile to a public phone and called 911. The first law enforcement officer arrived about fifteen minutes later and saw "a bunch of hair on the floor. . . . People sitting all around . . . and they all were crying. His [Raymond's] hair had chunks cut out, he was bleeding . . . both on the left and right side. He had . . . cuts or scrapes whatever down both sides of the top of his head."[17] Andy explained, "I'm bald. My dad is not. He had a full head of nice gray hair, pretty nice and thick for his age." After the shearing, "some spots on his head were bare . . . it was all chopped."[18] More important, his white mid-chest-length beard was also gone, with only an inch, at best, remaining.

October 4: "It's Probably Bergholz"

Leaving the farm Mike Kanoski drove the truck back home toward Bergholz. About an hour later, as they entered Carroll County, Johnny asked to make another stop. They arrived at the second site at 10:45 p.m. It was a newer, more modern Amish house with a small shop-barn along an isolated gravel country road. Again, the same five men walked to the house in darkness and returned in about fifteen minutes. And, again, none of the passengers left the trailer. As Mike turned on the headlights and started to leave, a barefoot Amish man ran in front of his truck and glanced at the license plate.[19]

■ ■ ■

In 2001, Myron Miller (no relation to Marty, Barb, or Levi F. Miller) was ordained a bishop at the young age of thirty-six. The parents of eight children, Myron and his wife, Arlene, live in Carroll County, Ohio, about twelve miles northwest of Bergholz. In addition to his church duties, Myron is a self-employed carpenter. For several years, Myron and Arlene assisted Bill Mullet, the youngest son of Sam Mullet, when Bill had some difficulties with his marriage and his father. Bishop Mullet, who enforced strict church rules in Bergholz, was concerned that Bill would be led astray through his association with Bishop Miller's more progressive church. Moreover, Bishop Mullet viewed the Millers as meddling with his family. The situation created friction between the two bishops.

On the evening of October 4, the Millers went to bed at about 9:30. At approximately 10:45, their daughter, who was not asleep, roused her parents to report that someone had knocked at the back door that led out to the patio. Arlene whispered, "It's probably Bergholz." Like many other Amish people, the Millers had learned about the September beard cuttings through newspaper accounts and conversations with relatives in other areas. Some people had even warned them that they might be victims; yet, Myron did not think that Sam's enforcers would ever do something like that to him. Nevertheless, the Millers had decided that they would press charges if they were ever attacked.

Myron could not find a flashlight, so he went to the back door without one as Arlene trailed close behind. He opened the door a few inches and peered out. A voice in the darkness said, "Hey, Myron, we want to talk with you." Uncertain who the visitors were, he opened the door a few more inches. In a flash, Johnny Mullet grabbed Myron's beard as other arms wrenched him down and pulled him through the door and down two steps to the patio. Myron was able to grab Johnny's beard and yanked hard enough that Johnny yelled out in pain.

Four or five men held Myron down. "I saw a flash of the scissors right here by my head and I knew right away what they were going to do and I was powerless to stop them," Myron recalled. He struggled to get free, but in a minute, his beard was sliced off. Johnny repeated his "let's go" mantra, and the barbers ran to the front of the house where Mike Kanoski's truck and trailer were waiting along the gravel road. Barefoot and in his nightclothes, Myron followed them. Perplexed about the large livestock trailer in the shadows, he ran to the front of the truck to read the license plate and immediately sprinted back to the house and called the sheriff. His beard was severely shorn, leaving only an inch and a half on his chin. "It was humiliating. . . . I just pulled together and kept going, tried not to let it get me down."

■ ■ ■

The entourage arrived back at Bergholz about midnight. Mike dropped the group at Bishop Mullet's house and waited until they were ready to go home. About an hour later, their meeting ended. After Mike was paid for his services, he took them to their own homes. Perplexed about the long, exhausting day and the two late-night stops, Mike called his wife to say he would be home soon, adding, "Something happened today, but I don't know what." He arrived home about 2:00 a.m. to find two sheriff's cars in his driveway. The officers took him and the truck and trailer to the Jefferson County police station, where they interrogated him for several hours, photographed his truck and trailer, and inspected the vehicles for hair—human hair. Mike's twenty-eight-hour day finally ended at 7:30 a.m. when he drove his truck back to his farm. It was the last time he would ever haul any Amish.

November 9: "A Whole Bushel Bag of Hair"

For many years Melvin and Anna Shrock, both age fifty, lived in the Amish settlement near Fredericktown, Ohio.[20] In 2000, they moved to the Bergholz settlement along with several of their adult children because it seemed like a pleasant new Amish community. Things were harmonious for several years but eventually turned sour because, in Melvin's eyes, Bishop Mullet was teaching strange doctrines, saying God was talking to him, and excommunicating anyone who disagreed with him. In 2006, Bishop Mullet excommunicated the Shrocks in what Anna described as arbitrary, unbiblical, and not following normal Amish practice because the bishop did not consult with them in advance or provide a reason for his action.

After their excommunication, the Shrocks, along with two of their married children and their families, left Bergholz. Their son Emanuel, married to Linda Mullet (Bishop Mullet's daughter), stayed in the Bergholz community. Following their departure, Melvin and Anna wrote to Emanuel on several occasions, raising concerns about Bergholz and urging him to leave. He never responded and refused to speak with his dad even when they saw each other occasionally at the Mount Hope Auction.

To Melvin and Anna's surprise, Emanuel sent them a letter on October 17, 2011, which included these lines: "I'm beginning to wonder if perhaps you were right after all and we are some kind of cult? . . . The youngest ones [grandchildren] don't even remember you and keep asking about you. . . . I'm willing to listen to reason if you come, but don't ask me to come to Ashland or Michigan. . . . I have a hard time trusting anyone outside of Bergholz. Love and prayer, Emanuel."[21]

Melvin and Anna responded, expressing interest in visiting their son and daughter-in-law while also making it clear that they were worried about their safety. They had learned through newspapers and friends about the four recent beard-cutting attacks, including how David Wengerd was lured back to Bergholz and ambushed. Emanuel responded on October 24: "I can understand your fear of coming here. But, I'm still man at my own house and nobody, not even Sam Mullet, has a right in here without my consent. . . . Linda and I were talking, and we decided to invite you here for supper one evening. Just let us know which evening you will come. It suits us most anytime. We're living in *deceiving* times. . . . Hope to see you soon."[22]

Melvin's health was poor and, wishing to see his son and grandchildren while he was still able, he and Anna responded, saying they were interested in visiting although still somewhat anxious about their safety. On November 5, Emanuel reassured them in a letter: "I promise you that nobody outside the Shrock family, us, will be here if we know you're coming and you will be safe. . . . Plan on coming next Wednesday evening for supper and we'll be looking for you."[23]

At about 6:00 p.m. on November 9, Melvin and Anna and their non-Amish driver arrived in the village of Bergholz after a two-hour trip from Ashland. One of their sons who lived in Ashland had called Sheriff Abdalla to alert him that Melvin and Anna were coming to the Bergholz Amish settlement to visit Emanuel. Abdalla met the Shrocks in the village of Bergholz and then preceded them to Emanuel's house. Abdalla explained to Emanuel that his parents had arrived and that he would remain nearby to ensure their safety. Emanuel assured Abdalla that his parents would be fine. Their driver parked outside the house, and Melvin and Anna entered and had a friendly two-hour visit with their son, daughter-in-law, and grandchildren. Meanwhile, the sheriff waited some two hundred yards down the road at a historical marker.

As they were about to leave, Emanuel suddenly opened a drawer, grabbed a scissors, and began cutting his father's beard. Melvin resisted, so his two teenage grandsons quickly restrained him, covering his mouth when he began yelling for help. Meanwhile, Anna bolted toward the front door, but Linda caught her and covered her mouth when she started screaming. As soon as the shearing was done, the grandparents were released. They ran out the door to the baffled driver, who drove them down the road to the even more flabbergasted sheriff. Abdalla was astonished at what had happened despite his warning and surveillance. "I was furious," said Abdalla, "and ready to go back to Emanuel's house and drag him out and . . ." Melvin, who had been so excited about meeting his grandchildren, "was too embarrassed to even look up at me after the cutting when I talked with him in the car," the sheriff continued. Melvin refused to press charges but obligingly told Abdalla that he "will think about it," making the pursuit of an arrest difficult.[24]

The whole Bergholz community, aware of the setup, gathered later that night at Bishop Mullet's house to hear Emanuel Shrock announce, "We got a whole bushel bag of hair." Emanuel had kept only half of his promise: His family members *were* the only people in the house that night, but his mother and father certainly were not safe. Two months later, on January 10, 2012, Melvin Shrock died.

Fear Stalks Amish Country

The bizarre string of events left nine victims—eight men and one woman—in its wake, leading federal prosecutors to eventually charge ten men and six women with multiple crimes. The two attacks in September and the late-night assaults on two bishops in October inflamed fear across Amish country like a fast-moving brush fire spreading 150 miles beyond its center. Amish families who had never locked their doors now locked them. Some installed new locks, and others oiled their rusty ones to make them work. The sheriff's offices in both Jefferson and Holmes Counties received dozens of calls from Amish people asking about their safety and how to protect themselves. What was mace? What was pepper spray? Where could you buy them? Several bishops confessed privately that for the first time in their lives they carried pepper spray in their pockets, and others were certainly thinking about it. One defector from Bergholz, who lived 150 miles away, was so afraid that he never stepped outside his house at night for the entire fall of 2011.[25] According to Abdalla, a few Amish people were doing a very non-Amish thing:

loading shotguns in their homes at night to protect themselves from the Bergholz barbers.[26]

That the assaults left many peace-loving, forgiving Amish obsessed about being attacked by other Amish was a sad irony that escaped no one, not the Amish or the millions of outsiders around the world reading news flashes on their smartphones, computers, and television screens. Amish people across the United States were aghast. How did it ever come to this, they wondered, as the startling news spread across their communities. How was it that a small band of renegades raised in the gentle ways of humility and the peaceful precepts of Jesus, Sunday after Sunday—people of their own flesh and blood, people who had pledged to reject revenge at baptism—suddenly had trashed all of that and turned on their own people?

The bandits were not only ridiculing the Amish religion but also embarrassing and shaming the sixty thousand decent Amish people in Ohio. Even worse, they were not rebellious adolescents on *Rumspringa*, former Amish, or disgruntled rank-and-file members—they were, in fact, ordinary members led by two preachers in collusion with their bishop. The Bergholz community was waging a whisker war on their fellow brethren. Amish people had been the targets of bias and hate crimes before, but not from their own religious kin.[27] In the face of this terrible fact, in home after home, Amish people could only beg for God's help and shake their heads in utter disbelief and despair, saying, "Aye, Yi, Yi, Yi, Yi, Yi, Yi!"

The Bergholz barbers not only filled Amish hearts with fear and smeared the Amish reputation but also posed a difficult moral dilemma for their victims: Should they press charges? Committed to the nonresistant way of Jesus, who taught "resist not evil. . . . Love your enemies. . . . Pray for those who persecute you," Amish people have historically sought to resolve conflict quietly within their local congregations. Their religious persecution in sixteenth-century Europe has honed a sharp separation of church and state, a theological distinction between two kingdoms: the kingdom of Jesus anchored on peace and nonresistance to evil and the political kingdom of this world based on the use of force or, at least the threat of it, to maintain order. Since their origin, Amish leaders have taught their members to respect civil authorities, pay their taxes, pray for government leaders, and cooperate with law enforcement as long as doing so does not violate their religious conscience.[28]

Despite some reluctance, Amish people do report major criminal acts by Amish and outsiders to law enforcement. The first thing the Amish teacher did at Nickel Mines in October 2006 when an armed non-Amish neighbor entered her one-room school and threatened to take twenty-six children hostage was to run to the nearest phone and call 911.[29] Yet even if they are willing on certain occasions to inform and to cooperate with law enforcement, Amish people are reluctant to press charges against their own people or even against outsiders because, in their minds, that step violates Jesus's clear rejection of the use of force. They are also loath to file lawsuits for any reason and reluctant to testify in court or to serve on juries out of obedience to the teaching of Jesus: "Judge not, that ye be not judged." In humility they ask, Who are we to judge others? Let God be the judge.

Why Beards Matter

Diversity abounds in Amish society. There are some forty Amish affiliations with different practices and more than 2,100 congregations, each of which establishes its own regulations.[30] For example, the color of buggy tops varies by affiliation, ranging from yellow to burnt orange to white, black, and gray. Some congregations permit cell phones, indoor plumbing, power lawnmowers, LED lights, and fax machines. Others prohibit all of these amenities. Yet across all these diverse Amish groups, one constant is the beard. All Amish men sport this public symbol of cultural and religious identity. Typically, men begin wearing a beard when they marry. In Bergholz and in a few other settlements, however, young men begin growing a beard when they are baptized, which is usually in their late teens or early twenties. Beard wearing is so firmly entrenched in Amish tradition that it rarely needs to be justified or encouraged.

The roots of Amish teachings on the beard reach back to the origins of the Amish, when the group separated from other Anabaptists in Switzerland and France in 1693. Jakob Ammann, their founder, spoke about the beard in his earliest writings: "If there would be someone who wants to be conformed to the world with shaved beard . . . and does not acknowledge that it is wrong, he should in all fairness be punished. For God takes no pleasure in the proud."[31] Two church rulings—one in France in 1752 and another in Germany in 1779—forbade trimming and cutting the beard. That religious taboo continued in the nineteenth century in church regulations in Pennsylvania in 1809 and in Ohio in 1865.[32] These were not merely friendly admonitions; the church disciplined men who violated the norms, and if they were unrepentant, they faced excommunication and shunning.

In 1983, an Amish bishop wrote a short essay titled "The War of the Whiskers" for an Amish family magazine. In it, he notes that, in the world, "beards come and go as fashions and styles ebb and flow. . . . As Amish people, we have always worn beards. We have not worn them because fashion dictated it—we have felt that our reasons for wearing beards went deeper and were less fickle than that. . . . We feel that Bible principles and common sense support a consistent wearing of a beard." He then offers two reasons for wearing one. First is the principle of sex distinction: It is wrong to blur the clear line between men and women. Facial hair, he argues, is a universal mark of masculinity. "The second major Bible principle supporting the wearing of a beard," according to the bishop, "is that the creature should be subject to the Creator. God created mankind so that women have smooth faces. Men are created so that the beard grows over much of his face. Did God make a mistake in making this distinction and difference?"[33]

An Amish publication that offers answers to questions about the Amish way of life advocates beard wearing for three reasons: (1) it was a common practice in the Old Testament, (2) Jesus wore one, and (3) God created men this way to differentiate between men and women. The manual also notes that Leviticus 19:27 and 21:5 prohibit the marring of the beard and "to have one's beard cut was humiliation (II Sam. 10:4, 5), a form of punishment (Isa. 7:20), or a mark of sorrow and distress, the same as wearing sackcloth (Isa. 15:2; Jer. 48:37)."[34] Chapter 4 explores the meaning of these biblical texts regarding humiliation and sorrow in more depth.

The Amish church draws on the teachings of the Apostle Paul in I Corinthians 11:3–15 as a basis for women having uncut hair and wearing a prayer covering, typically referred to as a *Kapp*. The covering is a symbol of reverence and submission, as described in verses 3–10. Long hair, usually worn in a bun in daily life, is a symbol of the woman's glory—her beauty and dignity—and it is shameful if she is shorn or shaven (I Cor. 6–7).

Barb Miller, the only woman whose hair was cut in the attacks, said, "I wear my cap to show submissiveness, to keep the glory of my hair covered so we are not prideful. And when we pray to God we believe that we need our hair, our heads covered. . . . We're told not to cut our hair, that's what Scripture tells us." Having her waist-length hair cut short was a profound shaming, one that she would recall every morning for several years as her hair slowly grew back.[35]

Without exception, all of the victims of the Bergholz barbers were humiliated and disgraced. "Beard cutting," said a well-respected Ohio bishop, "is degrading, it's just shaming!" A young Amish man explained, "It's like someone holding you down and tattooing you on the face and you couldn't hide it in public. It shames a bishop, because he has to sit in the front of his church where everybody sees him."[36]

Bishop Hershberger, forcibly shaved on October 4, could not muster up the courage to face his congregation and preach again for six months. He was so embarrassed by his unseemly looks that he did not attend the wedding of his grandson two days after the shearing. And when his grandchildren first saw him after the attack, they all cried.[37]

Man after man, the male victims all confessed that they shied away from public appearances for weeks, if not months. Beard cutting was a clever way of doing short-term damage that struck at the heart of Amish identity and caused several months of public embarrassment.

Faintly reminiscent of the enmity between the Hatfields and McCoys (1863–1891) in West Virginia, the Bergholz unrest pointed to family feuds. Although violent aberrations of Amish ways, the attacks appeared to some observers as petty family spats between adult children and their parents (and between in-laws in David Wengerd's case)—just an odd Amish dispute. If the assaults were simply a grown-up version of Amish pranks, were they worthy of the attention and resources of an outside system of justice?

Regardless, these attacks, unprecedented in Amish history, were even more egregious because they were directed and at times executed by clergy, who supposedly embodied the religious virtues of Amish life.[38] Such off-the-charts behavior provokes a series of questions: What motives spurred these despicable acts? Why did a gentle, peace-loving, forgiving people turn violent? What sorts of beliefs provided the logic—the rationale—to justify this behavior? And what sociocultural factors had nurtured these unusual beliefs and behaviors at Bergholz?

The Bergholz Amish school.

TWO

THE CLAN

Stopping the Drift

Samuel E. Mullet was born in 1945 and grew up in the Middle-field Amish settlement forty miles east of Cleveland. He lived near Mesopotamia, a small hamlet in Trumbull County that locals simply call Mespo. His father, Eli, an ordained preacher, became a bishop in 1961 when Sam was sixteen years old. Three years later Sam was baptized into his local *Gmay*, a Pennsylvania Dutch shortcut for *Gemeinde* (church community). Each Gmay, or congregation, consists of twenty to thirty families who live near one another in a church district with geographical boundaries. In that baptismal ceremony, Sam confessed his faith in Jesus Christ and promised on his knees to God and all the witnesses that he would remain faithful to the teachings of the church for the rest of his life.[1]

As was typical in the Middlefield Amish community in the early 1950s, Sam completed four grades in a public elementary school and four in an Amish private school before ending his formal schooling after the eighth grade. As a conscientious objector during the Vietnam War, he served a two-year stint in a government-approved program of alternative service in a state hospital. Some Amish young men received farm deferments, but Sam was ineligible because his family was involved in lumbering. He performed his alternative service as an orderly with mentally ill patients and was responsible, in his words, "to shave

them, give them haircuts, see to it that they took their baths . . .
just general care, maintenance and orderly work."[2]

Sam was the third of a dozen children born to Eli and Nancy
Mullet. When he turned twenty, a typical age for marriage in
conservative Amish groups, he married eighteen-year-old Martha D. Miller, who had sixteen siblings. Martha and Sam had six
children within the next seven years. Their family culminated in
nine boys and nine girls, an unusually large number for an Amish
family, which typically averages six to ten children, depending
on the particular group.[3] Two of their children died at an early
age—Henry died of pneumonia at age eight, and Emma died of
cancer at age twenty-five.[4]

At about six feet, Sam was a tall man with a commanding
presence. "He was friendly, easygoing, and could be very con-
vincing and persuasive," said a man who knew him well. "He was
smart and knew how to make things happen."[5]

For the first twelve years of marriage, Sam and Martha lived
in Trumbull County on the eastern edge of the Middlefield
Amish settlement, just east of the Geauga County line. Shortly
after their marriage, the Middlefield community had split over a
controversy about how to treat ex-members—a religious ritual
the Amish call shunning. Amish affiliations differ widely in how
they practice this ritual and how offenders can be restored to
membership. Sam and Martha's congregation, where his dad was
bishop, aligned with the most traditional faction, which adhered
to a strict type of shunning.

Sam had a conservative bent and disliked the modernizing
changes creeping into the churches around him, so in 1977, the
Mullets moved about sixty miles west to a new four-year-old
Amish settlement in Fredericktown, Ohio—which was even
stricter than the settlement they left behind. Martha explained
their reason for leaving Middlefield: "When we moved out we
wanted to step back in *Ordnung* and the use of material things. It
[change] was just going too far [in Middlefield] and so we moved
to Fredericktown."[6] By stepping back to a more conservative
Ordnung (church regulations), the Mullets were seeking a more
traditional lifestyle.

A strong-minded, opinionated, and conservative man who wanted to hold tightly to the old customs, Sam had several run-ins with church leaders in Fredericktown over the years.[7] Although he was nominated for ordination, he was never selected for a leadership spot. One of Sam's children explained, "He has problems getting along with anybody over a period of time if they're not family. Through the years, he has never been able to get along with anybody hardly."[8] Another family member described it this way: "Sam didn't like the bishop there, and he wouldn't accept church votes [decisions]. He didn't want to hear the voice of the church. He was vocal, aggressive, and intimidated people. . . . It was either his way or no way."[9]

The Mullets lived in the Fredericktown settlement (an affiliation of a dozen like-minded congregations) for eighteen years. Looking back on that time, Martha wrote, "In those eighteen years it had drifted so far [toward the outside world] it was scary to go along anymore. The drift is still going and is a *lot worse* since we moved to Bergholz."[10] Sam and Martha were not alone in worrying about Amish people slipping into modern society. Elmo Stoll, a prominent Amish bishop, writing in *Family Life*, described it this way: "Drift is like a snowball rolling downhill—it gains speed and size as it goes. And one reason that it is so hard to stop is that as drift and worldliness make inroads into our churches . . . [they] rob us of the power and authority of God's word.[11]

Unhappy with the trends in Fredericktown, Sam decided to pursue his dream of building a new settlement of his own. In 1995, he acquired land in the mountainous area of the Yellow Creek Valley in Jefferson County a few miles east of Bergholz, a village of six hundred residents near western Pennsylvania. Martha explained, "We bought 800 acres of land when we moved to Bergholz. . . . Most of it was stripped for coal and we have five nice pits [water-filled surface mines] with a lot of good fishing and a lot of woods for hunting."[12] As new families arrived, some bought land from Sam, and others purchased it from non-Amish people nearby. Bergholz was not a compound or reservation on a single parcel of land; it was a number of properties, some adjoining one another and others with non-Amish properties in between.

Far from the large, modernizing Ohio Amish communities in Holmes and Geauga Counties, the site offered seclusion for a new community that wanted to cling to old Amish ways and stop the drift into modern life. "When we moved to Bergholz," noted Martha, "we wanted to step back in time a little and live more like our grandparents, because the *drift* in the Amish church is so plain to see, we just couldn't stay there [Fredericktown] anymore. So we stepped back in times, no bathrooms, no pressure water, no modern or power tools for carpentry work, only allowing dark-colored dresses etc., *no* box shaped or fancy caps [for the women] which is way out of hand in most settlements and is out of control."[13]

Building a New Community

Sam's long experience in lumbering and carpentry served him well in leading the process of carving out homesteads in this wilderness area. Almost five years after their arrival, Martha noted that nine families with a total of twenty-five children had moved in, and four others were expected in the spring of 2000. For her part, she was "busy with the family and busy helping the marrieds, etc." Several of Sam and Martha's children were living in Bergholz at that time, but by the fall of 2011, when the attacks occurred, eleven of their sixteen surviving children were living there.[14]

As the settlement took root, the Bergholz clan constructed and began operating its own school staffed with teachers from its community. After sending their children to one-room public schools for many years, Amish communities across the country started building their own small private schools in the 1960s and '70s. This movement accelerated after 1972 when the US Supreme Court, in *Wisconsin v. Yoder*, granted Amish parents the right to terminate the formal schooling of their children at age fourteen.

Some people predicted that Sam's venture at Bergholz would fail. No one would follow him, folks said, and at first very few did except for his own children. With a smile, Sam told one re-porter, "Everybody thought, 'Nobody would move with Sam Mullet because he's too strict.'"[15] But Sam had the grit and the guts to grow the settlement, and he proved the naysayers back in Fredericktown wrong as more families joined the fledgling community, including a handful without any Mullet ties.

The Amish church in North America has no pope or national executive office and hence no guidelines for establishing new settlements. Typically, several families scout for desirable land. Each household purchases its own acreage nearby, but often not adjoining, one another. The new settlers encourage friends and relatives to join them. An embryonic community normally seeks to affiliate with other like-minded congregations whose preach-ers will travel to the new outpost and whose bishops will periodi-cally administer baptism, conduct weddings, supervise biannual communion services, and handle any disciplinary matters.

Since Sam had emigrated from Fredericktown, those preach-ers and bishops were the obvious ones to assist Bergholz until it ordained its own leadership. Fredericktown preachers occasion-ally visited Bergholz, but Sam declined any bishop supervision from his former community. Instead, he turned to Eli Yoder, the bishop of a tiny Gmay in nearby Salinesville, Ohio. Yoder soon moved to Enon Valley, a small unaffiliated Gmay in western Pennsylvania.

The Fredericktown bishops met in February 2001 and de-cided that they no longer could fellowship with Bergholz because Bishop Eli Yoder was a lone ranger leader who had no ties to other Amish groups beyond his own congregation. Sam Mullet, who was a preacher at that time, was invited to attend the meet-ing but declined. A Fredericktown leader explained, "After that meeting the Fredericktown ministers and bishops did not go down to Bergholz anymore."[16] Thus, for a number of years, Bishop Yoder was Bergholz's only link of fellowship and account-ability to other Amish groups.

As a new settlement takes root, it ordains its own ministers (typically, two preachers, a bishop, and a deacon) from within its ranks. These ministers, serving without training or compensation, provide spiritual direction for the members and function as an informal executive committee to guide the Gmay. When selecting their leaders, the Amish follow an old biblical ritual of "drawing lots" from a pool of prospects. Members of the congregation, both men and women, nominate men into the "lot," the pool of nominees. Hymnbooks, equal in number to the number of candidates in the lot, are shuffled before the ordination. A slip of paper inscribed with a Bible verse is placed in one of the books before they are shuffled. During the ceremony, each candidate selects a book, and the supervising bishop opens each one until he finds the hidden slip of paper. The new shepherd of the flock is immediately ordained. The entire service from nomination to ordination takes less than ninety minutes. Bishops and ministers from other Gmays attend the ordination, not only to observe but also to ensure its integrity.[17]

Sam Mullet was ordained the first preacher of Bergholz in May 1997, two years after the settlement began. Sam and two of his sons, Johnny and Danny, were the three nominees in the lot. Sam was the lone ordained official until 2000 when three other leaders were selected within eighteen months to provide a full ministry team. Because only preachers are eligible to become bishops, several preachers needed to be ordained before a bishop could be selected. In April 2000, the congregation nominated two men for preacher: Sam's twenty-six-year-old son Johnny S. Mullet and forty-two-year-old Levi F. Miller (unrelated to Sam), who moved to Bergholz from Ashland, Ohio. The supervising bishop, Eli Yoder, found the slip of paper in Johnny's hymnbook. Six months later, in October, Levi was the only nominee in the lot, and so he became the third preacher. In May 2001, thirty-eight-year-old Laverne Troyer (unrelated to Sam), one of three nominees, was ordained deacon. Troyer and his family had moved to Bergholz from Holmes County.

With a full bench of preachers and a newly minted deacon, the Gmay could proceed to ordain a bishop. In October 2001, all three preachers were nominated for the lot. Eli Yoder, the presiding bishop, found the slip of paper in Sam's hymnbook and proceeded to ordain him bishop of Bergholz.[18]

Some skeptics raised questions about the ordination process. First, given the Amish tradition of humility, campaigning for the office of preacher or bishop is unusual. In the two weeks preceding the bishop ordination, according to one member of Bergholz, "Martha, and some of their children were saying, 'It's got to be Sam. He's the oldest. He must have it.' It was very unusual promotion."[19] In fact, in most Amish communities, such campaigning by family members would virtually eliminate a man from nomination for the lot because to display any interest in holding office is a bold sign of pride unbecoming for a prospective servant of the church, who should fully embody humility.

Unwritten tradition in Amish circles stipulates that at least three bishops observe the ceremony and lay their hands on the head of the newly chosen servant as he kneels for the ordination, which represents the transfer of bishop authority within the Amish church.[20] Frequently, more than three bishops as well as numerous preachers from other congregations attend these emotionally intense ceremonies. In a few rare cases, only two bishops have observed or presided over an ordination. At Sam Mullet's ordination, Eli Yoder was the *sole* bishop in attendance. One Amish historian recalled that the only other time this happened was when a bishop was ordained in Paraguay in the 1960s, and US church leaders agreed to send only one supervising bishop because of the high cost of transportation.[21] The Bergholz breach of the age-old Amish tradition of at least three bishops observing an ordination troubled outside Amish leaders.

With no other bishops present to verify the ordination process, rumors of misconduct were rife across Amish communities. One ex-member opined that a slip of paper may have been placed in *each* book and that Bishop Yoder knowingly opened Sam's first. Another defector who had witnessed the ceremony thought it was credible but was troubled by the absence of other bishops to observe and assist. One outside bishop wondered whether somebody had "monkeyed with the books," but concluded, "We really don't know the truth."[22] The credibility of this sacred ritual, far from a simple lottery to the Amish, rests on their enduring conviction that God reaches down from heaven to call the next shepherd of the flock. This deeply ingrained belief grants enormous legitimacy to the one who is chosen.

Some outsiders saw a troublesome pattern emerging in Bergholz. Typically, in a new settlement, each pioneer family buys its own land. In this case, a strong leader had purchased eight hundred acres and sold land to some families to build their own homes. (Other families had purchased property from non-Amish landowners.) The location was isolated from other Amish settlements both in distance and by the majestic mountains that framed the valley. The founder, who was quickly ordained preacher, was now the bishop. In the opinion of one former member, "Sam rushed to have the first minister ordained when only family members were living there so they could be in control of the new settlement."[23] A lot of power was coalescing onto Sam's lap. Despite these concerns, Bergholz still attracted newcomers staking their future on this venture, which, from all outward appearances, was thriving—at least until the tumult of 2006.

The Purge

Any harmony in Bergholz dissipated quickly during the twelve months following September 2005. According to one ex-member, things started falling apart one late October evening when Eli, one of Sam's married sons, had a psychotic break.[24] An eyewitness described it as "a mental fit." "He was basically blowed out, you know, where he didn't know what he was doing." Various members of the community sat on him and tried to cover him to "keep the devil out of him." His brother Johnny, the preacher, "jumped on him and Eli started screaming and it was fierce!" Again and again throughout the evening, Johnny declared that Eli was the devil, and eventually, Sam pontificated that "Johnny is the Holy Ghost and Eli's the devil." The struggle to purge the devil from Eli continued throughout the night. Johnny and others held him down on a gravel driveway for several hours, hoping that if they held him down until sunrise the devil would flee. "His coat was all torn up. It was ripped down the back and both sleeves on the seam." Somehow during the episode, Eli found a rifle, which he thought was loaded. He aimed it at his father, sitting a few feet away, and pulled the trigger only to hear a click because it had no bullets.

At one point, Eli escaped screaming into the mountains. The next morning, seeing him walking into the driveway, Sam declared, "Here comes the devil." Eli asked if he could hug his wife, but Johnny stopped him, staring him in the face while Eli kept saying that he "didn't want to live anymore." The sad episode continued for several days. After he was "running loose" for almost a week, according to one eyewitness, someone at Bergholz called an emergency squad to take Eli to the hospital, where he received treatment for mental illness. Through this experience, his community gradually learned that medical rather than spiritual issues caused his condition. Although the Amish typically do not believe in demon possession, there are scattered cases when they have viewed mental illness that way.

By the spring of 2006, Deacon Laverne Troyer had become gravely concerned about Bishop Mullet's mode of leadership. Sam's way of doing things did not fit what Laverne had seen in other Amish congregations over the years. Privately, Laverne consulted with several outside leaders, who confirmed his observations and fears. One of those was Bishop Atlee Miller, who lived in Potter County, Pennsylvania, near the small town of Ulysses. Losing confidence in Sam and worried about the future of Bergholz, Laverne decided to move to Ulysses, but Sam said, "No way."[25]

Nevertheless, Laverne bought a farm in Potter County without telling Sam, who was outraged when he learned of it.[26] Laverne then sold his farm in the Bergholz area through a Realtor, who listed it on his website as he did with all properties. Adamantly opposed to using the Internet, Sam excommunicated his deacon. Soon after Laverne and his family moved to Ulysses, Sam hunted him down there, "furiously waving his arms and saying that he had 'scriptural reasons'" for Troyer's expulsion. He told one Ulysses church leader, "People lie, yell, and call me anything except a white person and Amish! You can have Laverne Troyer. I'm tired of all of this."[27]

The sudden expulsion of their deacon, a rare event in Amish circles, baffled many members, and the prospects of a thriving community began to crumble. Some who opposed the excommunication were soon expelled themselves. Others tried to leave quietly but were excommunicated nonetheless. Some who contemplated leaving or had already left were intimidated in various ways (detailed in chapters 3 and 4).[28] In the spring and summer of 2006, at least nine families, more than a third of the Bergholz community, fled into exile, marked with the stigma of excommunication. Vernon Mast, who stayed behind, reported in a letter to the *Budget* that "seven families moved out since April, each to a different community."[29]

For the Bergholz clan, the widespread exodus was a public relations disaster because it sent ripples of concern throughout the Amish communities of eastern Ohio and beyond. It certainly was not a good omen for recruiting new families to the Yellow Creek Valley. The expulsions also created a vexing problem for other Amish congregations: what to do with the families that Sam had excommunicated.[30]

Amish congregations follow an established process of discipline for those who transgress church teachings and practices. Offenders are given the opportunity to confess their faults and, if contrite, are pardoned and restored into the full fellowship of the Gmay. Transgressors who show no remorse and refuse to heed the counsel of ministers will eventually face a slow, patient process of excommunication, which requires a vote of the membership upon recommendation of the bishop.[31]

Amish people describe excommunicated members as being "in the ban," meaning that they are banned from participating in Holy Communion, members' meetings, and some other church functions. They are also shunned. Amish leaders did not invent this practice, which is described in several New Testament passages and used by non-Amish churches.[32] Shunning does not forbid members from talking with ex-members, but it does prohibit them from certain activities such as accepting rides in the cars of former members and eating at the same table with them at wedding or funeral meals. Shunning, in short, involves rites of shaming to remind transgressors that they have broken the baptismal vow they made to God on bended knees when they promised to uphold the precepts of the church for the rest of their lives. As described in Article 17 of the Dordrecht Confession of Faith, shunning should be done with a spirit of love to win the wayward soul back into full Christian fellowship.[33] Offenders are welcome to return to the fold upon confession and a pledge to recommit their lives to the church.

The Amish world divides into two camps on the proper way to "lift the ban" to restore sinners into fellowship. The most traditional communities practice *strict* shunning, which requires that ex-members return to their "home" bishop—the one who excommunicated them—to confess their transgressions in order to rejoin that Gmay. Later, depending on their behavior, they may be able to transfer to a different congregation. The other half of the Amish world practices a milder, more lenient shunning. These churches will lift the ban and stop shunning an ex-member who joins any Amish Gmay that accepts him or her into membership. In brief, lenient congregations do not require offenders to return to their home bishop to confess their sins.

Most of the Bergholz families originated from strict-shunning congregations. Those who were expelled in the spring and summer of 2006 had nowhere to go because other strict-shunning Gmays could not accept them unless they first went back to Bishop Mullet. The ex-members were in Amish limbo. They adamantly declared that, because they had not violated any biblical teachings, their excommunications were arbitrary and capricious. Most of their friends and relatives were members of strict-shunning churches, but they could not join those congregations without first confessing to Bishop Mullet sins that they claimed they had not committed. The only way they could remain in the Amish world was to join a more progressive, lenient-shunning Gmay whose way of life they could not embrace because it was too permissive.

The impasse also posed a predicament for the bishops of strict-shunning congregations who wanted to receive the Bergholz exiles but could not. Many of these leaders doubted the legitimacy of Bishop Mullet's expulsions, and yet they could not sidestep the long-standing rule requiring a confession to the home bishop lest they too commit a transgression. So, what to do? In a series of meetings over the summer of 2006, a group of church leaders found an answer.

Rebuffed by the Elders

In June 2006, a large number of ministers (bishops, preachers, and deacons) from strict-shunning churches met near New Wilmington in western Pennsylvania to discuss a variety of matters. At the end of the meeting, someone asked, "What are we gonna do about Sam Mullet?"[34] After some discussion, the leaders agreed to appoint an investigation committee of five bishops to visit Sam and explore options for reconciliation. One of the bishops on the committee explained that "putting people in the ban is death to the soul. It's very, very serious. There must be a good reason for doing it. It should not be used as a tool. Sam seems to use it to keep people there in Bergholz."[35]

A few weeks later the investigation committee traveled to Bergholz and met with Sam and the preachers, Johnny Mullet and Levi F. Miller. According to one of the visiting bishops, when Sam was asked why the people were excommunicated, he "just talked in circles. Everything was for Sam. He was afraid people would move out. At one point, Johnny got very agitated and jumped up out of his chair."[36]

Next, the committee met with some of the expelled people to hear their side of the story. Committee members thought the ex-members' complaints about excommunication without scriptural or other justification seemed valid. Thus, in August, the five bishops returned to Bergholz with a message for Sam: "We don't think these people should be placed in the ban. Please lift it." Sam retorted, "I cannot do that until these people stop spreading gossip and bad stories." It was, in the words of one committee member, "a very short meeting. It was not very pleasant. We could almost feel the presence of the devil."[37]

Despairing of their ability to resolve the impasse with Sam, the investigation committee informed other church leaders, who agreed to convene a large ministers' meeting on September 13, 2006, at Atlee Miller's farm in Ulysses, Pennsylvania. Calling an all-day meeting of elders to grapple with the practices of one leader, several Amish bishops noted, is extremely rare. Some three hundred bishops, preachers, and deacons from five different states, representing more than sixty strict-shunning congregations, met in the upper floor of the barn on Miller's farm. Sam was invited to the meeting to give his side of the story, but he declined. "The checkers have already been played," he said.[38]

After an opening devotional, seven bishops were appointed to serve on a listening committee and, based on what they heard, to prepare a proposal for action by the end of the meeting.[39] These bishops were deemed impartial because their congregations were not considering accepting ex-members from Bergholz. The five-member investigation committee reported on their visits with Sam, and then the gathered assembly engaged in open discussion.

Over a lengthy lunch recess, the listening committee convened in the house and drafted a statement for the full group to consider. After citing several pertinent scriptures, the statement advised the five-man investigation committee to return to Sam and give him one more opportunity to reinstate the ex-members. If he refused, the statement read, other congregations would be free to admit the Bergholz exiles into full fellowship. The statement, which was signed by all seven bishops on the listening committee, was read to the full assembly, which unanimously approved it. Bishop Raymond Hershberger, the beard-cutting victim from Holmes County, Ohio, was a signatory to the statement. The action that day did not overturn the long-standing tradition that required an ex-member to return to the home bishop to lift the ban and cease the shunning. The decision at Ulysses, however, did make a onetime exception to the rule for anyone Sam Mullet had excommunicated.

With some anxiety, the investigation committee of five bishops headed back to Bergholz to deliver the statement on September 19. Sitting on chairs in Sam's yard, they waited for an hour until Sam and Johnny appeared. One of the bishops recalled that "Sam was not civil. He did not shake hands like he did at the first two meetings." Again, the committee asked him to lift the ban and again he refused, citing "the gossip and false stories circulated by ex-members." One of the visiting bishops noted, "It wasn't a sit-down meeting. We couldn't get out of there fast enough. It was awful."[40]

The collective voice of the church leaders, spoken unanimously by the three hundred ministers on September 13, was a pivotal point in the history of Bergholz. Until then, Sam could hold the threat of excommunication over any members who challenged his authority because he could expel them and they had nowhere to go. Now, he could no longer coerce them into compliance with that threat. He could still excommunicate, but ex-members were sure to find a friendly welcome in another strict-shunning Gmay. The action of three hundred elders in Ulysses had eviscerated Sam's power to excommunicate. The leaders were unable to remove him from his bishopric because of the autonomy of Amish congregations, but what they could and did do was severely shrink his power.[41]

Sam's increasingly volatile behavior and emotional outbursts were a growing and grave concern for certain church leaders and for some of Sam's children living outside of Bergholz.[42] After they spoke with court officials and documented their concerns in writing, the Jefferson County Court ordered Sam to undergo a psychological assessment in the fall of 2006. Court deputies served the order on Sam on a Sunday evening. He stayed at a medical facility overnight and was evaluated and released the next day without any requirements for therapy or medication.

Those who had pressed for the assessment—including an Amish bishop who had footed the $1,600 bill—were dismayed. Although they had explained their concerns in writing, family members were not included in the diagnostic session. "If we had been there to contradict him. . . . They would've seen the reaction he has when we talk to him and disagree with him. It would have changed the whole situation," lamented one of his children.[43] In the words of one of his sons, "Dad was smart enough to outfox them."[44] Martha, rising to Sam's defense, wrote, "Sam is not mental and never was. What is wrong . . . is the disobedience of the people. Sam works and stands by the Word of God."[45]

The Custody Dispute

Bishop Mullet's sanction by the Amish elders and his mandatory psychological assessment were followed by a lengthy custody battle over two of his eighty-plus grandchildren. The two children were born to his daughter Wilma, who, in November 11, 2004, had married Aden Troyer, son of the exiled deacon, Laverne Troyer. The custody dispute ran from September 14, 2007, to June 2010 when an appellate court let stand the Jefferson County Court's decision to grant Aden custody of the children.[46] The prolonged entanglement generated considerable animosity.

The story of Wilma and Aden's relationship is convoluted and complicated. The four-year drama began in the summer of 2006. Only a year and a half after their marriage, Wilma and Aden's relationship was disrupted when his parents moved to Ulysses, Pennsylvania, under the stain of excommunication. By that time, Aden was so troubled by the rancor within Bergholz that he also wanted to move to Ulysses. Bishop Mullet insinuated that Aden had engaged in some immoral behavior and then prohibited him from seeing his wife and child and threatened to expel him unless he signed a statement confessing his sin. Aden wrote a false statement of confession just to make peace with Sam so that he could be reunited with his wife, Wilma, and his young daughter. (He later told the court about this event and passed a lie detector test regarding his account of it.) Nonetheless, Aden, who had already moved close to his parents' home in Ulysses, remained separated from Wilma for several months. During that time, their second daughter was born. Aden and Wilma were reunited in May 2007 for several weeks, and during this period, they went to Indiana for counseling and then to Ulysses.

Meanwhile, Sam Mullet's son Eli and his nephew Eli Miller traveled 245 miles to Ulysses to search for Wilma and bring her back to Bergholz. They broke into Deacon Laverne Troyer's home and assaulted him. Both men were arrested and charged with breaking and entering. At the preliminary hearing for the

two men in Coudersport, Pennsylvania, Wilma testified that
Aden had not mistreated her, that she felt safe with him, and that
she wished to stay with him rather than return to Ohio. However, shortly after the hearing, several of Wilma's family members, who had come to Coudersport in a van, placed the two
young girls in the vehicle and coerced Wilma into returning to
Bergholz with her children, telling her that she would go to
hell if she refused. Aden, fearing reprisals from Bishop Mullet,
decided to stay in Ulysses.

Aden Troyer filed a Complaint for Allocation of Parental
Rights and Responsibilities in the Jefferson County Court of
Common Pleas on September 14, 2007.[47] The court designated
him the residential parent of both children and directed Sheriff
Abdalla to remove the children from Bergholz and place them
in Aden's custody. Furthermore, the court order prohibited four
men—Bishop Mullet, and his sons Johnny, Eli, and Christ—
from having any contact with the children. The sheriff, who had
received three death threats from the Bergholz clan, feared a
violent confrontation, so he formed a SWAT team to accompany him when he served the custody order on Wilma in the
one-room Bergholz school where she taught.

As the SWAT team watched from a public road, Abdalla and
two assistants walked up to the schoolhouse. When the sheriff
stepped onto the porch, he heard a voice say, "You're dead, Fred!
You're dead, Fred!"[48] That taunt prompted the SWAT team
to run to the school as the sheriff served the custody papers.
The SWAT team then proceeded to Sam's house where the
children were staying and placed them in Aden's custody without incident.

In May 2008, the Jefferson County court designated Aden as
the residential parent and legal custodian of the children and gave
Wilma periodic visitation rights at locations outside of Bergholz.
An appellate court later upheld the decision of the county
court.[49]

Bishop Mullet was outraged that the state had intervened,
removed his grandchildren, and forbidden him any contact with
them. He was so incensed that he closed the school for a year

and invested enormous energy and financial resources in a legal fight to bring the children back to Bergholz.

In radical defiance of Amish beliefs, Sam, the teachers, and the parents of the twenty-nine children in the schoolhouse that day filed a $35 million suit against the Jefferson County Sheriff's Office in September 2008 requesting compensation for violation of their rights and punitive damages. The charges included surrounding the schoolhouse with a fully engaged SWAT team armed with automatic weapons, which deprived the plaintiffs of their freedom and liberty and subjected them to "fear, intimidation, ridicule, derision, humiliation, embarrassment and mental, bodily and physical distress."[50] The legal action was time consuming, requiring sixty-six depositions due to the large number of plaintiffs, which included the children. After several motions and countermotions by both sides, the case ended with a financial settlement of about $85,000 for the plaintiffs. About half of that went to pay attorneys' fees, and the remaining amount was allocated to several of the children. According to Sheriff Abdalla, Sam "tore up the check," and the funds were retained in a custodial account held by the county for the children.[51]

Bishop Eli Yoder, who had ordained Sam Mullet and was his sole supporter over the years, had learned about the suit in a news article. Surprised by the unprecedented action of a bishop filing a lawsuit, Yoder ended his affiliation with Bergholz, leaving it without fraternal ties to any other Amish group. Meanwhile, a new deacon was ordained in May 2008 to replace Laverne Troyer, who had been excommunicated two years earlier. Eli Hostetler was a woodworker from Enon Valley who had married Sam and Martha's daughter Emma. They had settled in Bergholz in 1999, and Eli remained in the community after Emma's death in 2003.[52]

■ ■ ■

Two humiliating rebukes—the first by three hundred elders in the highest court of the Amish world and the second by an appellate court of the state of Ohio—fueled some of the animosity that led to the beard attacks. Long-simmering resentment over the loss of the custody battle was verbalized in snide references to "the two girls" during the beard cutting at Marty and Barb Miller's home on September 6, 2011, suggesting that the Bergholz community falsely linked the Millers to the custody dispute.

The vision for a flourishing settlement continued to fade, and the Bergholz flock gradually shrank in size. Writing in the Amish newspaper *Die Botschaft*, Lovina Miller summarized the 2010 year-end statistics for Bergholz. Their numbers had dwindled to 17 families, 9 babies, 38 schoolchildren, 7 fourteen- to sixteen-year-olds, 7 Rumspringa-age youth, and 40 members, for a total of 101 souls.[53] With the exception of Preacher Levi F. Miller's family, everyone was related in some way to Sam and Martha. Unlike other Amish congregations across the country, which are rarely stocked so heavily with relatives, Bergholz had become a clan, and its leader was Bishop Mullet.

Sam Mullet outside his home in Bergholz, Oct. 10, 2011.
(AP Photo/Amy Sancetta)

THREE

THE BISHOP

"Can't You See What's Happening?"

Big changes were afoot in Bergholz as its first decade came to an end. In early August 2006, Rebecca, an Amish woman residing in a different community, wrote a despair-filled letter to her married brother Andy living in Bergholz.[1] "Dear Bro," she began. "Greetings from above where all is Love. I have been trying for so long already, to keep from doing this for the sake of the others down there [in Bergholz] who were trying so hard to make peace. But now that they had to give up and because of all the *terrible* things, my mind, my head, and my heart are so full I can't keep my mind on my work—I just walk around in a daze. And sometimes I think maybe they will have to load me on an ambulance and take me to the hospital for having too much stress."

Rebecca then asked the question that was haunting her: "Andy, oh Andy, can't you see what is happening? I could write a whole page full of *Oh Andy, can't you see what's happening??* Where is the Andy I grew up with? I often stepped in your room . . . before going to bed at night, sharing all the everyday happenings and personal struggles. Where is the love when people actually are afraid to even go to church?"

Some ex-members considered the rough-up of Eli Mullet during his psychotic break in the fall of 2005 the pivotal point, yet others thought the changes creeping into the settlement came to a head with the purge of Deacon Troyer in 2006.[2] Nonetheless, most of the defectors linked the big changes in Bergholz to Bishop Mullet's growing intolerance for dissent. Unlike the shared decision making typical in most Amish congregations, in Bergholz members had to agree with Sam or leave.[3]

A woman who had lived in the community said, "If anyone disagreed with him or did not do as he wanted, [he said] they were living in sin. They had sin somewhere in their lives. Everyone who was sin-free would just automatically be able to agree with Sam." One of his children explained it this way: "Dad said he is for God, and God's with him. . . . If I disagreed with him, he pointed his finger at me and said, 'Then Satan lives in you.' He was trying to tell me that he is all right and has no wrong; that God is with him." Anna Shrock, who had lived in Bergholz for several years, disliked the fact that Sam said God was talking to him. "We don't believe that [God talks directly to people]," she said.[4]

What was happening at Bergholz? In the five years since his ordination as bishop in 2001, Sam Mullet was consolidating his power inch by inch. Outsiders heard only tidbits about some of the "terrible things," but those with direct family connections like Rebecca were keenly aware of changes.[5] One ex-member described the mutations as incremental—one small step, one small incident at a time, as people gradually slipped under Sam's authority.[6] Another defector who lived in Bergholz both before and after the purge saw "big changes in Sam's behavior after 2005. He had more trouble with anger."[7] By August 2006, many of the dissenters, most of whom had found contentment in Bergholz when they first arrived, had been expelled or had left on their own. The loyalists who remained were casting their lot with Bishop Mullet and his way of running the church.

The ordained men who lead a Gmay are viewed as servants of both God and the congregation. Their German title, *Diener*, translates literally as "servant." According to one Ohio elder, "A bishop is a servant, which means 'house grandfather.' It's a term of endearment, not a 'lord.' The bishop speaks first and last. He is considered the first servant in the congregation."[8] The ordained leaders, who have no professional credentials or special training, serve for life and are not paid but earn their living by farming, carpentry, or other occupation.

A bishop is the spiritual head of a Gmay. He officiates at baptisms, weddings, communions, funerals, and members' meetings. As spiritual captain of the leadership team and the incarnate symbol of church authority, he interprets and enforces church regulations. If disobedience or conflict arises, he is responsible to resolve it.

Sam Mullet described his responsibilities this way: "It is the same as the duties of a father in the house. To see to the flock, make sure things are peaceful and work with God's word, what the Bible teaches us, what our forefathers taught us, and what we promised when we were baptized, to serve the order [Ordnung] and to see to it that the members obey."[9] On several occasions, Sam compared his role to that of the president of the United States. On one occasion he told a magistrate in court, "I don't like to be called bishop . . . because the title comes from God and we don't like to use that as a front. I don't want to hide behind that, in other words."[10]

As noted in chapter 2, Amish leaders are selected by drawing lots.[11] This ritual may seem like a game of chance to outsiders, but for the Amish, the mystery-filled rite confers divine blessing on church authority. The process grants bishops considerable spiritual clout because the Gmay believes that God directs the rite, reaching down from heaven as it were, to select a new shepherd of the flock. If members are unhappy with the outcome, their only recourse is to argue with God. Despite their belief in divinely sanctioned leadership, the Amish are well aware that their leaders are fallible humans. Nonetheless, the role of bishop carries heavy responsibilities and exerts wide influence over the life of the Gmay.

With more than 2,100 diverse Amish congregations in North America comes diversity in leadership style. Some bishops are dominant and heavy-handed. Others are gentle and gracious. Some hold authority tightly in their own hands, while others consult widely before making decisions. Because a bishop controls the agenda, he has considerable latitude to decide what issues to bring to the Gmay for a vote and when. Although bishops have muscle, several checks and balances restrain their reach. First, a bishop needs the consent of the Gmay to proceed with major actions. (In some situations, though, members may grudgingly accept a proposal to avoid stirring up trouble.) Second, a bishop's attempt to promote or obstruct a proposed action—discipline of an errant member, change to the Ordnung, or acceptance of a new technology, for example—will only be effective if the other ministers support it. An additional bridle on a bishop's power is the sentiment of other bishops in nearby or affiliated congregations. Finally, if a Gmay is paralyzed by conflict, members may ask outside bishops to mediate it—unless they are afraid to request such assistance.

Although he is selected by God, the bishop is responsible to his congregation. He brings proposed actions, including excommunication, to members for a vote. Sam agreed with this policy in principle. He even explained to a magistrate that Amish polity requires members to vote on key matters, not just leave them to the bishop's discretion. However, several members of Bergholz could recall only one time when anyone had spoken against one of Bishop Mullet's proposals and that person was soon expelled. One ex-member explained, "They [members] all knew what Sam wanted to hear so no one ever spoke up against him in church if they disagreed."[12]

For unknown reasons, Bishop Mullet took a very unusual step at a members' meeting in 2006. He asked the congregation to vote on this strange question: Do you believe that I was ordained by God? Two people—Melvin Shrock, the oldest member of the congregation, and one of Melvin's sons—agreed but said that they did not like how Deacon Troyer was treated. According to one former member, "This made Sam super mad. He looked at Mel and said, 'If you don't like how I run the church, why don't you run it.'"[13] The bishop of another congregation noted that within weeks Melvin was "in the ban" (expelled).[14] Five years later Melvin Shrock was assaulted when he returned to Bergholz at the invitation of his son Emanuel.

A Prophet

By the fall of 2006, Bishop Mullet's emerging ideology and self-identification had crystallized. Several weeks after the gathering of three hundred Amish elders in Ulysses, he sent a hand-drawn illustration—created by one of his teenage daughters with colored pencils—to Bishop Atlee Miller, who had convened the leaders at his farmstead.[15] The title at the top of the drawing reads: "!!Atlee and his helpers!!" Beneath the title stands an altar, inscribed with the words "Prophets of Baal" and surrounded by eleven stick figures. A second altar with flames of fire swirling heavenward appears in the lower half of the illustration. The Old Testament prophet Elijah stands beside the altar. The inscription reads, "Prophet of God (Elijah)." Beside the figure of Elijah are the words "Sam Mullet."[16]

This particular story, found in I Kings 18:1–46, features a contest on Mount Carmel between Elijah, the prophet of God, and 450 false prophets of the idol Baal to see which god could send fire from the skies to ignite a fire on the altar.

The prophets of Baal construct an altar, slaughter a bull, and place it on the altar as a sacrifice to Baal. For most of a day, the 450 prophets cry aloud and plead to Baal to light their sacrifice with sparks from heaven but to no avail.

When his turn comes, Elijah likewise builds an altar and slaughters a bull. Both the bull and the altar are consumed by fire as soon as the prophet prays to God. When the Israelites, many of whom had been worshiping Baal, see the fire, they fall on their faces saying, "The Lord indeed is God." Having proved himself as the true prophet of God, Elijah instructs the people to seize all of the false prophets and kill them.

The text on the part of Mullet's drawing directed to Bishop Miller reads, "You thought you were on the top of the latter [sic]!!! You Atlee fell all the way down to the bottom using the sheriff to try to get me!!!!!!! The dirtiest trick of all. It didn't work. Again—I'm still free. Ha Ha Ha Ha Ha Ha Ha Ha Ha Ha Ha."

The takeaway is clear. Like Elijah, Sam is a true prophet of God. Bishop Atlee Miller and three hundred Amish elders are

!! Atlee and his helpers!! the goo Bishop's?? At Your Deiner Vorsammlung You weren't satisfied with that!! You Thought You were on top of the Latter —!!! You Atlee Fell all the way down to the Bottom using the Sheriff to try to get me !!!!!!! The dirtiest Trick of All it didn't work Again — I'm still Free. Holt Ha Ha Ha Ha Ha Ha Ha Ha Na Sam & mullet

Prophets of Baal

Prophet of God.(Elijah)

Sam Mullet

false prophets. And to any doubters: beware the fire. This simple drawing illustrates Bishop Mullet's religious ideology, his self-understanding, and his view of Amish leaders outside the Bergholz environs.

Explaining why he did not go to the all-day ministers' meeting, Sam told a magistrate, "It was just a trap to get me to come. If I go to their meeting, I have to agree to obey their rules. I didn't go, because I didn't have to go. They shut the door in our face. They didn't want nothing to do with us, but yet they wanted to decide what to do with this case. That is why this picture was made, because according to our Articles of Faith of 1632 [more than] 400 years ago, it tells us plainly that if anybody is excommunicated like Laverne Troyer, nobody is to give them any help for spiritual things. So he, Atlee, by doing that [helping Troyer], it makes him a false prophet. That was the idea of the picture."[17]

When he first saw the illustration, one senior bishop simply said, "Aye, Yi, Yi, Yi, Yi, Yi, Yi!" Shaking his head in disbelief, he lamented, "Sam somehow got his people to hang with him. He got his people to believe him. It's just a shame, a shame, a shame. He always wanted to be on top, even at Fredericktown before they moved to Bergholz."[18]

According to one of Sam's children, "Dad thought he was a prophet like Elijah. He was the only one allowed to read the Bible. He was the only one who could interpret the Bible because they [the Bergholz members] thought he was God. They looked up to him as a god. Whatever he said, they would do."[19]

"We're Not Christians"

The simple pencil drawing also points to Bishop Mullet's strong reliance on the Hebrew Bible or Old Testament, which Amish people call the "Old Book." Since their beginning in 1693, Amish faith has focused on Jesus and in particular on his teachings in the Gospels, especially the Sermon on the Mount in Matthew's Gospel. This cluster of teachings categorically rejects revenge and admonishes the disciples of Jesus to love their enemies, forgive wrongdoers, and pray for their persecutors. Although Amish preachers frequently cite stories and wisdom from the Old Book, they accent the New Testament. Two-thirds of the biblical scriptures read at Sunday services come from the four Gospels, the books that recount the life, teachings, miracles, death, and resurrection of Jesus Christ.[20]

In interview after interview, people confirmed Bishop Mullet's use of the Old Testament to justify some of his actions. One ex-member described it this way: "He wanted to go back to the Old Testament, to the time of Abraham, because God spoke directly to people through the prophets, men could have multiple wives and use physical punishment."[21] One of Sam's children explained, "Dad used Old Testament passages as a way for him to support his ideas. He talked about going back to the Old Bible because there you can hit people. He picked out those verses to match his actions." Said a bishop in another settlement, "Sam wanted to use the Old Book because you can use the fist." And a woman who had lived in Bergholz explained that Mullet's use of the Old Testament encouraged an atmosphere of "violence. Angry. Hateful. More the eye-for-an-eye syndrome. . . . 'If he does that to me, I'll do that and worse to him.'" When speaking about how Bishop Mullet punishes members, a bishop who knew him well said, "He uses the Old Testament to support what he does."[22]

Given the tilt toward the Old Book, it was not a complete surprise that the Bergholz barbers announced, "We're not Christians." Yet such a bold denunciation of their faith shocked the Amish world. During the beard-cutting attack at the Millers, Marty and Barb chanted, "Forgive them, God." In response, one of the assailants snickered, "It sounds like we have a Christian over there." When Bishop Raymond Hershberger was under attack, he struggled to free his arms. Preacher Johnny Mullet admonished the elderly bishop: "A Christian shouldn't fight back like that." Raymond replied, "Christians don't do what you're doing." And Johnny retorted, "We're not Christians."[23]

This whack at the Christian pillar of Amish orthodoxy opened the door to other changes in the Bergholz community. In a move almost as shocking to the Amish mind as the denunciation of their Christocentric faith, the Bergholz clan stopped holding church services. One of the bishop's children explained, "One Sunday Dad got up to preach and was speechless. He just had nothing to say. He tried and tried but had nothing. So the congregation just sang and sang at the service. I think God left him that day." An ex-member said that Sam blamed the silence on "the church members because they didn't pray enough for him. And so he said they'll just stop having church services. Sam thought it's better to quit having services because he wanted

to be different and not have church like the other Amish do."
Sam described church services as "a phony cover for sinful daily
living."[24]

One observer noted, "Bergholz quit having church and instead they sit in a circle in Sam's yard. He's in the middle of the
ring trying to convince them of his power." Explained another
informant, "Instead of church services, they had group meetings
Sunday, Wednesday, and Friday nights. And they would talk way
into the night. Sam was trying to get everyone under his influence. They just sat in a circle and nobody said nothing. Sam was
the center of the conversation." One defector added, "When we
met in his house, Sam would sit on his chair like a king." In addition to the community gatherings, prayer meetings were held
every other Sunday at the home of various members.[25]

Replacing regular worship services with three social meetings
each week at the home of the bishop was unheard of in the Amish
world. Congregations across North America hold worship services on Sunday mornings every other week, rotating the gatherings from home to home. The substitution of social meetings
for Sunday worship services signaled a sharp break with Amish
tradition.

Bergholz also discarded other basic Amish practices. Several
people reported that some of their prayer books, New Testa-
ments, and *Ausbund*s (the standard Amish hymnbook) were on
sale at a public flea market. They also "stopped having morning
and evening prayers . . . and they have no silent prayer before
and after meals," said one ex-member. They got rid of these
things, explained another, because Sam wanted to go back to the
Old Book.[26]

Most Amish families have a copy of Martin Luther's German translation of the New Testament in their home and use it
regularly for devotional reading. Amish households typically
have a prayer book in their home as well, and families read from
this compilation during morning and evening devotions. Because
ministers do not compose extemporaneous prayers in worship
service, prayers from the prayer book are also read in the Sunday

services. The Bible, the hymnbook, and prayer books are the
classic reservoirs of Amish spirituality.

Giving Up

Sam was a man, the founder of the community, the oldest member, the bishop, the patriarch, and *Dawdy* (Grandpa), a term of
affection. In addition to these roles, Bishop Mullet had a bundle
of communal Amish values at his disposal as well. Amish bishops
do not operate in a cultural vacuum. They hold an esteemed role
in a society permeated with collective values that can be mobi-
lized for the spiritual health of the community or exploited for
other purposes.

The deepest canyon in the cultural landscape between Amish
life and modern society is individualism. Although Amish people
do not squelch individual expression, they emphasize the importance of community and yielding to the collective order. Values
such as self-denial, humility, submission, and obedience are core
themes in Amish spirituality. The accent on community starkly
separates the Amish world from the modern one, which trum-
pets individual choice, rights, and achievements at every turn.

The Amish speak of *uffgevva* (giving up), aligning ambition
and personal desires with the will of God and the wisdom of the
group. The Amish see uffgevva exemplified by Jesus Christ, who
willingly surrendered his life for the sake of others. Explained an
Ohio deacon, "He submitted himself to God so completely that
he never tried to do his own will by using his power to ma-
nipulate and force others." In other words, "the first step to true
brotherhood . . . [is] overcoming selfishness."[27]

In the spiritual realm, uffgevva means yielding to God's will.
Although self-surrender may sound repressive to modern people,
the Amish believe that those who forgo personal advancement
for the sake of family and community make a sacrifice that hon-
ors God and the church, the body of Christ. "Yielding and sub-
mitting is at the core of our faith and relationship with God,"
said one member. Self-denial means "sacrificing our own selfish
interests and desires in our service to God," according to another.
One leader writes, "We are part of a group, and as such we must

be willing sometimes to make personal sacrifices for . . . the overall benefit of the group."[28]

Children learn to give personal ambition a back seat to scripture, tradition, and family. Training in uffgevva begins at an early age. Parents teach it as they hold a toddler's hands together for prayer before meals so the child cannot reach for food. Growing up in large families teaches children self-denial as they learn to share food, toys, and bedrooms with their siblings. A common sign in Amish homes and schools proclaims that true JOY comes from putting Jesus first, Others next, and Yourself last. These small practices and a multitude of others prepare Amish children for living in community.

Although Amish society discourages assertive individualism, it certainly does not extinguish individual expression. Amish people have distinct likes and dislikes, personal preferences, and sometimes strong opinions. Despite the many constraints in Amish life, there is also room aplenty for individual choices and creativity. "The church doesn't tell us to wear boxer shorts or briefs, to go to McDonald's or Burger King," said one father. "The idea that Amish give up all freedom of choice, and let the community decide everything, is a myth. Even if you do decide to let the church decide, that in itself is a choice."[29] Still, while Amish people do not expect everyone in their community to think and act alike, the range of diversity pales alongside that in postmodern society.

"Obedience is the most important word in the dictionary," said one Amish elder. Early childhood socialization is crucial to acquire the habits of obedience. Children learn to "give up" and "give in" at an early age. They are taught from the Bible to obey their parents. "By the time the child reaches the age of three, the mold has started to form and it is the parents' duty to form it in the way the child should go," a leader advised. And in the words of a grandfather, "The children of parents who teach obedience are much more likely to remain in the church."[30]

Members are expected to accept church decisions. Spouses typically discuss issues together, but a wife is expected to defer to her husband if they come to an impasse. Preachers defer to bishops and younger bishops to those with seniority. And even older bishops bend to the counsel of their peers and the authority of scripture and tradition. Although obedience is expected, it is usually couched in a spirit of loving concern throughout the entire social system. Parents should not discipline their children in anger. Only with the Gmay's support may a bishop excommunicate a member. Calls to obey typically echo a concern for one's eternal destiny.[31]

One of Sam's children recalled that when his father left Fredericktown, "He had problems adjusting to other people's advice. If things weren't done his way, he'd be upset. He was not willing to *give himself up* to the church."[32] Another child who lived in Bergholz said that he was restrained physically, "because I was not *giving up* to Dad. That's what was said, anyway."[33] Sam expected his children and his church members to obey, to "give themselves up" to his authority.

Bishop Mullet had a package of values at his beck and call that could enhance the well-being of the Gmay or, if exploited, do it great harm. This package included deeply ingrained beliefs that men have the last word in home and church; that age is privileged—older people are wiser and should be respected; that church leaders are selected by God and have the authority to mete out discipline to help members stay on the heavenward path; that yielding to community—giving up and giving in—is necessary to purge selfishness and sinful ambitions; and that obedience is written on the ticket to heaven because disobedience signals rebellion against God.

Making It to Heaven

The ultimate goal of Amish life is "making it to heaven" at the end of one's earthly journey. In a court hearing in 2008, Bishop Mullet explained that obedience is key to achieving this eternal goal: "Excommunication is the same as when you're a father in the home and your child *disobeys*. Solomon says in the Bible, 'Spare the rod and spoil the child.' We don't want our children running out on the streets. That's why we use punishment. That's why we use excommunication. That's why we still spank our children. The goal of excommunication is the same thing as if you spank a child. . . . You tell them first and everybody knows . . . [that at baptism] you promise to *obey* the church and then if they don't *obey*, there's no other way, if they won't *obey* the rules of the church."[34]

Turning to an example that he thought the magistrate might understand, Sam said, "Just like the rules of the state on the road, we can't go out and drive on the wrong side of the road, we'll get killed and that's what will happen spiritually if they don't *obey* the rules of the church, that they promise to *obey*, not to the bishop, not to the church, but to God and the church. God is always first. The idea is to get the sin out of the soul so the soul can go back to God who gave it in the first place."

Bishop Mullet concluded, "If we don't *obey* the Bible and God's rule, we're just not going to make it to heaven. That's all there is to it. . . . You can't serve God and the devil both, in our faith or in any religion. It's not just the Old Order Amish. In any religion, you have to *obey* the rules of the church. . . . Catholic, Protestant, Church of Christ, the rules are pretty much the same. . . . It's just whether you enforce the rules or you let them [members] go wrong."

Explaining that bishops who are too lenient will have a problem, Sam said, "If I don't punish members and I just let it [disobedience] slide or if I find excuses [such as] it's my kids, my sons, my daughters, I won't have a congregation very long. . . . The members will not stay in a church if you just let everyone do what they want. You just can't let every sheep just run and get the best grass that's around. You have to have a fence, a ruling, and the bishop is not the ruling. He just enforces it like the president, like the judge. If the members or the other ministers don't agree with the bishop, there's nothing he can do."[35]

Bishop Mullet linked his views of punishment to his interpretation of "what the Articles of Faith say about shunning. If we don't practice that, we're not following God's Word. . . . Our older people [ancestors] were a lot more strict, a lot stronger than most of us are. That is the main reason things are held against me, I guess if I may say so, because we are still stricter than most people. If it's their own children, they kind of look through their hands and they don't want to punish them. We can't do that. If I do that, my other members that are obedient to the church want to leave." In Bergholz, the strands of bishop, church, scripture, and God were woven into a tight fabric of authority.

Another bishop observed that "Sam didn't want anybody to leave Bergholz, to move out, because it looked bad for him. If those who left were saying bad things about him, then others wouldn't want to come to Bergholz."[36] Previous members with firsthand information about the goings-on in the clan were a menace to the bishop because they could mar the community's reputation, and indeed, some of them were attacked in the fall of 2011. According to one defector, Sam was stuck on the horns of a dilemma. New families were needed for the settlement to grow; yet, it was difficult to tolerate dissent, and those who were exiled would spread toxic "rumors" sure to discourage any prospects.[37]

Consequently, the clan broke off relationships with former members and relatives outside the community to diminish the flow of information, a decision that ironically only fueled the curiosity about what Rebecca had called the "terrible things" happening in Bergholz. One way that ties with relatives were cut involved screening some of the mail. A woman who eventually left said, "Most of the people, most of the time, we would get permission from him [Bishop Mullet] before we sent a letter to anybody. He would often read them before we sent them. And if somebody got a letter from somebody else, quite often they would give it to him to read."[38] The sweep of that surveillance is not clear, but ex-members say that some of their incoming mail was opened before they received it.[39]

One mother lamented in 2013 that she had not received a letter from her daughter living in Bergholz since 2005. This echoed the experience of many other parents and relatives with children and siblings living in Bergholz.[40] The parents of a daughter who was married to one of Sam's sons decided to visit her in the summer of 2010. They had not seen her or their grandchildren for four years. When they knocked on the door, she declined to shake hands, saying, "We don't shake hands anymore with strangers." According to the parents' account, Sam arrived at his daughter-in-law's house a few minutes later, "white in the face and mad, saying, 'You hypocrites get out of here, right now!'"[41] The visit lasted a mere twenty minutes. Cutting ties to outside relatives isolated clan members, making them ever more insular and dependent on their little society in the Yellow Creek Valley.

The Magic

Some members of Bergholz thought their world was enchanted with spirits and incarnations of the devil. Most Amish people believe that the devil is an active force for evil in the world—a being who tries to obstruct goodness and righteousness. Candidates for baptism pledge that they will "renounce the devil and all of his subtle ways."[42] An Amish devotional guide warns readers that Satan has cunning ways to ensnare people and lead them astray.[43]

The orthodox Amish view of the devil was intensified along the Yellow Creek. There, Satan was personified in animals and in certain people. One person with close ties to Bergholz described it this way: "They believe more by signs, like things happen, and they go by that, the signs. They see visions and they go by those visions."[44]

Church members believed that Bishop Mullet was endowed with the mystical power to decode the meaning of certain spiritual manifestations. As a prophet, he believed that many events, including how a dog or cat would lie on the floor, were signs from God. Sam explained that the devil can come in the form of a snake, as he did in the Garden of Eden, or as a wolf in sheep's clothing, "ready to tear the flock apart."[45] Sheriff Abdalla, for example, was deemed the devil on at least one occasion.[46]

One day when Sam saw a stray white cat, he declared that it was Aden Troyer who had returned to snoop around. One of his children said, "Everything has a special meaning—for example, a black cat would be the devil." Another time a white pigeon sitting on a roof embodied the devil. Sam's son Eli's dog was Satan incarnate. Eli and his brother Billy, on separate occasions, were held down to flush the devil out of their bodies. And one night, Preacher Johnny Mullet used a baseball bat to chase the devil out of a barn.[47]

Once in a wedding sermon, Sam described a vision from God. Explaining his vision in court in 2008, Sam said that God intended the dream "to get people's attention, to wake up," because God was coming back. "People were glad to hear that story that God gave me a horse and he gave me a gun, because people cried in church when they heard the sermon, that God is telling us, 'Wake up, before your chances are gone, it won't be long.' "[48] Some may have cried, but others were frightened because they thought this meant that God had given Sam the authority to kill and a list of whom to kill.[49]

In addition to his power to read spiritual signals and interpret dreams from God, the bishop's piercing eyes could peer into a heart and take a spiritual MRI. He could detect deep sins from the past, especially sexual ones. Several former members described Sam's eye-to-eye stare and his uncanny ability to see the dark sins hidden in the crevices of their lives.[50] "If you disagree with Sam, then you had hidden sins, said one defector."[51] The bishop sometimes asked individuals to write down their sins and confess them to him, to the Gmay, or to both. On one occasion, Sam asked everyone to write down all the bad things they had done in their lives.[52] In response, they brought "these letters to me—some wrote 100 pages," Sam said. He placed them in manila folders.[53] According to one defector, "The more you wrote, the better Sam liked it."[54] A woman who left Bergholz recalled that Sam talked about the end of the world being near and emphasized the need to "get all our sins out, put them on paper. Don't wait until tomorrow."[55] One member reported that some people complied by jotting down a minor sin or two or wrote about contrived sins to satisfy the request and avoid punishment.[56] On one occasion, married couples were asked to write down five things they liked and five things they did not like about their spouse and give their notes to Sam.[57]

Afraid to Leave and Afraid to Stay

Threats of excommunication were another way to exert control. When a member told Sam that someone had tricked him, the member recalls the bishop saying, "Shut up! If you say that one more time I'll excommunicate you!" One woman, a former member, explained, "If you didn't agree with him you would be punished about it and he would have you confess in front of the church that you would agree with him. . . . He told people what to do. If they didn't do it, he would hold a grudge against them. He would shun them from the church. They would be excommunicated, and they would not eat and drink with them [other members] for maybe two or four weeks."[58]

Ex-members tell of various attempts to thwart their plans to leave the community. Instead of fences, guns, or security cameras, Bergholz loyalists used verbal threats, condemnations to hell, and physical obstructions to prevent people from moving out. When one of Sam and Martha's sons wanted to exit, "Sam talked with him all night trying to convince him to stay," according to one member.[59] A different tactic was used against another son and his wife. The couple moved some of their belongings one day, and when they returned for the rest on another day, they found large, fresh-cut trees lying across their driveway, the doors on their house boarded up, the windows screwed tightly closed, new locks on the doors, and the basement deliberately flooded, "all because we wanted to move, we wanted to leave."[60]

Some families had purchased property from Sam. In at least two cases, he did not give deeds to the owners, although they had paid for the land or were in the process of paying for it. When such homeowners left the community, they were not able to sell the property and recoup their investment because they did not have the deed.[61]

Another mode of control involved probing questions about sexual relationships. In one case, Sam asked a married couple "to confess the things that [they] do in [their] bedroom that are not pure." He also asked evocative questions about intimate details of their sexual practices. "He said if we confess and make our things right in the church then we'll be closer to God and not close to Satan. We got hounded all the time from him. He said we wouldn't *give up* because we wouldn't tell him those things," said a married woman.[62]

The bishop's demeanor varied somewhat by his mood, according to one ex-member. "If things were going his way, he would be very compassionate." If they were not going his way, he became "angry. Very angry. Screaming, yelling. Nobody could do anything right. And you never knew what would set him off."[63] Reflecting on his response to similar accusations, Sam noted, "[Some people] say I get mad and wave my arms and holler. I don't know, maybe I do."[64]

Numerous people testified in court about their fear of Bishop Mullet.[65] A woman who had lived in Bergholz described her anxiety this way: "Well, I had a fear of Sam. The look on his face, it was not a nice, friendly look. And whenever we had to talk about something, we had to stare him in his eyes, and he'd stare me in my eyes. That was the only way we could talk about something. I felt intimidated by him."[66] Another woman said, "I'm scared of Sam Mullet . . . he did not threaten me . . . but he threatened a lot of people. I've heard him make threats on people's lives . . . on two of his sons. . . . He said he wouldn't stop at nothing until he got revenge [on them] for coming and taking Wilma. He said he wouldn't stop at nothing until he sees them put behind bars or killed."[67]

The women were not alone in their fear. A man who left in July 2006 said, "I was afraid to leave and I was afraid to stay." When he told Dawdy that he was planning to leave, Sam threatened to excommunicate him and forbade him from talking to his brother. "He didn't want me to talk to my brother because he didn't want us to leave. I couldn't talk with my brother for a month. I was afraid of Sam. That is why I stopped talking with my brother." This same man, who had witnessed the mistreatment of Sam's son Eli, said that he did not object at the time, "because I was afraid of Sam." He eventually wrote a letter to the sheriff because he was worried that Sam would "harm more people."[68] One of the bishop's close relatives who lived in another county was so fraught with anxiety about a possible attack that he built escape exits into his house.[69]

One couple fled Bergholz at night without using any lights because they were afraid of Sam. The defectors called the Jefferson County sheriff at 11:00 p.m., "asking for help because they were scared to death." Later their belongings were removed under the protection of a police escort. Even so, the husband had visions "that they all would come after me and beat me and thrash me."[70]

"People were scared because Sam would punish them and threaten to excommunicate them," said an ex-member. "At first we just thought it's a windstorm, and there will soon be a sunny day. But it only got worse and worse."[71] Indeed, the sun never did break through the clouds, and the gale winds only grew stronger.

David Wengerd (*left, black hat*) before and (*right*) after his beard-cutting attack in the pasture.

FOUR

THE CULT?

Intimate Encounters

Stories of sexual misconduct at Bergholz had been swirling around for several years before the attacks.[1] Christ Mullet, for example, was convicted of three counts of unlawful sexual conduct with a minor in 2008 and sentenced to six months in jail.[2] Reports of sexual impropriety did not surprise a van driver who frequently transported the Bergholz clan. He noted an unusual pattern. When they traveled in his van, the women sat on the seats near Sam at the front while the men sat at the back. The driver, who understood some Pennsylvania Dutch, was startled one day when the women gigglingly asked Sam which one of them would sleep at his house that night.[3]

This story did not surprise one of Sam's offspring, who described the situation in Bergholz this way: "As for sexual matters, they felt that everyone could run together and have sexual relations with others. It was okay if sex happened with other people.... The regular Amish bishops would have stopped that kind of sex."[4] Former members had observed several adult women in Bergholz living at Sam's house for extended periods at one time or another, and several other accounts insinuate that Sam had intimate ties with women.[5] Yet the exact nature of Bishop Mullet's involvements with women is shrouded in secrecy, because very few women have spoken about their experiences to outsiders.

In the general allegations of the indictment that charged Bishop Mullet with hate crimes, the US government contended that he "misappropriated the wives of other members of the community and 'counseled' them on how to be sexually satisfied in their marriage." Furthermore, it noted that "the women were expected to leave their husbands and children and live in Mullet's house where they were further expected to be sexually intimate with him." Those who "disobeyed or resisted this practice were ostracized from the community."[6] The intimate encounters were described as "marriage counseling" to help wives solve their marital problems by learning how to improve their sexual relations with their husbands.[7] At least one of the women received a book on sexual intimacies as part of her counseling. Through his attorney, Bishop Mullet has adamantly denied that he ever had sexual relations with any woman other than his wife.[8]

An Amish woman who had resided in Bergholz for a time was shocked to see how Sam interacted with women. There was "too much intimate behavior," she said. "Close sitting. Looking into each other's eyes, having a conversation where a word could be understood just between two people." This was "totally foreign" to the practices of other Amish communities. A former member recalled, "One time Sam hugged me on the sidewalk outside his house, and asked if I wanted to be his daughter. If I had said yes, that would have led to sitting on his lap and kissing. At another time, he asked me, 'Do you believe God gave me the calling to be a bishop?' I didn't answer because if I had said yes, then I would've had to do whatever he asked me to."[9]

Deviating sharply from the taboo on bishops and ministers meeting with women alone, Sam talked privately and at length with a teenage girl, trying to persuade her to join the church. Although Amish family members often encourage their children to be baptized and join the church, the decision is voluntary. Sam was upset, explained an ex-member, because this particular teenager had reservations about joining the Gmay. "He did not allow her to talk with others. Sam forced her to join the church. He met with this seventeen-year-old alone. That should never be done by a bishop. A bishop never meets alone with a young woman like that."[10]

Nor should an Amish bishop meet with adult women alone or ever discuss sexual matters with them. But Bishop Mullet did. In one instance, he visited the wife of a couple who were planning to leave Bergholz. She did not want more pregnancies for medical reasons. Sam urged her to have more children, recalling that his "mother said a woman like that would go to hell." Moreover, he asked explicit questions about her sex life with her husband, including their physical positions in bed.[11] Bishop Mullet met with her several times privately, making her feel guilty for wanting to abandon the community.

Couples were sometimes separated for several weeks or even months while the wife lived at the bishop's home and her husband lived in the couple's home or with another family.[12] A former member explained the process of dividing couples: A few women would tell the wife "bad things about her husband, running him down." Eventually, "the wife would be convinced that her man is no good." The husband would then be punished in some way and separated from his wife for some time while she lived in the bishop's house to "learn how to improve their marriage."[13] Although they lived apart, husbands and wives could see one another throughout the week. For weeks at a time, Sam's wife, Martha, lived in the homes of her adult children, helping to care for her grandchildren.[14] In the opinion of a knowledgeable bishop, "Sam's wife goes away to take care of children so he is free to have sex with other women in Bergholz."[15]

Helping Eli

In the spring of 2008, Eli Mullet was back in the hospital for another round of mental health treatment.[16] After receiving proper care and medication, he returned to Bergholz. Later that summer, he checked himself into the hospital again, because, according to his wife, Nancy, he "was very upset because he found out that Mr. Mullet asked me to sit on his lap." Nancy stayed at Sam's home while Eli was in the hospital the second time, and the bishop told her that perhaps "one of the reasons that Eli got sick [was] because he was not satisfied with how our marriage was."

According to Nancy, Sam would hug women and expected them to hug him back. If they were reluctant to hug him or if he felt their embrace was reserved, he would suggest they were hiding something from him. "What is wrong, what are you hiding?" he would ask. "At least I'm not kissing you, I'm just hugging you." According to Nancy, the hugging would eventually lead to sitting on his lap and to kissing.

Nancy did not want to hug her father-in-law, but eventually, she agreed to "because he would tell me that we have to do this so Eli can get better, and he would tell me that *the other ladies* are doing the same thing. I was always afraid [not to do] those things, in my mind, I was thinking that if this is what it takes to *help* Eli, I will do it," she said. She wanted to go back to her own home, but "they said I can't go by myself because the devil is going to get a hold of me if I go home and stay by myself."[17]

On one occasion when Nancy was sleeping in an upstairs bedroom at Sam's house, she was awakened in the middle of the night by one of Sam's married daughters, who told her, "Dawdy wants you to go down to his bedroom." Nancy refused. The messenger returned a second time: "Dawdy said just to obey him." In Nancy's words, "If I didn't want to obey, he would say things like 'I can't understand why you can't obey me. The other ladies can.'" And so, "I always gave up [uffgevva], I was afraid not to . . . . He would also say, 'Don't you want to help Eli? Don't you want him to get better? This is the only way we can help him.'"

Another night, according to Nancy, Sam "was upset because I had not come down that evening, and he wanted me to. So he sent his wife back to get me, and he said, 'I cannot understand why you can't obey and just do as I tell you to? I have witnesses sitting right here that tell me what I am doing is helping their marriage.'" He had assembled four couples in the kitchen, who "nodded in agreement."

Eventually, Nancy's fear fled, and she refused to go to Sam's room and comply with his wishes. Shortly thereafter he came to her house when she was alone and asked her for the book "about the intimate things that he was doing with the ladies" that he had loaned her. Nancy remembered him saying that he would "give it to somebody else to *help* them." And then he said, "I'm done *helping* you." After walking out to his buggy, he returned with a word of farewell. "There is one more thing I want to tell you. I just got done talking with [two of his daughters] and we all decided that you're a whore."[18]

The next day, Nancy recalled, "I told my husband, 'I'm not staying here.' I was getting to be a nervous wreck. . . . I told him, 'If you don't take me away from here, I'm going to run away.'" Eli called a driver and they left with their children and a "few suitcases of clothes." Nancy never returned to the Yellow Creek Valley.

Bishop Mullet, speaking to an outsider, described his role as a helper: "They say I went to the women—but they come begging to me for help. 'Help us get out of this hole.'"[19] On the subject of sexual matters, Sam sometimes cited the Old Book. On one occasion, he explained to another bishop that King David was forgiven even though he had many wives. Exasperated by such a cavalier attitude toward marital infidelity, the bishop declared, "If Sam is a prophet of God, who can criticize him?"[20]

The Winter of Lament[21]

By 2009, a dark cloud had stretched over the Bergholz community.[22] Sam and Martha's son Eli and daughter-in-law Nancy had fled in 2008 to start a new life in Pennsylvania. The clan had lost the custody battle over Aden and Wilma's two young children. The $35 million suit against Sheriff Abdalla and Jefferson County had fizzled, resulting in only a meager settlement. And like the three hundred elders had done three years earlier, Eli Yoder, the bishop who had shepherded them for several years, had also cut them off, leaving Bergholz stranded without fraternal ties to any other Amish churches. Moreover, Amish people in other communities were spreading lurid "lies and rumors" about the Bergholz clan.[23]

In the face of all these setbacks, folks in the Yellow Creek Valley wondered whether God had forsaken his little flock in

Jefferson County. As they considered their predicament, the word *hypocrite* came to mind. Perhaps, they thought, they were not practicing what they preached.[24] During the Winter of Lament (2009–2010), the people of Bergholz began to acknowledge that they were hypocrites living sinful lives and that they wanted to get back on the right path with God.[25]

"We realized some of us were living in sin or God wouldn't have allowed this to happen," Sam told a reporter.[26] As they floundered in this sea of despair, the clan sought hope in rituals of remorse, solitude, self-deprecation, and bodily depravation. It was a time of repentance and contrition. But it also was a time of renewal as they searched for a fresh start, for ways to reset and recharge their spiritual lives. During this season of regret, some unique ritual expressions emerged. These rites of remorse in the winter of 2009–2010 involved extended exclusion in small animal pens, paddling of adults, and cutting of hair and beards.

Amish Jails

About a dozen men and several women spent time in small chicken houses, dog kennels, and pens inside barns, which the clan dubbed "Amish jails."[27] The nickname was pure hyperbole: these jails had no locks, keys, electric fences, guards, guns, or surveillance cameras. They were small primitive structures for housing animals. Three of them were inside or attached to barns; others stood alone on a farmstead. The size of the chicken coops varied, but some were roughly ten-by-twenty feet. They were furnished with fresh straw and blankets for the penitent as well as with some curious chickens. People stayed in these homespun prisons from several days to several weeks. Some men were "incarcerated" for two-week stints on two separate occasions. The gates of the jails "were not locked," explained one man, "but no one left because all of them were afraid of Sam."[28]

This practice of exclusion may have begun as early as 2007 when a woman was relegated to a horse box stall in a barn for several weeks on a bread-and-milk diet without access to a regular bathroom.[29] In the fall of 2008, a man stayed in an outside dog kennel under the trees for three nights because he was "blamed for having bad thoughts. The real reason," according to a member of Bergholz, "was so Sam Mullet could have his wife," who went to live at Bishop Mullet's house for three months or more.[30]

In another case, Emanuel Shrock spent two weeks in a goat pen because he was "blamed for having dirty thoughts."[31] On the advice of his four brothers, Raymond Miller was the first person to enter a chicken coop, "to clear his mind . . . because he was having problems keeping his mind where it should be, thinking good thoughts, and he wanted to turn his life around.[32] Individuals either voluntarily committed themselves or, like Raymond, entered a jail on the advice of friends or family members. Other members of the community brought the "inmates" food. A few of the men worked during the day and returned to the pens for evenings and weekends. The jails were not heated, and many of the stays occurred in cold weather, leading at least two men to sustain frostbite.[33]

In addition to the men, three women spent time in the jails: Sam's wife, Martha, who was in her mid-sixties, their daughter Mary, and their daughter-in-law Mattie, wife of Preacher Johnny Mullet.[34] Johnny entered the chicken coop in his barn on his own initiative, and later, he encouraged Mattie to spend some time there as well. Bishop Mullet explained to a reporter the value of jailing: Participants told him that "their mind is clear and they write things down." Furthermore, he said, "There's plenty of straw and hay and plenty of blankets."[35] A member of Bergholz explained, "[We were told that] the devil has these men tied up and won't let them confess their sins. And by sitting in a goat pen, dog kennel, or chicken coop, he [the devil] would let them loose so they could write down and confess *all* of their sins."[36]

Preacher Levi F. Miller stayed in a chicken coop several times, trying "to turn his life around so he could be the father and husband that God intended him to be."[37] Meanwhile, Levi's wife lived at the bishop's home.[38] Sam explained to an outside bishop that "it took a while to get Levi to see things my [Sam's] way."[39] Bishop Mullet himself did not spend time with the chickens. He did visit Levi, however, during one of Levi's stays in a jail; otherwise, he did not make pastoral visits to the penitent. When occupants ended their time of remorse and reflection, they would typically visit with Sam that evening to discuss their experience.[40]

Why were people sleeping on straw beds in primitive animal pens during Ohio winters cold enough to produce frostbite? One member explained that people "went in there to straighten up their lives, to live a different life."[41] Participants and witnesses recited a cluster of reasons highlighting lament, sorrow for sins, repentance, cleansing, and renewal.[42] The rites of remorse, they said, helped to make things better, helped to change their lives around, got their minds on a different track, and rid their minds of dirty things, of sins. In short, the jails offered a quiet place to clear their minds, to think, and to try to live better. The experience supposedly provided the penitents with a fresh start and a chance to turn their lives around, and they felt it helped them.

Spare the Paddle and Spoil the People

During the Winter of Lament (2009–2010), numerous adults participated in rituals of paddling. This practice originated from a confrontation between Emanuel Shrock and Christ Mullet. According to one member, when Emanuel was in the goat pen inside his barn he became agitated with Christ and hit him with a broom handle. When he left the goat pen a day or so later, Emanuel went to Bishop Mullet's house where Christ, using an ax handle, beat him hard enough to fracture some ribs.[43] To prevent future altercations, the clan started using a paddle when people became frustrated with one another. "It was my idea to get the paddle," Bishop Mullet said.[44]

Sam turned to Deacon Eli Hostetler, a skilled woodworker, and asked him to fashion a paddle, drill some one-inch holes in it, and attach the paddle to an ax handle. "The holes make it sting more," said one Amish man.[45] Nineteen-year-old Johnny

Mast, a grandson of Sam, recalled paddling two of his brothers. Some people took turns paddling one other, typically at a community gathering. At other times, the paddlings were not reciprocal: a brother paddled another brother, a daughter paddled her mother, wives spanked their husbands, and individuals paddled other individuals. A woman might spank her husband, for example, if she thought he was showing too much interest in other women. It was something people did if they held a grudge or bitterness against someone or if they wanted to rid themselves of the anger they had toward a family member.[46] "The paddlings hurt," said a member who had been hit hard by another man who held a grudge against him. "We weren't just playing around."[47] Knowledgeable people, including relatives, allege that on one occasion three of Martha's daughters spanked her so hard that she had difficulty walking.[48]

The paddlings occurred for about a year. They reflected and applied the wisdom of Solomon—spare the rod and spoil the child—to adult life in the Bergholz community. In the mind of the clan, it was a way for people to discipline one another without aggressive fights, a way to help rid people of the devil and to help them stop hypocrisy.

Although it's not unusual for Amish parents to spank their children, physically punishing adults is very rare in Amish society. In the words of a prominent bishop, "Physical punishment is never, ever, ever part of [adult discipline]."[49]

During this season of lament, the clan was jolted by the sudden departure of Deacon Eli Hostetler and his family, who slipped away one night in November 2009. They left because they were afraid of what might happen to them in Bergholz: "We had to get out to have a happy, peaceful life and marriage."[50] Within three years, both of the clan's deacons had fled the Yellow Creek Valley.

Beards and Barbers

A third unique ritual—hair and beard cuttings—had begun in the fall of 2009 and intensified during the Winter of Lament. Unlike jailings and spankings, this practice has roots in the Old

Testament, where beard cutting has multiple meanings.[51] Several scriptures affirm that a long beard is a sign of God's honor and blessing. One verse instructs the men of Israel not to mar the edges of their beards lest they dishonor God (Lev. 19:27).

Cutting off someone's beard by force was an act of shaming and great disgrace. On one occasion, King David sent ambassadors of goodwill to Hanun, the new king of the Ammonites. Hanun suspected the ambassadors were spies in disguise so he shaved off half of their beards and sent them home. Because they were too ashamed to go back to Jerusalem in that state, King David permitted them to sojourn in Jericho until their beards had grown back. This mutilation of beards triggered a vicious battle involving some thirty-two thousand foot soldiers (II Sam. 10:1–7).

Two other meanings—grief and purification—are attached to voluntary beard cutting. When he was overwhelmed by great destruction and tragedy, Job tore his robe and shaved his hair and beard to signal his grief before God (Job 1:20). The death of a king prompted eighty men to shave their beards as a sign of mourning before bringing their offerings to the temple of the Lord (Jer. 41:5). These and other examples point to voluntary beard cutting as a sign of grief or mourning. Voluntary beard cutting was also part of a ritual of purification for lepers (Lev. 14:9) and the Levites (Num. 8:5–7). It was also included in the Nazarite vow of commitment and consecration, which forbade a novitiate from touching his head with a razor except under special circumstances such as when he unexpectedly encountered a dead body (Num. 6:9).[52]

Anchored on these examples in the Old Book, the Bergholz clan engaged in a voluntary rite of beard cutting that had two meanings: (1) it was a sign of grief and confession for past sins, including hypocrisy; and (2) it was a rite of purification, cleansing, and recommitment to live better lives.

During the long Winter of Lament, most of the women had their hair cut and about a dozen men had their beards, hair, or both cut, as signs of remorse and purification. These voluntary cuttings were done by other members. Some women cut the hair of men and of other women. Men most often sheared the beards of other men.

Nineteen-year-old Johnny Mast, who had purchased clippers to groom himself, became the head barber of Bergholz, so to speak. Although Johnny never had his own hair or beard cut, he estimated that ten or twelve of the adult men had. Most of the cuttings took place at Sam Mullet's house. Johnny did not do all the shearing, but he trimmed the ragged edges on some of the men to minimize any embarrassment created by untrained barbers. People had their hair or beards cut, explained Johnny, "because they weren't living their life the way they knew they should be and they wanted to turn their life around. It was to give them a new start."[53]

Bishop Mullet did not have his beard cut. He told a reporter that he would have "gladly cut" his beard. But, he said, "[my people] won't let me. They tell me, 'You haven't done anything to deserve that.'" Nonetheless, he agreed that the beard cutting "would help stop people from being hypocrites."[54]

Elizabeth Miller had her hair cut, as some other members did, to help "her get back on track with the Amish lifestyle." Her sister-in-law Nancy helped to cut Elizabeth's hair, so that she could "get help, to try to change her life around."[55] Two women first proposed that men should shave their beards if they are hypocrites and want to get a fresh start.[56] Preacher Miller agreed to have his beard shorn, because "he wasn't living a good Christian life." He had a problem with his temper and had mistreated his wife and children, and it was "a pretty bad problem," according to one woman in Bergholz, so bad that Levi was living apart from his family at Emanuel Shrock's home.[57]

Eighteen-year-old Daniel Shrock, Emanuel's son, said he had his hair cut because he was lying. His uncle, Lester Mullet, proposed this remedy and cut Daniel's hair at Sam Mullet's house with the bishop and at least ten other people watching. Daniel explained that having his hair cut "humbled" him. People agreed to have their hair and beards cut, he said, "to uncover ourselves, to show what kind of person we really are. So people know that we are in sin and want to live a better life," and to start over. Daniel's brother Melvin Shrock Jr. agreed that "if you're sinning, you get your hair cut and now you start all over again because now you are clean."[58]

All of the unique rituals enacted during the Winter of Lament—jail stays, paddlings, hair and beard cuttings—drew upon similar themes of remorse and renewal. One participant in these activities agreed that it was a period of self-reflection and purification, when the whole community turned inward. People "confessed that they weren't living right, that they were living in sin."[59]

One member, Barbara Yoder, concurred that during the long God-forsaken winter of 2009–2010 the community tried to find its way back "on the right path with God." This was a time when members acknowledged that they were hypocrites who were living sinful lives, that they were doing things that hurt their families, including angry behavior, fighting, and physical and verbal abuse.[60] Sam's wife, Martha, told the *New York Times* that at first she was "shocked by the beard cutting and other practices but that they 'seemed right for our people.' "[61]

By some accounts, these new ritual activities were voluntary and not directed by Bishop Mullet. Yet a former member explained, "Sam was behind whatever happened, but not directly involved in it. He always sent someone else to do his dirty work."[62] According to trial testimony, Bishop Mullet rarely prohibited any of these unusual activities, most of which ended after 2010.

The exclusions, paddlings, and beard cuttings inside Bergholz were not odd concoctions of crazy people—at least not for those whose minds had been marinated in these ideas. In their world, these rites, especially those drawn from the Old Book, seemed reasonable. These unpolished rituals were communal rites, even though not everyone participated in each activity. They were a defining experience, a turning point that conferred a new identity on the Bergholz clan, another sign of their break from Amish orthodoxy and a pivotal moment for what they called a new and fresh start.

Gossip, Rumors, and Hypocrites

Following the Winter of Lament, the symbolic boundaries separating Bergholz from the rest of the Amish world grew ever sharper and deeper. The bitterness of the past lingered, and mistrust abounded on both sides. The lines between good and evil, saint and sinner, pure and defiled, were sharply drawn. A former member, describing the long winter, said, "It was their way to cleanse themselves from wrong and to purify themselves. The Bergholz people started cutting their own hair because they were bad and sinners and it would help them start over and create a new life. Now they are pure and they want to cut the hair of others who are sinful."[63] Some in the Bergholz camp saw the struggle with other Amish as a battle of good and evil.

A close relative of Bishop Mullet complained, "[Sam] views the rest of us other Amish as so low down. He talks of how we other Amish are so crooked. Whatever we do, the Bergholz people don't do it because we're so bad."[64] Why, the Bergholz folks wondered, should they be like the other Amish, whom they now viewed as hypocrites. Having vilified some other Amish, the clan dropped certain traditional Amish practices and created alternatives to draw sharper lines of distinction. One example is their unique patterns of dress for women. "The headscarf of the women is unique to them," explained the wife of an Amish bishop. "The women's scarf at first was black. . . . Later they changed it to white in 2012. It's not like the standard Amish Kapp. They wear different colored aprons in public, and don't wear capes anymore. Some of the younger women wear sweatshirts." The woman noted, however, that the men dress just like other Amish. They wear wide-brimmed hats similar to those worn in conservative Amish groups.[65]

The clan was convinced that other Amish hypocrites were spreading rumors and falsehoods about the goings-on inside Bergholz. Visiting with an Amish businessman in August 2011, Bishop Mullet "ranted and raved about how other Amish people were spreading lies and gossip about Bergholz. He accused other

Amish leaders of being hypocrites." The entrepreneur urged him to "make peace with other Amish people and with God and ask for help from other leaders." Sam retorted, "The outside bishops just lie to us. I'm well satisfied with the way things are now in Bergholz."[66]

He would go it alone. In fact, he told one Amish bishop, "Noah went into the ark alone."[67] Speaking in court in 2008, Bishop Mullet explained that even if five thousand elders had voted against him at Ulysses, Pennsylvania, he would not have yielded. "There's nothing in the Bible, there's nothing in our Confession of Faith that tells me I have to listen to it [them]," he said.[68] Such defiance of church authority reflects a wholesale rejection of the Amish principle of uffgevva.

Other Amish people were annoyed by the self-righteous tone that they heard coming from Bergholz. When Rebecca wrote to her brother Andy in Bergholz (see chapter 3), she said, "People all over are talking about these things and shaking their heads because they just never heard of anything like it. . . . How can every other church district be wrong and *you* the only right one? There are many other districts working together for years and years and I'm sure you never classed them wrong before? So again, *who changed? You*, or the hundreds of other people?[69]

One defector explained, "At Bergholz, black was white and white was black."[70] A harsh critic of Bishop Mullet claimed that he "accuses the other Amish of exactly the same sins he does and is charged with. All sorts of sins he blames on others, such as sexual promiscuity, physical punishment, lying, etc. Sam always sees his problems as the fault of others."[71] Other Amish people, embarrassed and exasperated by the behaviors and rumors swirling around Bergholz, disowned the group with an inflammatory four-letter word: *cult*.

In early 2011, an Amish woman in Trumbull County wrote these words to the staff of an Amish newspaper: "Please *do not* print letters from Bergholz. We were shocked they'd write. They are a cult and don't even go to church. They all look up to their leader."[72] In 2010, some Amish people, especially those in Indiana, Michigan, and Ohio, were reading a book about Wilbur

Hochstetler: *Out of Deception: The True Story of an Amish Youth Entangled in the Web of a Cult*. Hochstetler grew up near Shipshewana in northern Indiana. As a fifteen-year-old Amish youth in 1988, he became involved with a small handful of Amish and ex-Amish led by Wilbur Lee Eash. Hochstetler tells how he gradually came under the influence of the thirty-five-year-old Eash, a self-appointed prophet of God. Hochstetler, whose involvement lasted for five years, explains his eventual doubts about Eash's beliefs and his difficulties breaking away from the young prophet. At the end of the book, Hochstetler describes the dangers of a cult.[73]

An Amish preacher and his wife who had read Hochstetler's story said, "It fits one hundred percent to Bergholz. At the end of the book, it says there are three things in deception: the abuse of power, money, sex."[74] An ex-member of the clan who had also read the book said, "The Hochstetler cult was but a mere shadow of what happened at Bergholz."[75] The wife of an Amish bishop with intimate knowledge of Bergholz, unapologetically labeled it a cult and declared that "demonic forces have a hold on these people."[76] To distance themselves from Bergholz, Amish people, as well as law enforcement officers and non-Amish taxi drivers, dubbed the folks in the Yellow Creek Valley a cult with little hesitation.

Helping Other Hypocrites

Several clan members recall that a new idea emerged during the Winter of Lament: perhaps beard cutting could help Amish hypocrites outside Bergholz. The idea wove together two strands of meaning connected to beard cutting in the Old Book—shaming and the judgment of God. Several scriptures mention cutting beards as a sign of the severity of God's judgment on the disobedience of the Israelites. Isaiah prophesied that because of the people's disobedience, the Lord will shave with a razor and sweep away the beard. Later the prophet warns that God will destroy Moab because of disobedience, and every head will be bald, and "every beard shorn," and everyone will wail and melt into tears.[77]

Cutting the hair and beards of Amish hypocrites beyond Bergholz would not only shame them but also warn them of God's impending punishment and doom because they had strayed from the true path of Amish faith. The beard attacks on other Amish people would echo the passages in the Old Book where beard cutting was a sign of God's judgment for the disobedience of his people.

The five Miller brothers—Lester, Marty Jr., Alan, Eli, and Ray Miller, sons of Marty and Barb—brainstormed about this idea one day with their uncle Sam in the barn across the gravel road from his large house. The brothers were agitated about their relationship with their parents, especially their dad. Their sister, Nancy, thought her parents were "bad parents. They didn't really practice what they preached. They said one thing and did another. They were hypocrites." They were "belittling" to her brothers, she said, "always putting them down, they were never good enough."[78] The Miller boys thought their father, Marty, was a hypocrite because he would confess faults in the church and then repeat them again in his daily life. In these discussions, the Miller boys wondered whether perhaps giving their parents a haircut "might help them" in their spiritual life.[79]

Then, for a year, the idea was forgotten. It flared up again in the summer of 2011 when several of the Miller brothers met their father at a machinery auction. He chastised them for having cut their beards. Using words to this effect, Marty told his sons, "If God is with you, your beard wouldn't have been cut. If God is with me, my beard will never be cut."[80] It was an enticing challenge; one that was hard to toss aside.

In the months before September 2011, the term *hypocrite* was increasingly bandied about for critics of Bergholz. According to his daughter Barbara, who lived in Bergholz, Bishop Mullet used the label not only for Marty and Barb Miller but also for Myron Miller and for Emanuel Shrock's father, Melvin. Sam also suggested that beard and hair cuttings would help to stop people from being hypocrites.[81] Daniel Shrock, a grandson of Dawdy who had heard talk of cutting the beards of other people to help them, said, "I *finally* was seeing it as the right thing to do."[82]

Drowning in a Sea of Disobedience

Inside Bergholz, a set of ideas—a narrative—had gradually gelled since the Winter of Lament. The emerging story made sense and offered a meaningful, albeit alternative, worldview for the people living there.[83] The story line went something like this:

- Bishop Mullet stands for the Word of God. He stands against the drift into the larger sea of disobedience. His teachings rest on four-hundred-year-old Amish traditions that other Amish are discarding. Like Noah, Sam went into the ark alone, and only the few that came with him will be saved. The rest of the Amish world, as in the time of Noah, is drowning in a sea of disobedience and headed for hell. The wayward hypocrites have slipped off the old Amish path. The only way to get to heaven is to stand rock solid on the Word of God, sticking with the old traditions and clinging to the truth. Even the three hundred Amish elders at Ulysses lost their bearings when they uprooted centuries of Amish teachings and tradition. If, perchance, as many as five thousand elders had voted against him, Sam would still have steadfastly upheld the Word of God because Almighty God holds him responsible to discipline and punish those who stray. The end of the world is near, and the disobedient must be reminded that obedience is the only way to make it to heaven.
- Like a prophet of old, Sam voiced a lonely, solitary plea in the wilderness against God's rebellious people. Like the Old Testament prophets Elijah, Jeremiah, and Micah, who were called to announce God's punishment on the idolatrous Israelites, Sam is called to preach against the swelling tide of disobedience in the larger Amish world, warning those who have lost their way to repent or else drown in a sea of despair.
- Amish hypocrites who tell lies and gossip—people who have been tricked by the wiles of the devil—have persecuted the faithful little flock at Bergholz. They cannot get

justice or a fair hearing from their relatives, from other
Amish leaders, or even from the government. No one treats
them fairly; no one understands them. Yet as a prophet of
God, Sam stands stalwartly for the truth.

■ Sam is not only a prophet announcing God's judgment on
the wayward Amish, he is also a servant helping his followers. He is the one who helps them in every possible way:
helps them identify and confess the sins that obstruct their
journey to heaven; uses discipline to help them purge those
sins and to start their life anew; helps couples who have
marital problems; helps women learn how to be better wives
and enjoy more fulfilling lives. His flock is even willing to
help other Amish hypocrites to see the truth and turn their
lives around, to get back on the old road to heaven before it
is too late.

In the Bergholz mind-set, the beard-cutting episodes that began in the fall of 2011 were warnings of the devastation to come
from God's hand if the Amish hypocrites did not repent and turn
around, as the Bergholz flock had done during the Winter of
Lament. In that sense, the shearings were prophetic acts of compassion to help other Amish get back on the old road to heaven.

Still, there was a sinister word underlying this yarn that was
spun along the Yellow Creek. That word was *revenge*. The narrative that the clan constructed blamed many of its troubles on the
outside Amish hypocrites. And now, with a compelling ideology
legitimated by religious belief, the little flock felt justified to exact
vengeance on those they thought had treated them unfairly.

Imputed with this righteousness, their narrative carried a
deep sense of moral obligation. Acting on their convictions was,
in short, the right thing to do. It was this set of beliefs that
spurred the Mullet clan forward in the events that began to un-
fold on September 6, 2011.

Township Road 280 leading to the Mullet home and several others.

FIVE

THE FBI

Better to Be Beaten Black and Blue

On Tuesday evening, October 4, 2011, Detective Joe Mullet (no relation to Bishop Mullet) was hanging out in the parking lot of the East Holmes Fire Company.[1] At 9:46 p.m., a 911 call flashed on his monitor regarding an incident at a home on Township Road 606 in Salt Creek Township near Fredericksburg. As a drug agent for the Holmes County Sheriff's Office, Mullet normally did not take routine calls. At that moment, however, all the other officers were busy, so he took the "jump call" and investigated the incident, having no idea of the location or who lived there. He sped over to the site, seven miles away, arriving in exactly ten minutes.

Although Mullet had grown up Amish in Holmes County, he had never joined the church. When he turned into the driveway of the farm on TR 606, an Amish man named Levi met him. The detective greeted Levi in Pennsylvania Dutch and, excitedly, Levi explained, "Them guys came right in and took Grandpa down, held me down, and held Andy down, and cut Grandpa's beard and hair."

Entering the house, Detective Mullet found hair lying on a chair by the doorway. He listened as family members recounted how the attackers grabbed Grandpa (Bishop Raymond Hershberger) and his son Andy and cut their hair, tackled Levi, and restrained the bishop's thirteen-year-old granddaughter, Miriam. The detective thought the bishop looked "deathly scared." When asked how it felt to have his hair and beard cut, he "started sob-bing and said, 'I'd rather have them beat me black and blue than take my hair.'" Bishop Hershberger declined to have his picture taken but agreed to photographs of the evidence in the small kitchen and living area. The Hershbergers were certain the of-fenders were from Bergholz. Detective Mullet had never heard of the town, so he returned to his cruiser to search for it on a map.

The detective was surprised that, despite Raymond Hersh-berger's hurt and humiliation, he did not want to press charges by signing a statement, but he did agree that his sons Andy and Levi could sign "a paper" for themselves.

Holmes County Sheriff Timothy Zimmerly soon arrived at the Hershbergers' to assist in the investigation and collection of evidence. He phoned the Jefferson County Sheriff's Office to advise them to be on the lookout for a red pickup truck pulling a livestock trailer and to stop and identify the subjects. About the same time, the Jefferson County officials received a call from Bishop Myron Miller in Carroll County reporting the license number of a truck that stopped in front of his house after he suf-fered a similar assault that night.

At 11:15 p.m., an hour and half after he had arrived, Detective Mullet left the Hershbergers' farm and returned to the Holmes County Sheriff's Office to file his reports. The detective was still completing his paperwork at about 2:00 a.m. when he re-ceived a call from Jefferson County Sheriff Fred Abdalla saying that his deputies had apprehended the truck driver and taken him (and the truck) to the sheriff's office for questioning. De-tective Mullet and Sheriff Zimmerly immediately drove the ninety miles to Steubenville and began interviewing the driver, Michael Kanoski, at about 3:30 a.m. He identified four of the five men who rode with him in the cab as Lester Miller, Levi F. Miller, Johnny Mullet, and Lester Mullet. Investigators gath-ered multiple samples of hair from the seats of the truck before releasing it to Kanoski later that morning.

Detective Mullet left Jefferson County at about 8:00 a.m. and, while driving home, received a call from Andy Hershberg-er's wife, who said, "We decided now we don't want to press charges after all." Mullet was astonished: "You've gotta be kidding, I've just worked all night on this case and so has Sheriff Zimmerly." The detective knew that if the Hershbergers withdrew their charges it would be difficult to arrest any of the suspects. Having a signed statement by a victim was the easiest way to move forward because, in his words, "If no one is willing to sign a paper, then you don't have a victim. And if you don't have a victim; you don't have a crime." After nearly twelve hours of work, the case was about to crumble.

"We'll Stand behind You"

Still without sleep, Detective Mullet and Sheriff Zimmerly arrived back at the Hershbergers' at about 10:30 a.m. on Wednesday, the day after the attack. Preacher Andy Hershberger came out to meet them. "Are you sure you want to drop the charges?" Mullet asked. Andy's facial expression hinted that he did not want to drop them but was under pressure from his father to do so. As the bishop had said, "I only got a haircut. Look what Jesus went through. He was beaten up and died hanging on a cross. But he never fought back."[2] As his forebears had done, the bishop had preached the message of Jesus—the supreme example of nonresistant faith—throughout his life. If he wanted to follow in the steps of Jesus, he felt he had no choice. He could not fight back, could not press charges. Although most Amish people will cooperate with law enforcement, they are loath to press charges. Those in more progressive groups may be willing to do so but even then only at the urging of the police.

Andy mentioned that several senior bishops had arrived to meet with his dad. So later that morning around the kitchen table in Andy's farmhouse, the bishops, the Hershbergers, Detective Mullet, and Sheriff Zimmerly discussed what to do. They spoke in Dutch, and the women, listening from the adjoining living room, occasionally stood in the doorway to hear better. Eventually, Bishop Hershberger repeated his words about Jesus not protesting when he was tortured. Detective Mullet reminded the bishop, "The only way we can help you is if you help us. If somebody else gets hurt down the road, what will you do? Now they're just cutting hair but what they do next might be even worse. We don't want this case to fall apart now."[3]

These words—which carried special weight for Bishop Hershberger because they were spoken in Dutch by an officer born into his own faith—were pivotal in the discussion. Fortunately for the detective and the sheriff, they had met periodically with the bishops sitting around the kitchen table to discuss various issues involving the Amish and the sheriff's office. Thus, on that Wednesday morning in the Hershberger kitchen, Mullet and Zimmerly had credibility—they knew the bishops around the table and the bishops trusted them. The officers were tapping the reservoir of social capital they had gradually accumulated over the years.

As the conversation drifted toward an end, the bishops unanimously agreed that it would be okay for Andy and Levi to sign the statements "so that no one else gets hurt by the Bergholz people." As the detective and sheriff stood to leave, Bishop Hershberger and his preacher son, Andy, told them, "We'll stand behind you." They had agreed to hold the perpetrators accountable for their acts and to protect potential victims, while still grappling with their community's age-old ethical quandary of how to respond to violence with love.

After agonizing over their moral predicament, the Amish leaders agreed to press charges, not to get revenge against Sam Mullet and the Bergholz Gmay, but "so other people don't get hurt in future attacks." Bishop Myron Miller, following his attack the previous night in Carroll County, had arrived at the same decision.

Reflecting on Raymond Hershberger's struggle sometime later, Detective Mullet mused that "one reason the Hershbergers had agreed to press charges was because all the pieces of the puzzle seemed to be fitting together."[4] An Amish-born detective was nearby and available to take the 911 "jump call" when all other officers were busy. The detective could speak Dutch. The bishops arrived the next morning when the officers were there. And Detective Mullet already had a relationship with the bishops. The emerging plot, in the eyes of the Amish, pointed to a providential plan, implying that they had received a blessing from high in the heavens.

Later Wednesday afternoon Detective Mullet and Sheriff Zimmerly met with the Holmes County prosecutor, Steve Knowling, to discuss next steps. At first, the prosecutor was reluctant to press charges because he was not persuaded the case was significant enough to pursue. Eventually, he agreed to proceed, hoping the prosecution might stop the perpetrators. Prosecutor Knowling filed charges against the four assailants identified by the driver the night before and obtained warrants for their arrests. They were charged with first-degree felonies (the highest in the Ohio criminal code) for kidnapping and burglary. The kidnapping charge applies when someone is restrained and the burglary charge pertains to entering a property by force or deception.

The prosecutor filed the charges, and by 4:00 p.m. that day, the arrest warrants were available with a $50,000 cash bond. The Holmes County officials informed Jefferson County Sheriff Abdalla, who served the warrants straightaway, arrested the four men (Levi F. Miller, Lester Mullet, Johnny Mullet, and Lester Miller), and transported them to the Jefferson County jail in Steubenville that evening. Detective Mullet and three other officers from Holmes County once again drove the ninety-five miles back to Jefferson County to interview the detainees in prison that night.

During the interviews, they discovered a case of mistaken identity: Lester Miller was not in the cab of the truck and did not participate in the attacks. Miller explained, "I was in the trailer but I didn't help with the attack. But I did go to Trumbull County (September 6) and participate in that attack."[5] Later that night he was released. When the interrogations were finished, the detectives verified that the five men riding in the truck were the two preachers (Johnny Mullet and Levi F. Miller) and Danny Mullet, Eli Miller, and Lester Mullet. Prosecutor Knowling then issued arrest warrants for Eli Miller and Danny Mullet.

To their surprise, the investigators discovered during the interviews that Levi F. Miller, Johnny Mullet, and Lester Miller seemingly had no remorse. In fact, they described with satisfaction their successful forays into Holmes County and Carroll County and boasted that they were stronger than the victims and were able to hold them down—a condition that met the legal description of kidnapping. Johnny Mullet was "proud and defiant about what he had done."[6] However, Bishop Mullet's twenty-six-year-old son, Lester Mullet, was sobbing and very sorry.

Late that evening Detective Mullet and Sheriff Zimmerly made the two-hour trek back to Holmes County, concluding a twenty-four-hour nonstop investigation.

Ready to Cut More Beards

The two preachers—Johnny Mullet and Levi F. Miller—as well as Johnny's younger brother Lester were held in the Jefferson County jail in Steubenville from October 5 to 11. During that time, they made several calls back to Bergholz. When prisoners place outgoing calls, they hear a message that the call will be recorded. All of the conversations between the men and the people in Bergholz were in Pennsylvania Dutch.[7] Detective Mullet, who translated the calls, learned that in one conversation a prisoner, referring to him, said, "That Amish guy here is an [expletive]!"

In one call, Johnny Mullet said, "They are trying to get me to admit it was Grandpa's [Bishop Mullet's] idea to do this." Asked if he admitted to that, Johnny replied, "No, I stuck to my story that it was all me." Bishop Mullet, also on the line, noted that the newspapers said that cutting hair is a "religious degrading and they [law enforcement] are not allowed to do anything about it." In response to comments about getting most of the victim's hair, Johnny exclaimed, "Good!" and laughed.

Bishop Mullet then asked Preacher Levi F. Miller, "Did they wear you down?" Miller answered, "Yes," and noted that the officer had asked him about his stay in the chicken house—one of the so-called Amish jails. Sam Mullet replied, "Watch what you say, [because] you were in the chicken house and chicken shit for a long time." Preacher Miller replied, "Well, they asked me about that. I studied for a little bit and then I told him I was in for about twelve days. He [investigator] does not know that I was in before. I only told him that I was in once. I hope he don't find out I was in there multiple times." Miller then pondered, "How do they find this stuff out? I want you to know he [Detective Mullet] is one smart man. He don't forget nothing."

On one of the calls, Lester Mullet pleaded, "I want to tell them I'm sorry I did this." A woman on the line from Bergholz said, "Bullshit that you are sorry." Lester sobbed, "Yes, I am sorry, I don't believe in it [cutting beards]. Bishop Mullet replied, "You better wake up, kid. The heck with being sorry. I will get you out of there, don't worry." Lester then confessed that he told the investigators by mistake that they [the attackers] had a camera. Sam retorted, "Well, they won't get ahold of the camera cause Eli is going to tell them he threw it away, cause we are keeping it here."

The bishop then admonished his son: "They are telling you that to break you. Holy shit, Les, you can take more than that. They are just trying to get you to talk, so they can get me and then they can tear this [conspiracy] apart, that's what they're after. Those things they are telling you are not that bad, they are just making it sound bad. . . . You can take more than that. I know it is rough. You've been in there for a while. I know it's not funny. They are doing this so you break down." Sam then encouraged Lester to "stay strong," telling him, "We're going to bull our way through this thing."

In several of the phone calls, Bishop Mullet informed the jailed men of future plans, in words to this effect: "Ray and the men are ready to go again [cut more beards]. . . . The men are ready to go again and do it tonight. . . . By the time we're done, there will be a lot more [beards] taken off." Clearly, the clan was not deterred by the arrests and a little jail time for three of their comrades.

A Halloween Prank

After spending six days in the Jefferson County jail, Johnny and Lester Mullet and Levi F. Miller were brought to the Holmes County jail overnight for arraignment. The next day, Wednesday, October 12, Eli Miller and Daniel Mullet were escorted from Bergholz to Holmes County and all five were arraigned there. Bishop Sam Mullet accompanied Eli and Daniel to the arraignment. Their driver asked Sheriff Zimmerly to explain everything to him and said he would inform the bishop. The sheriff refused and interviewed Sam Mullet himself. After assuring the sheriff that the attacks would end, the bishop paid $250,000 in bond—$50,000 for each defendant—either in cash or a lien against his property. Following the arraignment, the five defendants were released on bond to return to Bergholz for some temporary freedom.[8]

With all the defendants now free on bail, the anxiety in Amish country spiked higher than ever. The Jefferson County and the Holmes County sheriff's departments received a growing number of calls from Amish people about safety. Those with any cause to fret were locking their doors and taking various precautions. Some jittery men and women called to ask where they could buy pepper spray and were told it was sold at True Value hardware stores. The police also received many tips from relatives, neighbors, and non-Amish people with connections to Bergholz, who reported allegations of various types of abuse there.[9]

The angst persisted through October. A Halloween prank in Holmes County almost turned violent. A group of youth from a more progressive, car-driving Beachy Amish church played a prank on one of their friends in a traditional horse-and-buggy-driving Amish family. The Beachy Amish arrived at their friend's home one night pretending to be from Bergholz. The Amish family, not realizing it was a prank, called 911, and the Holmes County officers responded to what they assumed was another Bergholz attack. One of the unarmed pranksters, who initially refused to obey police orders, was nearly shot by an officer.[10]

A Federal Overreach?

During the week of October 11, the FBI received a call from the Holmes County Sheriff's Office. After several calls back and forth, the FBI also spoke with law enforcement officers in Carroll County regarding the assault on Bishop Myron Miller. On October 19, police and prosecutors from Carroll and Holmes Counties and representatives of the FBI and the US Department of Justice met in Holmes County to determine whether any federal laws had been violated.[11] Were the attacks in fact motivated by religion?

Some observers were surprised that the federal government might become involved in what at first glance looked like a petty intramural Amish quarrel. Was it really worth spending federal resources to investigate a simple Amish spat? Why not let county officials conduct their own prosecutions?

The case was quite complicated because the victims and attacks involved five counties (Ashland, Ashtabula, Carroll, Holmes, and Jefferson), and without FBI assistance, it would have been more difficult to bring charges against Bishop Mullet. The Holmes County prosecutor could charge the five men who rode in the pickup truck during the attacks that took place in his jurisdiction and possibly put them behind bars for seven to ten years, but he could not charge Bishop Mullet. Federal authorities, however, *could* prosecute Mullet and could also request longer prison terms for the other defendants.

Unlike local prosecutors, federal attorneys could use quotes Sam Mullet made to television reporters explaining that the beard cuttings were all about religion. Both federal and county prosecutors could compel uncooperative witnesses to appear before a grand jury, but if Holmes County had convened a grand jury and subpoenaed Amish witnesses, "it would've been a political nightmare with the Amish and they would never cooperate again in any of our law enforcement efforts," said one Holmes County officer.[12] Holmes County Sheriff Zimmerly requested federal assistance because it was a multicounty problem. Furthermore, Ohio's assistant attorney general certified the state's request for the federal government to assume jurisdiction of the case to secure substantial justice.[13]

As a result of their consultation on October 19, federal justice officials, in cooperation with local and regional law enforcement, agreed to prosecute all of the attacks in a single case, citing these reasons:[14]

- The initial arrests and imprisonment of several perpetrators after the October 4 beard cuttings in Holmes County did not stop the attacks. In fact, the recorded prison conversations revealed that future attacks were very likely.
- Because the perpetrators and the victims lived in five different counties, separate prosecutions in different counties and judicial districts were not economical or efficient. In short, the case was too big, too complex, and too costly; it would severely burden smaller counties.
- Separate local prosecutions of specific attacks would minimize the full extent and magnitude of the malicious behavior and the harm done to the victims.
- County courts would handle the cases in disparate ways, resulting in unequal treatment of defendants and uneven punishment of convicted offenders.
- Federal officials, partnering with county officials, could deal with *all* the attacks, locations, offenders, witnesses, victims, and evidence in a single prosecution.
- A federal prosecution would avoid the complexity of having witnesses testify multiple times and eliminate any custody issues involving the passing of evidence from one district court to another.
- Early in the investigation, it was difficult to determine whether the attacks were random events or whether all of them were driven by an ideologically motivated conspiracy.
- Federal legal statues related to hate crimes, if applied to some of the attacks, would transform them from simple assaults into more serious charges, resulting in more severe sentencing options.
- Federal courts would provide greater and more uniform post-conviction and post-incarceration control over offenders.
- A coordinated and uniform federal approach would offer deference to Amish sensitivities for testifying and better protect them from additional harm.

- Finally, the federal government had greater power to convene a grand jury and subpoena witnesses who might otherwise be unwilling to testify.

Collaboration between local authorities and the FBI is not always smooth. Detective Mullet noted, however, that he had never seen "such goodwill between different agencies" as he did in this case: "The cooperation between local and federal authorities was excellent."[15]

"We're the FBI"

The FBI officially opened the Bergholz case on October 24, 2011, and agents began interviewing knowledgeable people. In bold defiance of law enforcement and a breach of Bishop Mullet's promise to Sheriff Zimmerly that the attacks would end, they did not. Melvin Shrock was lured to Bergholz and ambushed on November 9. This event spurred on the prosecution and bumped the beard case to the top of the FBI's priorities in northern Ohio. Federal agents and prosecutors prepared an affidavit to issue criminal complaints, and search and arrest warrants were authorized by a judge.

In cooperation with some former Bergholz members and other people, the FBI gathered information on the location of properties and their interior layouts, including a floor plan of Sam Mullet's house. After consulting with informants, the FBI decided to enter Bergholz and arrest seven people and search five different locations for evidence on November 23, 2011, the day before Thanksgiving. This date ensured that the targets of the arrest would likely be in Bergholz, and the weekend afforded time to process those arrested. On November 22, a judge signed arrest warrants for seven people, including Bishop Sam Mullet, and search warrants for five of his properties.

At 5:00 a.m. Wednesday morning, seventy to eighty law enforcement officers from the FBI and county sheriff's offices met for a briefing at the Bergholz Volunteer Fire Company, three miles west of the Amish community. Emergency medical personnel and victim assistance specialists were also on hand. Organized into several teams, the officers were prepared to conduct simultaneous arrests and searches. Each team met to discuss its plan. The operation required so many officers, explained the lead FBI agent, Mike Sirohman, because "at each arrest we like to have eight to ten law enforcement personnel. . . . We want to have enough personnel so that we can control the situation because we never know what we will encounter."[16]

When the tactical forces drove into the Bergholz settlement at 6:00 a.m. that Wednesday morning, "it was very dark. . . . There were no lights on inside or outside the houses." According to Agent Sirohman, "We make it clear that we are from law enforcement. We wear markings, whether it's a jacket or a vest and we also have police cruisers turn on their lights . . . so there's no question as to who's there. . . . We announce, 'We're the FBI' or 'It's the police,' or both."[17]

When no one answered their knock on the front porch door of Sam Mullet's house, the officers entered the large enclosed porch and then opened the unlocked door to the kitchen, announcing again and again, "We're the FBI."[18] At Sam's first-floor bedroom, which was locked, they repeated, "We're the FBI," as they knocked on the door. A voice from the bedroom said, "I'm getting dressed," or something to that effect. A few minutes later the bishop emerged from the bedroom followed by twenty-eight-year-old Lovina Miller, wife of Eli Miller, a nephew of the bishop. (Lovina and Eli had participated in the first attack on September 6 in Trumbull County.) Two of Sam's daughters, who had been sleeping upstairs, came down, and one of them lit a gas lamp so the officers could see as they handcuffed the bishop and interviewed him. At first, the women refused to speak with the agents, but when Sam permitted them to cooperate, they did.

Bishop Mullet was notified of his rights and signed the advice of rights at about 6:40 a.m. The agents interviewed him, and, according to one of them, his demeanor "was very friendly, very charming. He was easy to talk to." Later, he was charged with lying to the FBI because of some of his answers to the agents' questions that morning.[19] In Bishop Mullet's residence, the officers found drafts of contracts for gas and oil leases for his large landholdings, and in a search of his barn, the agents discovered a scissors and clippers as well as a small quantity of marijuana seeds and some cocaine.[20]

In addition to Bishop Mullet, six other people were arrested that morning: Eli Miller, Anna Miller, Lester Miller, Danny Mullet, Johnny Mullet, and Emanuel Shrock. At the Shrock residence, the officers entered the kitchen announcing their presence. Emanuel opened the door of a room, and a minute or so later, came out with a small child but then suddenly turned and ran back into the room, closed the door, and refused to come out as ordered. Considering it a barricade situation, the agents called in a supervisor and Sheriff Abdalla. The sheriff opened the door, entered the room, and asked Shrock to release the child and come out. Emanuel complied, diffusing the tense situation.[21]

A few days after Eli Miller was arrested, he realized that the small disposable camera he had purchased at the beginning of the attacks was still at the Shrock residence, where he had been living. Worried that the FBI would find it if they searched the house, he called Emanuel's wife, Linda, and asked her to remove it. She elicited the help of her son Daniel, one of Sam's grandsons, and he found the camera containing the undeveloped film in a bureau drawer. Daniel gave it to his cousin Johnny Mast during deer season in early December, telling him to "either hide it or get rid of it."[22] Johnny took it with him into the woods, sealed it in two plastic bags, covered it with leaves, and placed it beside a tree, which he marked.[23] They decided not to destroy the camera, Daniel said, "because we wanted to look at the pictures later."[24]

The prosecutors had assumed that the camera, which had been used during three of the attacks, was destroyed. Later in the investigation, the prosecutors learned that the camera had been hidden, not destroyed. When they retrieved it, they expected poor-quality photos, given that they were taken by amateur photographers in dimly lit Amish homes at night. Surprisingly, the photos were good enough to provide compelling evidence at the trial.[25]

A First Amendment Firewall?

The November arrests at Bergholz triggered a series of legal events over the next nine months that ended in a trial by jury in the federal courthouse in Cleveland. Within a week of the arrests, a preliminary examination and detention hearing was held. The government then convened a grand jury, which heard evidence and returned an indictment several days before Christmas. The indictment officially charged the defendants with crimes and opened the door to proceed with a trial. Meanwhile, although the lead defendants were behind bars and the threat of attacks was waning, Marty and Barb Miller woke up on December 8 to find a sign in their yard announcing, "IT'S NOT OVER." The culprits were never found, and the Millers did not receive other threats or attacks.[26]

The grand jury added additional charges in a superseding indictment on March 28, 2012. The government built its case around the Matthew Shepard and James Byrd, Jr., Hate Crimes Prevention Act (Shepard-Byrd Act) enacted by the US Congress in 2009.[27] The attorneys for the defendants filed motions to dismiss the charges, contending that they were unconstitutional because the First Amendment protected the defendants' right to freely exercise their religious beliefs. The prosecutors pushed back, arguing that the hate crimes statute specifically prohibits "all religiously-motivated violence, regardless of whether the perpetrators and victims are members of different religions, the same religion, or no religion at all." Moreover, they asserted that the Shepard-Byrd Act targets and criminalizes violent behavior, which the First Amendment does not shield.

In short, Shepard-Byrd does not regulate religious speech or expression. What it does is criminalize violent conduct motivated by religion. Thus, the First Amendment does not protect any violence, even if it is driven by religious motives.[28] In other words, the First Amendment safeguards one's right to hold and practice sincere religious beliefs, but it does not protect religious-driven violence toward anyone inside or outside that religion. In his May 31, 2012, order denying the defendants' motion, Judge

Dan Polster agreed with the prosecutors, thereby leaving the government's case intact.[29] One Amish man opined that some people at Bergholz "always thought God stood between Sam and the police." With these developments, God had vanished from that spot, at least temporarily.[30]

There was some good news for the defendants during their long wait behind bars. In the spring of 2012, Bishop Mullet received the first payment of a $3.5 million contract from gas and oil leases on his land. This windfall was made possible by the new hydraulic fracking technology used to access deep gas and oil reserves. Amish landowners in Ohio and elsewhere have long been permitted to have small wells on their land for tapping oil near the surface. With the advent of fracking, numerous Amish property owners signed lucrative leases for access to deep gas reservoirs on their land. The fracking technology arrived just in time to provide financing for the legal defense and for the daily operations of the Bergholz community while their leaders were in prison.[31]

Several new legal issues emerged during the summer of 2012, including a defense motion to ban the word *cult* from the trial because of its potential to bias the jurors' judgment. Although Judge Polster supported that request, he rejected another defense motion when he allowed a witness to describe her intimate relationship with Bishop Mullet to illustrate the span of his influence over the Bergholz community.

As both legal teams prepped for the trial, they considered possible plea agreements for the defendants, who now numbered sixteen.[32] On Monday, July 29, all sixteen defendants were offered plea bargains that would have given most of them short prison terms and possibly granted probation to others.[33] One by one, Judge Polster looked them in the eye and told them it was their decision and their decision alone. He asked the defendants how many children they had and their ages, and he carefully explained the risk of long prison terms if the case went to trial.[34]

One of the lead defendants insisted that the devil was behind the proposed offers, and he urged his comrades not to bargain with the devil.[35] In the end, all rejected the plea bargains. To plead guilty would have contradicted their deeply held conviction that what they had done was right and their confidence that their version of the truth would prevail.

According to his defense counsel, Bishop Mullet, for reasons unknown, offered "to cut his [own] beard." He made the offer several times, "even though he didn't do any [criminal act]." His offer was never accepted.[36]

In an August 2012 letter from prison, Preacher Johnny Mullet wrote, "We never know how it will turn out if we go to trial. But looks to me like it [the case] will get throwed [sic] out yet. Our lawyers have been after us quite a few times already to take a plea, but I can't see taking a plea as if we do, it would dissolve the reason we did what we did. That is why the government is after us to take a plea. That way everything would settle back down again but still we wouldn't have justice. I know God will do the justice part, but we also have to do our part." Turning to the Old Book for support, Johnny continued, "If Noah wouldn't have got up and build [sic] the ark, he would have drowned with everyone else. I know what we did was something that's unheard of but then what were we supposed to do? We also know that what they [the three hundred elders] did by taking those out of excommunication wasn't right."[37] In this letter, Johnny suggests that revenge—not genuine concern about saving wayward Amish from drowning in a sea of disobedience—seemed to be a primary motive for the attacks.

In retrospect, one of the prosecutors who observed the almost robotic rejection of the plea bargains reflected that it may have been wiser to have each defendant consider a plea bargain privately before the judge, rather than to have all of them in the courtroom at the same time under the watchful eye of Bishop Mullet.[38]

Not one to flee adversity, Johnny Mullet, who had already served nearly nine months behind bars, was ready to extend his stint in prison for the sake of the truth. "So we're going to go to trial and if we get convicted then we'll just go to jail. We've been through too much already and we know what we know. . . . So why do we want to change what we learned and go somewhere

else or do something different? And I know all the other families feel the same way. So all we can do is keep going and do
what we know is right and hope for the best."[39]

The defendants' hopes for the best were about to be tested
on the anvil of justice by the evidence surrounding the attacks,
the testimony of witnesses, and the judgment of twelve jurors in
a three-week trial.

From left, Johnny Mullet, Lester Mullet, Daniel Mullet, Levi F. Miller, and Eli Miller in the Holmes County Municipal Court, Oct. 19, 2011. (AP Photo / *The Daily Record*, Mike Schenck, File)

SIX

THE TRIAL

Brazen and Malicious

It was Monday afternoon, and I was the next to last of twenty-six witnesses at the trial in the Cleveland federal courthouse, which stretched from August 28 to September 20, 2012.[1] As an expert witness for the government, I was there to answer questions about Amish history, social practices, and religious beliefs posed by lawyers on both sides.[2] Following my testimony, Bishop Raymond Hershberger, one of the victims, was the last witness to take the stand before the jury began its work.

With a nod to the First Amendment, the prosecutors told the jury that the defendants had openly defied "the principle that every person in America has the right to practice their religion as they see fit" without fear of assault. The defendants, in the words of the government lawyers, were "brazen" because they ambushed their victims—invading three homes in the dead of night to attack them and luring others to visit Bergholz on the false promise of safety, only to greet them with vengeance. Moreover, the defendants were "malicious," according to the prosecutors. They struck their victims "in the most offensive possible way, by desecrating a sacred symbol of their Amish faith, their beards and head hair." Every one of these assaults, the prosecutors asserted, took a whack at "a symbol of the Amish faith," the beards and head hair of the victims, which symbolized their commitment to God.[3]

I peered over a large audience from my perch on the elevated witness stand at the left side of the front of the courtroom. To my left, Judge Daniel Aaron Polster sat at a raised desk behind the judicial bench. In addition to his fourteen years of judicial experience, his knowledge of religious traditions (including the wearing of beards), informed by his Jewish heritage, gave him keen insight into the Amish case.[4] At a desk immediately in front of him, court stenographers dutifully keystroked every word. On my right, twelve jurors and three alternates sat in two rows.[5] They had already absorbed hundreds of details about the case from two dozen witnesses and numerous exhibits of evidence.

On the floor of the courtroom, thirty-two people were clustered at several tables—sixteen plain-dressed Amish defendants and sixteen defense attorneys, one for each client. About twenty feet in front of me was a podium where the attorneys from both sides stood to address Judge Polster and the "ladies and gentlemen" of the jury and to interrogate witnesses like me. In the back third of the courtroom, several rows of benches, divided by an aisle, provided seating for about sixty observers. This public area was primarily filled with Amish people, both supporters and critics of the defendants. A delegation from Bergholz observed the proceedings every day. The judge, jurors, and all the defendants and their attorneys had monitors on their tables to view the images and documents presented as evidence. Large monitors were also available in the public area for the observers.

A Legal Maze

The case was very complex because it involved sixteen trials wrapped into one. The prosecution, at least, considered it one trial of sixteen defendants, although some of the defense attorneys viewed it as sixteen separate trials, and one defense attorney argued that it was actually four trials, one for each day of the attacks. Regardless, it was complicated. There were not only ninety different legal charges, twenty attorneys, nine victims, five attacks on four different days but also sixteen defendants with overlapping names: four Mullets, nine Millers, two Shrocks,

Table 1. The Ten General Counts

Count 1	Conspiring with others to commit a crime
Counts 2–6	Assaulting a victim (that causes bodily injury) because of their religion
	2. The attack on Marty and Barbara Miller in their home, Sept. 6
	3. The attack on David Wengerd in Bergholz, Sept. 24
	4. The attack on Bishop Raymond Hershberger (and family) in his home, Oct. 4
	5. The attack on Bishop Myron Miller in his home, Oct. 4
	6. The attack on Melvin and Anna Shrock in Bergholz, Nov. 9
Counts 7–9	Obstructing justice
	7. Directing that a bag of hair be destroyed
	8. Hiding a camera with pictures of the assaults
	9. Concealing the shears used in the assaults
Count 10	Lying to the FBI

and one Burkholder. Moreover, four married couples were among the defendants (Emanuel and Linda Shrock, Lovina and Eli Miller, Lester and Elizabeth Miller, Raymond and Kathryn Miller).

All of these factors created a legal web that one defense attorney called a "litigation minefield."[6] To reduce any confusion that could entangle the jurors and possibly invite error into their verdicts, the prosecution provided spiral notepads and a three-ring binder for each juror with a section on each defendant that included the person's name, a color photo, the charges against him or her, and blank pages for note taking.

The government brought four major charges pertinent to the different defendants and the attacks, as shown in table 1.[7] The general counts included (1) *conspiracy*—knowingly and willfully planning and agreeing with others to commit a crime; (2) engaging in *assaults* motivated by religion that caused bodily injury (hate crimes); (3) *obstructing justice*—altering, concealing, or destroying any tangible object to impede the investigation; and (4) *lying* to the FBI.

Table 2. Mullet Trial Indictments

Defendant	Counts	Relationship to Sam Mullet
Samuel Mullet	1–8, 10	
Johnny S. Mullet	1, 4, 5	Son
Danny S. Mullet	1, 4, 5	Son
Lester S. Mullet	1, 4, 5, 8	Son
Levi F. Miller	1, 3, 4, 5, 8	None
Eli M. Miller	1, 2, 3, 4, 5, 8	Nephew
Lester Miller	1, 2, 4, 5, 9	Nephew
Raymond Miller	1, 2	Nephew
Anna Miller	1, 2	Married to nephew
Lovina Miller	1, 2	Married to nephew
Kathryn Miller	1, 2	Married to nephew
Emma Miller	1, 2	Married to nephew
Elizabeth Miller	1, 2	Married to nephew
Emanuel Shrock	1, 3, 6	Son-in-law
Linda Shrock	1, 6	Daughter
Freeman Burkholder	1, 2	Married to niece

The assault charges were governed by the Shepard-Byrd Act and were the most complicated and challenging charges to prove.[8] To persuade the jury to convict the defendants of the assault charges, the federal attorneys had to prove three elements beyond a reasonable doubt: (1) that the defendants acted willfully to cause bodily injury, (2) that the attacks were motivated by the actual or perceived religion of the victim, and (3) that the defendants used some instrumentality of interstate commerce—traveling in vehicles, using the US Postal Service, or using tools or weapons that had crossed state lines.

Eight defendants faced only two of the ten counts, while Sam Mullet had nine directed at him, including lying to the FBI. All were charged with conspiracy. (See table 2 for a listing of the defendants and the counts against each.)

It's All about Religion

In their opening statement to the jury, the prosecutors reviewed the attacks and the reactions of some of the victims, including the words of seventy-seven-year-old Bishop Hershberger, who sobbed shortly after his attack that "I'd rather have them beat me black and blue than take my hair."[9] The government's lawyers argued that the Bergholz barbers attacked their victims because of how they were practicing their Amish faith. The prosecutors seized on Sam Mullet's own words, "It's all religion," a statement he made on camera to a journalist to explain the beard attacks in 2011.[10] For Sam, those three words implied protection under the First Amendment for the defendants, who were "practicing" their religion. The words stretched a religious canopy over all aspects of the attacks, including the motivation that spurred them. His statement was also code for reporters and law enforcers alike to "stay out of my business."

Pressing on, the prosecutors argued that "in the Amish faith, a man's beard and a woman's hair are considered sacred religious symbols. . . . It is their outward symbol to the rest of the world that God is present in their lives." And they borrowed the words of a defendant, Lester Miller, to hammer home the point that "the beard and the hair are symbols of Amish righteousness." The prosecutors told the jurors that they would see evidence that the attack on Bishop Hershberger was revenge for his signature on the statement endorsed by the throng of Amish leaders at Ulysses five years earlier. All of the attacks, the prosecutors claimed, were aimed at "Amish hypocrites," Amish people living outside of Bergholz whom the defendants considered lax and wayward in their faith.

Speaking directly to the jury, Assistant US Attorney Bridget Brennan said, "I want you to listen to the victims as they tell you how these people attacked them. I want you to listen to their community members tell you what they did to these victims and how and why it was about religion, because of the victim's religion. I want you to listen to their own admissions. And I want you to listen for Sam's words, 'We know what we did and why we did it. This is all about religion.'" In conclusion, Brennan explained that the defendants were "on trial for physically attacking people because of religion, obstructing the investigation, and lying about it. That is what this trial is about."

The sixteen defense attorneys took their turns making opening statements on behalf of their clients. Assistant Federal Public Defender Ed Bryan, the lead defense attorney who represented Bishop Mullet, presented a long summary argument.[11] The defense did not challenge the factual evidence related to the beard attacks. Indeed, they said, "There is little difference between how we view the facts and how the government views the facts. The difference is what is the motive or intent of the heart." Numerous attorneys articulated similar ideas again and again: Their clients were "motivated by compassion" for other Amish people who had strayed "from the true Amish path," and the beard cuttings were "purely symbolic," a "shaming" to warn, discipline, and reform the wayward souls.

A consistent theme from the defense was that three of the attacks (the two deceptions in Bergholz and the nighttime attack on Marty and Barb Miller) were not spurred by religion. They were just flare-ups in family feuds, with relatives reprimanding one another. The beard cuttings, in short, were nothing more than a fight among kin. The defense argued that the attacks were independent events, not the result of a conspiracy, and that Bishop Mullet never participated in, ordered, or coordinated any of them. Attorney Bryan admonished the jury *not* to take the evidence and "tie it all up into a little package with a little bow that the government is trying to present, but look at it in the manner in which it truly happened and apply the law. . . . Apply the law to the facts in this case."

Shears, Photos, Recordings, and Pain

Prosecutors provided various forms of evidence to the jury: recorded jailhouse calls back to Bergholz, the battery-powered clippers and the shears used in the attacks, and other pertinent physical items such as sales receipts. The most surprising evidence was the photographs of some of the attacks taken by the Bergholz barbers themselves. Since Sam Mullet did not directly participate in the cuttings, the pictures were taken to provide him and other community members with before-and-after shots of the victims as well as images of the actual hair cuttings.

The prosecution called twenty-six witnesses to testify and confirm evidence. They included seven victims, seven law enforcement officers, three taxi drivers, three of Sam and Martha's grandsons, two of their children, one daughter-in-law, and one niece, as well as the salesman who sold the horse mane shears used in the cuttings. Some witnesses were subpoenaed to testify. All except Sam Mullet's daughter-in-law, Nancy Mullet, and me were directly involved in activities related to one or more of the assaults. None of the defendants took the witness stand, nor did the defense present any expert witnesses to testify on their behalf.

For the witnesses who had relatives in the Bergholz community, testifying was an excruciating emotional ordeal. After six years of painful separation from her family, Barb Miller took the witness stand to testify for the prosecution against her brother (Sam Mullet), three of her sons (Lester, Eli, and Raymond), and her five daughters-in-law (Anna, Emma, Lovina, Kathryn, and Elizabeth)—all of whom carefully watched her as they sat with their attorneys in the courtroom. The pain of a mother's heart, already broken many times, was poured out in public. There she stood, called to tell the truth as she knew it, as the stenographers listened and recorded every word in the public record forever. "It was," she said, "the worst thing I have ever done."[12]

Nancy (Miller) Burkholder, daughter of Barb, was compelled by law to testify. Still living in Bergholz, she was married to one of the defendants, Freeman Burkholder. Standing at the front of the courtroom, she answered questions from the prosecution that could incriminate her husband and her uncle Sam, as well as her three brothers, five sisters-in-law, and the other defendants, all of whom, with the exception of Preacher Levi F. Miller, were her relatives.[13]

Nancy Mullet, married to Sam's son Eli, was now living with him far from Bergholz. She stood and spoke, over strident objections from the defense. At the request of the prosecutors, the court permitted her testimony to illustrate Bishop Mullet's "control over the members of his community." Nancy testified about her father-in-law's sexual intimacies with her. In Amish communities, the three-letter word *sex* is taboo, only spoken in the bedroom (if even there), yet here she was, speaking about it in public. Although Nancy spoke truthfully, her words seemed laced with shame.[14]

Anna Shrock, wife of Melvin (who died in January 2012), was called to testify. Fully aware that her words could impact the jury's view of her son Emanuel sitting in front of her, Anna described her visit to Bergholz when Emanuel and two of his sons attacked her and Melvin and cut his beard while Emanuel's wife, Linda, held her, covering her mouth so she couldn't scream for help.[15] At the sentencing several months later, Judge Polster recalled, "For as long as I live I won't forget the haunting testimony of Ms. Anna Shrock. . . . She was stooped, she was frail, she was crestfallen, and I think she was my age. She looked a heck of a lot older, and I think I would have probably looked like that if I had gone through what she did. She described how her children and grandsons attacked her and her very ill husband and what it was like."[16]

And then Anna's grandson, nineteen-year-old Melvin Shrock, who was never baptized into the church, walked up to the podium. He had recently left the Bergholz community because "I was tired of it," he said. Melvin knew the intimate details of the daily routines of the Bergholz clan because he, with two of his cousins and a brother, had lived in the upstairs apartment of the shop attached to Sam's barn. He recalled numerous conversations in which various members of the clan planned the attacks, and he rode in the livestock trailer during the late-night attacks at the homes of two bishops. His testimony would help to incarcerate his father, Emanuel, and his maternal grandfather, Sam.[17]

The list of agonizing testimonies went on. Two of Sam's adult children, thirty-two-year-old Christ Mullet and twenty-five-year-old Barbara Yoder, both still living in Bergholz, also took their turns at the witness stand.[18] Gazing out at the sea of defendants and the Bergholz delegation in the back, they saw their kin, their neighbors, the very people they had lived, worked, and worshiped with for many years—all sitting a few yards from the witness stand, listening as they spoke words that could incriminate those they dearly loved.

Daniel Shrock, son of Emanuel and grandson of Bishop Sam Mullet, explained how he had helped in two of the clippings by restraining his grandfather, Melvin Shrock, and David Wengerd when those men were lured into a Bergholz ambush on separate occasions. Daniel also rode in the horse trailer during the two late-night attacks on October 4. He provided an eyewitness account of four attacks, which helped to convict his father, grandfather, and many of his relatives.[19]

Twenty-two-year-old Johnny Mast, whose mother, Mary, was a daughter of Bishop Mullet, also spoke. Johnny, also one of the "shop boys" who lived across the gravel road from his grandfather's house, had witnessed some of the attacks, hidden the camera in the forest, and observed the beard cuttings and paddlings during the Winter of Lament. He also described how he and about a dozen other men listened to the phone conversation when Levi F. Miller invited David Wengerd to the ambush in Bergholz. And he recalled hearing a loud noise, "like a mad bull," as he sat in the darkness inside the trailer during the attack on Bishop Myron Miller. His nearly five hours of testimony provided firsthand accounts of activities that would eventually incriminate members of his family—sitting just twenty feet from him as he spoke.[20]

The pain and pathos were palpable as the search for justice required blood relatives under oath to tell the truth as they remembered it. One by one they testified: mother against daughter, son against father, grandson against father and grandfather, and cousin against cousin, not out of malice, but out of duty, voluntarily or in some cases compelled by law to speak the truth with candor. Surely, some defendants must have lamented tossing aside the generous plea bargains offered only weeks earlier, deals that would have saved them from this shame and humiliation.

Five Hours of Testimony

I was spared the emotional anxiety of having any relatives or even close friends in the courtroom during my five-hour testimony, which straddled two days.[21] For the first two hours of direct examination, I answered questions from Assistant US Attorney

Thomas Getz, one of the prosecutors. I gave a short explanation of Amish history and described some of the practices of different Amish groups. I then explained the significance of the September 2006 decision by the three hundred Amish leaders to nullify Sam Mullet's excommunications. In my view, I said, he was a lone ranger bishop who had never developed close fraternal ties with other Amish congregations, thus weakening the checks and balances on his leadership.

In reiterating Amish beliefs, I cited the Dordrecht Confession of Faith, especially Article 14, which categorically rejects revenge. I also quoted a phrase from "Rules of a Godly Life," an Amish devotional guide that reads, "We should do no harm to anyone in any way." In summary, I noted that, at the core of their faith, Amish people "reject revenge, reject force, reject any coercive activities."[22]

At the request of the defense, the judge had barred the prosecution from calling the Bergholz community a cult during the trial, unless that label was introduced by the defense, which inadvertently happened prior to my testimony. Thus, Prosecutor Getz, quoting the words of a defense attorney, asked if I agreed that a cult could be defined as "bizarre and abnormal."

Without labeling Bergholz a cult, I listed a number of "red flags" sometimes associated with cults from a sociological perspective.[23] I left it to the jury to determine whether any of the flags I mentioned—an autocratic leader with special spiritual powers who does not tolerate dissent, uses threats of physical force to gain compliance, vilifies outside groups, and engages in sexual misconduct—fit the situation in Bergholz.

Following my direct testimony, I was cross-examined by five defense attorneys for nearly three hours.[24] Their task was to clarify or challenge things I had said, but most important, to raise doubts about my statements and to poke holes in the credibility of my testimony, so that my words would be less damaging to their clients. The cross-examination was in some ways both more interesting and more challenging, because unlike the direct examination, where I knew the gist of the questions in advance, the defense attorneys' queries were always a surprise.

Two attorneys interrogated me for over an hour, trying to drive a wedge between real religion and "pure Amish tradition" in order to advance the defense's argument that the attacks were not about religion. One attorney asked for specific Bible verses that pertain to the casting of lots to ordain bishops, the size of a hat, the use of modern appliances, and the use of buggies. Is plowing with horses a religious act? Is speaking Pennsylvania Dutch a religious act? Is wearing beards a religious act? All of these questions were aimed at severing Amish practices from the Amish religion. I explained that many Amish traditions are religion based because they are formulated and approved in church meetings and are everyday applications of the Amish interpretation of the biblical principle of separation from the world.

Another defense attorney spent about thirty-five minutes challenging the quality and accuracy of my scholarship. How could I speak with any authority about the practices in the Amish communities of Fredericktown and Bergholz if I had never conducted field research there? Why didn't I attend the meeting of three hundred elders at Ulysses in September 2006? If it was such an important meeting, why did I wait five years to investigate it—until I was hired by the US Department of Justice to work with the prosecution? How carefully did I verify my evidence with other scholars before I called Bergholz a "breakaway Amish group" when I spoke to the news media in the fall of 2011? And how can anyone have confidence in my research when a statement inside the front cover of my co-authored book *The Amish Way* says that the publisher and the authors "make no warranties with respect to the accuracy . . . of this book"? To that I replied, "Sir, that was written by a lawyer . . . the publisher puts it in every book . . . it's a standard procedure in the industry," prompting chuckles from the audience and even one from the judge.

The prosecution and defense attorneys interrogated the final witness, seventy-seven-year-old Bishop Raymond Hershberger, for about ninety minutes. In a quiet and faltering voice, he apologized for not knowing English too well as he answered questions related to the meeting at Ulysses and the attack at his home on

October 4, 2011. He explained that the bishop's role in the congregation is to "keep peace with each other, forgiveness and love,
to try to keep together." In the last moments of his testimony he
said, speaking of his attackers, "I can easily forgive them what
they done to me, but it's always in the back of my mind. I pity the
next man that would have to go through what I did."[25]

Over the two days that I was in the courtroom, the sixteen
defendants were attentive to the testimonies yet remarkably stoic,
showing little emotion as they heard the evidence against them
accumulate. After my and Bishop Hershberger's testimonies,
the prosecution rested. The defense attorneys chose not to call
any witnesses and rested. The prosecutors and defense attorneys
then delivered their closing arguments.

"A Campaign of Terror against Amish Hypocrites"

In their hour-long closing arguments to the jury, the prosecutors highlighted their key points.[26] They reminded the jury that
all sixteen of the defendants were charged with participating in a
conspiracy—a point they had reiterated throughout the trial. As
they planned their attacks, the defendants worked together, collaborating in a conspiracy, "a campaign of terror against Amish
hypocrites," in the words of the government's lawyers.[27]

Five of the defendants were accused of thwarting the investigation by knowingly concealing objects related to the purported
crimes. They destroyed a bag of hair from one of the attacks,
concealed the horse mane shears used in the cuttings, and hid
the camera they used to document their exploits. They took
photographs, argued the government's lawyers, to capture and
preserve their victims' shame, and when they decided to hide the
undeveloped film and camera from the FBI, they buried it under
a pile of leaves instead of destroying it, so they could later see
the pictures and relive their victims' suffering.

In their wrap-up, the prosecutors zoomed in on Bishop Mullet to pinpoint a key question hovering over the jury's verdict:
Were these attacks motivated by religion? They repeated once
again the words Bishop Mullet had proclaimed to the world on

television: that the assaults were "all about religion," and "We know what we did, and why we did it."

Mullet, sitting a few yards away, listened as US trial attorney Kristy Parker zoomed in even tighter on him in her summary: "Sam Mullet is different from everyone else because he didn't get any blood or human hair on his hands. And he didn't personally shear off any beards. But, let there be no doubt, none of the terror . . . that was unleashed on the victims last fall would have happened without Sam Mullet."

Looking straight at the jury, Parker continued, "[He] is the iron-fisted bishop who prides himself on strict control. Sam Mullet was the authority figure in this community. He said it himself. He was like the father in the house. It was his job to ensure that the flock, in his words, 'obeyed.' Sam Mullet is the person who controlled his community in Bergholz so tightly that the other members had to show him their mail before they sent it and allow him to read their incoming letters. He is the person who was able to coerce sex from . . . [female member] right under the nose of her husband, Sam's own son."

Sam is the man his sister "Barb Miller described as berating and hammering at people who disagreed with him until he got his way." And, finally, Parker reminded the jurors that "it was Sam Mullet's job to ensure that the members of his flock were punished if they acted improperly. . . . And that never happened here . . . . He didn't order the attacks in this case, but he also didn't stop them. And he certainly had the authority to stop them."

Wrapped in Strings of Bias

The closing statement from the defense stretched over three hours as, one by one, sixteen attorneys walked to the podium to defend their clients in fifteen-minute speeches. The lead defense attorney, Ed Bryan, representing Sam Mullet, gave an hour-long summation at the end. On several occasions, Judge Polster urged the defense attorneys to speed up and avoid repetition.[28]

The first attorney, James S. Gentile, clarified that the defense was not contesting the involvement of their clients in the particular

events. "Now, in this case, a lot has been said about these particular incidents, which really has not been disputed. These gentlemen admitted they were wrong. They admitted it from the very
beginning." The contested terrain involved the motivation and
meaning of the defendants' actions. In various ways, the defense
lawyers argued several core ideas on behalf of their clients.

First, they argued that "cutting hair and the beards were symbolic acts." The beard for men and long hair for women in Amish
culture are symbols. Moreover, the Bergholz men had voluntarily
cut their own beards as a sign of repentance and atonement—
reuniting with God "because they thought they had deviated from
the Amish path. They needed to come back to the Amish way, the
Amish path. These were symbolic acts for them that reawakened
them." Likewise, the beard- and hair-cutting ventures in the fall
of 2011 were symbolic means of atonement and repentance. They
were not intended to inflict bodily injury.

Second, "the intentions for cutting hair were pure. They were
acts of compassion, acts of love." Speaking about his client, Lester
Miller, attorney J. Dean Carro said, "Love was what motivated
him to cut his father's beard and for his mother's hair to be cut.
Love toward what end?" Simply, to help them get "back on the
Amish path, the path that Lester had experienced through his
atonement. They [the victims] were brought back to the path
through an act of love, plain and simple." The same purpose, argued the defense, propelled the attacks on Bishops Hershberger
and Miller on October 4: "What were the motivations for those
acts? There was a dispute. There was a power struggle, between
two or three communities." The defendants acted not "through
hatred, but through love, to bring these people back to the Amish
way. So their motivations were pure. They were acts of love."

Third, "there was no intent to do bodily injury. What were
their intentions? What were their motivations? These were acts
of compassion. These were acts of love." Miller's attorney explained to the jury, "You have heard ad nauseam, time and time
and time again, from witness after witness after witness . . . that
the intention was to cut the beard and to cut the hair. It was
never to injure the body." And he emphasized that "in order to

have bodily injury, there has to be injury to the body, to the body, to the body. That word [body] modifies everything else. It modifies injury. It modifies disfigurement."

Understanding that the definition of *disfigurement* was a key element of their defense, several attorneys pressed the point, noting that everyone in the courtroom "has cut their hair. Some people in this room have cut their beards. Using your common sense, have you cut your body? Have you injured your body? Have you disfigured your body? The answer to that is plain and simple [no]." Another attorney noted that on the body of his client's victim, "there's no abrasion. There's no bruises, there's no burns, and there's no disfigurement. You saw the cutting of the hair, and it grew back. That's not disfigurement . . . or impairment of bodily organs or mental faculty." He acknowledged that most of the victims "testified they suffered embarrassment," but reminded the jurors that "emotional and psychological effects are not covered by the law."

Fourth, numerous defense attorneys contended that three of the attacks were not motivated by religion—a basic prerequisite for a hate crime. Instead, they argued that these attacks were propelled by family conflicts, feuds, spats, and parent-child disputes. Religion was missing here; these were simply personal conflicts between individuals. They were "related to bad parenting and bad parenting alone is not about religion. These are personal issues" between individual people, not religious issues, argued one attorney.

In his summary, the lead defense counsel, Ed Bryan, told the jury, "The truth is, ladies and gentlemen, the package that the Government has tried to present to you has the strings of bias wrapped around it. They've used the strings of prejudice to wrap around it. They've used the strings of sympathy to wrap around it."

He proceeded to argue that the government's package was also, ironically, wrapped with a string of "anti-religious bias, not against the Amish in general, but against the Bergholz Amish community because, admittedly, they are different." To expand his point and to discredit the sole expert witness (which he was compelled to do), he noted that the government's "own expert, Dr. Kraybill, the most preeminent Amish scholar in the country, came in here and . . . sneered at the Bergholz Amish community, that they're a lone ranger group, they're a renegade group, they're a breakaway group. And every chance he got to try to put a dig in at them, he did."

In explaining the unique Bergholz rituals to the jury, defense attorney Bryan argued that they emerged when the community was under stress (2006–2009). The members worried that they were not living a proper Christian life and considered themselves hypocrites, so the men voluntarily engaged in cutting their beards as a sign of repentance and gave up conveniences to demonstrate the sincerity of their penance, "so they could start fresh." He pointed to the long tradition of self-sacrifice in Christian history, noting that "throughout centuries, men and women of faith have been denying themselves physically in an effort to get closer to God." During that period "of self-reflection and renewal . . . the Bergholz Amish community itself . . . used [the time] to come closer to God, to draw closer to God."

In the government's response, prosecutor Bridget Brennan made an incisive and vociferous rebuttal of core defense arguments.[29] She began by responding to attorney Bryan's claim that the government had wrapped the attacks into a package tied with strings of bias: "Ladies and gentlemen, what these victims suffered, what homes were invaded, people were kidnapped, what laws were broken, that's not a production, that is fact. . . . That's not made up, and it's not TV."

She contended that the attacks reflected a conspiracy of the "whole community's pledge to address Amish hypocrisy." Challenging the notion that Bishop Mullet was a passive bystander, she said, "No, he's not merely present; he's the bishop, he's encouraging, he's giving directions. . . . He's laughing, he's joking, on the jail calls, he's cheering them on. You can hear it."

Then she assailed the argument that the attacks were motivated by love and compassion: "Even if you think that these were loving attacks . . . you can't love someone to the point where you injure them because of religion."

Reiterating that the attacks were "all about religion," Brennan said they were aimed at cleansing the victims "of their religious hypocrisy [and] that is a religious event." Moreover, she noted, it matters not whether the attackers and victims have the same religious faith. "The question is whether you're doing it [attacking] because of religion. That's the question. . . . It actually goes to the very fabric of our country. That is why the Amish came here to begin with, because they were being persecuted somewhere else."

In her last words to the jury, Brennan said, "I'm asking you right now to defend the victims' rights to exercise their religion freely and peacefully without fear of violence. . . . You all took an oath, ladies and gentlemen, to apply the law. The facts here satisfy every element, of every charge, for every defendant." With those words, the prosecution rested.

With the closing statements over, the judge provided written instructions for the five women and seven men on the jury, who now held the weighty burden of sifting through all the testimonies, evidence, and legal guidelines as they searched for the truth in the hope of reaching a unanimous verdict. He reminded them that in making their decisions they can only consider what they saw and heard in the courtroom. "You absolutely must not try to get information from any other source . . . such as family, friends, the Internet, reference books, newspapers, magazines, TV, radio, a BlackBerry, an iPhone, Droid, or other smart phone, iPad, or any other electronic device."[30] For nine days, the jurors had been collecting and absorbing information. Now it was time for them to sequester themselves and deliberate until they reached a verdict.

What Is Disfigurement?

This was not a one-defendant case with a few counts of breaking, entering, and robbery. The jurors faced a multidimensional case with sixteen defendants, ten different charges, and seventeen defense attorneys, as well as three prosecuting attorneys and twenty-six witnesses. The complexity of arranging hundreds of details required systematic organization lest the case implode.

The first responsibility of the jury was to select a leader. The jurors selected a foreman who had demonstrated organizational skills and detailed courtroom note taking.[31] The foreman's ability to organize and track a multitude of data helped the jury members sort their notes and evidence and streamline their deliberations. He was permitted to tape sections of poster paper to the walls to summarize the testimonies, evidence, names, and charges. These visuals, noted the foreman, facilitated the jury's deliberations and decision making.

The jurors consisted of Caucasians, Hispanics, and African Americans with backgrounds in areas such as software, sales, and teaching. Overwhelmed by their task and the potential imprisonment for the defendants, especially the mothers of young children, some of the jurors, overcome by the moral gravity of their task, broke into tears on several occasions.

At the outset, the jurors reviewed their handwritten notes from the testimonies, asking, "Was this a reliable, trustworthy witness?" The grandchildren of Sam Mullet seemed very credible to the jurors in helping to piece together evidence of a conspiracy.[32]

A core issue looming in the minds of the jurors was whether the evidence was plausible enough to convict the defendants of a hate crime. The judge's instructions included the words of the Shepard-Byrd Act, which apply if someone:

> willfully causes bodily injury to any person, ... Because of the actual or perceived religion . . . of any person. Bodily injury means any injury to the body, no matter how *temporary*, and includes a cut, abrasion, bruise, burn, or *disfigurement*; physical pain; illness; impairment of function of the bodily member, organ or mental faculty; or other injury to the body, no matter how temporary. Bodily injury does not include solely emotional or psychological harm to the victim.[33]

One of the "big challenges," according to the foreman, focused on two words: *disfigurement* and *temporary*. The legal statute said that the definition of bodily injury included disfigurement "no matter how temporary." Was cutting a beard a form of disfigurement? One juror, "a stickler for defining *bodily*, argued, 'Hair is not my body. Skin is my body, but hair is not.'"

The jurors considered several hypothetical scenarios to help them decipher the meaning of bodily injury. If they forcibly shaved the head of one of the women jurors some evening, and she went to work the next day, would she be temporarily disfigured? Positing a different example, if a juror used a permanent marker to forcibly paint purple streaks on a male juror's face, would he be temporarily disfigured when he went to work? In a third, more extreme scenario, if a mountain lion attacked a woman and scarred her face, would that be permanent disfigurement? The jurors agreed it would be.

In the case before them, they needed to determine first whether cutting a beard was temporary disfigurement. Struggling to decide, they sent a note to Judge Polster asking for a definition of disfigurement. The judge reconvened all the attorneys and the jury in the courtroom, read the language of the statute, and told everyone, "This is exactly how it is stated in the law. The courts have not elaborated on the definition nor will I. You [the jury] must interpret what it means."

Eventually, the jurors reached unanimous agreement that cutting someone's beard or hair did constitute temporary disfigurement. Beards and hair can of course grow longer again. So after a second round of debate on the phrase "no matter how temporary," they agreed that snipping off a beard was temporary, but not permanent disfigurement. If the word *temporary* had been missing in the statute, the case for a hate crime may have crumbled or at least would have reduced the number of convictions. Some of the charges would have still applied because bodily injuries—burns, bruises, cuts, and bleeding—were apparent on some of the victims.

Another task involved the motivation that drove the attackers. Were they driven by the actual or perceived religion of their victims? More than half of the jurors did not practice any religion, so a religious worldview and perspective was somewhat foreign to them. During the initial deliberations, the jurors assumed this was "Amish on Amish" violence—just Amish people in the same religion. "For too long," said the foreman, "we were focused on the *attackers' religion* while we should have zoomed in on the *victims' religion*." What mattered according to the Shepard-Byrd Act was not the religion of the perpetrators, but whether their attacks were motivated by their perception of the victims' religion.

Some jurors wondered how Amish people, who appear to be so similar, could be arguing about faith. Was beard wearing just a tradition or was it real religion? Many Christian churches, the jurors reasoned, certainly do not agree on their interpretations of the same Bible.

Attack by attack, charge by charge, the jurors had to evaluate whether they had ample evidence, beyond a reasonable doubt, that the religion of the victims was the driving force behind the assaults. Eventually, the twelve agreed that the attacks were motivated by how the attackers viewed the actual and perceived religion of their victims. The jurors had a lengthy debate regarding the attack on Barb and Marty Miller: Was the attack retaliation for what the children considered bad parenting or was it about religion? The jury concluded that it was about religion because, according to the foreman, various witnesses testified that "the victims needed to be disciplined by force so they would get on the right path to heaven."[34]

Since all the defendants were charged with conspiracy, the jurors carefully sifted through the evidence "connecting all the different dots," in the words of one of them, to determine whether the defendants had schemed together to commit the crimes.[35] Specifically, they had to decide whether Bishop Mullet was a conspirator, even though he was not present at any of the crimes. Aligning all the evidence, the jurors unanimously agreed that he was central to the conspiracy.

The flow of events they had written on the poster paper lining the walls of the jury room helped the jurors sort through their decisions. They needed to review and vote on a total of ninety charges—two or more of the ten counts applied to various actions of each of the sixteen defendants. The jurors wrote the outcome of their first vote for each count on the forms provided by the judge and then voted again ninety times, count by count, to verify their decisions.

The jury deliberated for five days, and in the words of one of the prosecuting attorneys, "It was a nail-biting time for all of us." Was it taking so long because of the complexity of the case or was the jury stuck at an impasse? Then, at 2:09 p.m., on Thursday, September 20, the jurors returned to the courtroom where the judge had assembled the defendants and their counsel to hear the verdict: the defendants were guilty on eighty-seven counts.

The jury found both Sam Mullet and Levi F. Miller not guilty of count three for their involvement in the attack on David Wengerd. They also found Sam Mullet not guilty of count seven (obstruction of justice), ordering a bag of hair to be destroyed. Defense Attorney Bryan asked for a poll of the jurors, and one by one they verified their vote verbally. The fact that the jury did not render a verdict of guilty on all the counts attested to their diligence in sorting through the evidence.

Judge Polster thanked them with these words: "Ladies and gentlemen, you have been, I believe, the most attentive jury I've had in my fourteen years on the bench. You followed this testimony scrupulously through all the days and all the witnesses. I think we had more than twenty-five witnesses, notwithstanding a couple of breaks, and you obviously deliberated long and hard; five days of deliberation. So you have my thanks. You have the thanks of all the parties, and all the lawyers, and for that matter, of the public because this was a case of considerable importance."[36]

Amish people enter the US Federal Courthouse in Cleveland on Sept. 19, 2012.
(AP Photo/Scott R. Galvin)

SEVEN

THE SENTENCING

"It's Getting Scary"

The four-month interlude between the September verdicts and the February sentencing was an anxious time for the Bergholz community. Ten of their men—half of the married ones—were in prison, and the future was bleak. "It's getting scary," Elizabeth Miller, mother of eleven children, told the *New York Times*. Sam's wife, Martha, was hoping for another miracle akin to the $3.5 million deal for gas and oil rights on their property that had been finalized in early 2012. The hoped-for miracle this time around was light prison sentences for the defendants and perhaps none at all for the women. Martha "burst into tears as she bemoaned the upheaval" of what she considered the overly harsh hate crime convictions. "We're not denying that we did wrong," she said, but the victims can go on with their lives. "Their hair and beards will grow back. But they don't want our families to have any lives at all."[1]

Sam's youngest daughter, Lizzie, and her fiancé, Ferdinand Miller, son of Preacher Levi F. Miller, faced a dilemma. They had hoped to be married on Thanksgiving Day, but all the ministers were behind bars, and no one else in the Bergholz community was credentialed to conduct the ceremony. So they had a jailhouse wedding, likely the first in Amish history, at the Northeast Ohio Correctional Center in Youngstown, where Bishop Mullet was being held until sentencing. From behind a glass partition in the visitors' waiting room, he conducted the nuptial service via telephone, reading prayers and vows to the bride and groom and a small audience from Bergholz.[2] "It was the most bittersweet thing that I've ever experienced," recalled Lizzie.[3]

Nonetheless, there were also expressions of resilience along the Yellow Creek. "We're going to keep going. We are not going to disperse," Christ Mullet said. "We'll deal with whatever happens when we get to it." Despite the setbacks, they would cope and they would persevere. In the words of one of Sam's daughters, "We hang together because we have no one else." Moreover, their enduring loyalty to their father did not waiver. "No matter if he gets life in prison, he will still be our bishop here."[4]

Already behind bars for a year, the bishop had gradually adjusted to prison life. He told a reporter that the other inmates call him O. G., street slang for "original gangster." Sensing it was a cross-cultural compliment, he said with a smile, "I don't know what it means, but I guess it means something good." The new culture required some other adjustments as well. When the cells were locked down at night and the lights turned off, "some of the guys would holler back and forth, sometimes just cussing and screaming and carrying on for hours." Unable to sleep, Sam decided to start singing some of his favorite songs. He soon gathered an audience of inmates who would come to his cell in the evenings and listen to him sing until lockdown. One of his favorites was "Rank Stranger," the story of an old man who, upon returning to his childhood home, discovered his friends were gone and everyone was a "rank stranger." He was assured, however, that when he died he would meet his buddies in heaven.[5]

Several other things were also afoot following the trial. The defense lawyers sought to overturn the convictions by asking for a new trial for several reasons: The prosecution had presented no evidence that Bishop Mullet had participated in any of the attacks; permitting Mullet's daughter-in-law Nancy to testify about her relationship with him had tainted the jury and was irrelevant to the criminal charges; the court should have disqualified remarks Bishop Mullet made in an Associated Press story in October 2011. In early December, Judge Polster, citing various counterarguments, denied the request for a new trial.[6]

In the lull before the sentencing, the Bergholz clan did a very non-Amish thing: They welcomed and exposed themselves to intimate coverage by regional and national media, including the *Cleveland Plain Dealer* and the *New York Times*.[7] Amish leaders staunchly prohibit members from seeking publicity, from permitting their names to be used in news reports, and from posing for photographs.[8] The bishop granted two no-holds-barred jailhouse interviews—one to the *New York Times* and the other to the *Daily*. Just two days before the sentencing, his recently married daughter, Lizzie, spoke to an NPR reporter who visited Bergholz. She said that despite her father's imprisonment, "He's still the leader. He's still dad. He's still the bishop."[9]

No other Amish congregation in history has ever invited and received such unrestricted coverage in the national media. The exposure included not only interviews but also video footage and dozens of color photographs of people. The press reports of Bergholz showed idyllic scenes, with contented children playing and relaxed adults chatting in a pristine pastoral landscape.

This unprecedented exposure was likely orchestrated to counteract what defense attorney Ed Bryan called the government's "false narrative," which was designed to "not only influence the court, but influence public opinion" so that the prosecutors' severe sentencing recommendations would seem reasonable.[10]

"Not in Brazen Control"?

All the anxieties of the previous months came to a head on Friday, February 8, 2013, at the sentencing proceedings in the Cleveland federal courthouse. Each of the defense attorneys offered reasons to mitigate the severity of his client's sentence. The prosecutors had proposed a life sentence for Sam Mullet. The extent of his involvement in the crimes was a central issue that would weigh heavily on the severity of his sentence. US trial attorney Kristy Parker, arguing for the government, contended that "Samuel Mullet, Sr., was a leader and organizer of this conspiracy for all of the reasons that he was convicted at the trial." Even though he did not order the attacks, "the evidence shows that but for Samuel Mullet, Sr., none of the events and none of the crimes and the kidnappings, home invasions and terrorizing attacks and isolation [in Amish jails] would have taken place."[11]

Laying responsibility for the crimes at Bishop Mullet's feet, Parker said that he "was the leader of the community. It was his grievances that inspired the attacks. He was the person who came up with the concept of hypocrites and endorsed the idea of shearing the beards and hair of Amish hypocrites. He was the start and finish of each attack. He kept vigil and waited for each attack to occur. He was the person to whom everyone reported at the start and finish of the attacks each and every time." And by not punishing people, "he endorsed and ratified those attacks."

Moreover, she said, it was Sam Mullet himself who gave "assurances to the Holmes County sheriff that he was not going to allow these kinds of things to happen again. He not only exhorted the members of his community who were jailed at that time to keep the faith, he not only lauded them for what they had done, but he told them specifically that all of this was going to eventually blow over and that they would be able to go out and get more beards." She concluded by saying that "the evidence speaks for itself, and his role . . . shows him to be the leader that he was."

The bishop's attorney, Ed Bryan, offered a vociferous defense against life imprisonment. Bryan contended that there was no evidence that Bishop Mullet ever ordered anyone to go into a chicken coop: "He's not in brazen control over this community." Furthermore, Mullet's attorney said, the state of Ohio has milder sentences for kidnapping than the federal kidnapping guidelines—designed for much more serious cases—which "jacks up all of our clients' sentencings."[12]

Citing letters from two of the bishop's daughters-in-law, he noted that when they were growing up, "their fathers . . . were mean to them, would never have any time for them, but Samuel Mullet had time for them, he listened to them, listened to their concerns, listened to their problems, helped them with their problems." Bryan then recited the names of several terrorists (including Terry Nichols, the Oklahoma City bombing codefendant responsible for the deaths of 168 people in 1995) who were serving life sentences for murder. Sam Mullet's crimes, he argued, were but a tiny shadow compared to those and did not warrant life in prison.[13]

Finally, attorney Bryan recited the incident at the machinery auction before the first beard attack when Marty Miller chastised his son Alan for cutting his own beard and then declared, "If God is with me, my beard will never be cut." That argument, said Bryan, was the "true catalyst to all" the beard cuttings outside the community. The cuttings, he continued, were not "planned and toiled over and targets chosen or things like that. These things happened more by happenstance than anything else." The defendants "never dreamed in their wildest that a federal case would ever come of this. These were internal family disputes that began, that spilled over" to others.[14]

"I Never Dreamed It Would End Up Like This"

All the defendants gave a short statement before Judge Polster announced their sentences. Each of the four men whose wives were defendants offered to take his wife's sentence so she could stay at home with their children. Thirteen of the defendants offered statements laced with remorse and contrition and explicitly said that they were sorry for what they had done.

The three Miller boys apologized to their parents, Marty and Barb. Eli Miller confessed, "I'm scared. I never dreamed that it would end up like this. I'm sorry for what happened. I apologize to my mom and dad. I'm sorry. It will never happen again." Lester Miller apologized to his parents and added, "I didn't want to hurt you. I just wanted to *help* you. I hope someday you can forgive me." And Raymond, who had wanted to cut more beards after the first arrests, confessed to the judge, "I didn't realize the seriousness and I would like to apologize to you, sir, for all the trouble that this has caused and also apologize to my parents. I'm sorry for what I did to you."[15]

The daughters-in-law of Marty and Barb were contrite as well. Twenty-three-year-old Kathryn Miller said, "I just want to apologize for what I did and I'm sorry to my in-laws." She also thanked Judge Polster "for letting me be with my children this long, and I want to take my punishment and all the blame, whatever punishment you feel is fair on me." Elizabeth Miller, mother of eleven children, apologized "for all the pain and grief I've caused and I'm sorry for everything I did. I want to take my own punishment. Thank you."[16]

The tone of sincere contrition in the voices of the thirteen lay members was missing from the lips of the three ordained leaders. Preacher Levi F. Miller offered a tepid "I'm sorry" after defending his bishop in these words: "I knew Sam Mullet for over twenty-five years. First time I ever met him, I could see right off that he's a man that is walking in God's way. To this day . . . he's still doing that. And I've been a preacher for going on thirteen years. . . . I think it's way beyond reasonable doubt putting him in jail." Then Levi offered to "gladly" take Sam's place in jail, "so he can go home and be with his community. . . . I have no intention of ever cutting hair again. I'm sorry."[17]

Without apologizing, Preacher Johnny Mullet said, "I'll take my sentencing, what you think is fair. I'll take my dad's, too. If you give him life, then send me home or give me whatever, I don't know." Then Johnny concluded, "He's not the man that the government's putting out. All I can say is give me a sentence, send him home. I'll take the blame."[18]

When Bishop Mullet took his turn, he confessed, "I really don't know what to say. I'm being *blamed* for [being] a cult leader and . . . I'm an old man, I'm not going to live very long. I'd have a hard time fitting that eight hundred acres into a three-by-six hole when I die. *They* make it sound like I'm doing everything for myself. I'm not taking the farm with me. I'm not going to be here much longer. I'm not gathering things up for me."[19]

Then, summing up his life's mission, the bishop said, "My goal in life has always been to *help* the younger adult, to *help* people that are pushed back, frowned on, mocked. That's been my goal all my life. . . . *If* somebody needs to be punished for this, and I'm a cult leader, then I want to take the punishment for everybody. . . . Let these dads and moms go home to their families, raise their children, and I'll take the punishment for everybody. There's a lot more things I could say, but everything I say gets twisted and turned to mean something different than what I intend it to be, so I don't have much else to say. That's it."[20]

Sam presented himself as a victim of those who twist words, and he offered, as the shepherd of his little flock, to be the sacrificial lamb for them.

Wrestling with Justice and Mercy

After the defendants had spoken, all eyes in the courtroom turned to Judge Polster, who carried the burden of determining sentences within the statutory guidelines. He noted that sentences for violating the Hate Crimes Prevention Act could range from twenty-five years to life in prison, but that such sentences "are typically reserved for armed career criminals, career offenders, drug kingpins, terrorists" who take the lives of others, unlike the sixteen defendants before him who deserve some leniency.[21]

"Of course, what I've learned in my job," he reflected, "is that everyone wants justice when it's someone else; mercy when it's them or someone close to them. The two are irreconcilable. All any one judge can do is wrestle with them each and every time he or she imposes a sentence, and that's what I have to do. . . . It's the hardest thing any of us [on the bench] have to do."[22] He confessed that he had been struggling with how to determine fair sentences since the beginning of the trial.

Prior to the sentencing, Judge Polster considered fourteen letters from Amish people with ties to Bergholz or to the victims. All of the letter writers asked for either a lengthy prison sentence or life in prison for Bishop Mullet. The letters' themes included fear for the children's safety if the sentence is short, characterization of Bergholz as a cult, and gratitude to law enforcement for prosecuting the defendants. One writer, for example, said, "We have [adult] children living in Bergholz . . . which we feel is a cult and Sam Mullet Sr. has them brainwashed. Thanks to all of you [for] what you did so far. We think that Sam Mullet Sr. need[s] a long sentence for the sake of our children living in Bergholz, Ohio."[23]

The judge identified some of the factors he was wrestling with in meting out the sentences. The attacks "were calculated

to inflict the maximum emotional trauma and distress on the
victims, and that's what they did. For as long as I live," he said, "I
won't forget the haunting testimony of Ms. Anna Shrock who . . .
described how her children and grandson attacked her and her
very ill husband . . . [how] they were lured to Bergholz by lies
and deception. . . . [How] they didn't want to come, but their
son and daughter-in-law assured them, promised them that they
would be safe."[24]

He reminded the audience that the defendants took pictures
of the attacks so the Bergholz community "could see the victims
in their anguished and disfigured condition." Then he zeroed in
on what troubled him most: "Each and every one of you did
more than just terrorize, traumatize, disfigure your victims; you
trampled on the Constitution, and particularly the First Amendment, which guarantees each and every American religious freedom." Moreover, he noted that because some of the early settlers
to America "couldn't pray in the way they wanted to pray" in
their own country, "they got in some rickety little ships and went
across the Atlantic" in search of religious freedom that eventually became the First Amendment. "And," he said, "I took a very
solemn oath nearly fifteen years ago when I became a judge to
support, protect, and defend the Constitution."[25]

Speaking directly to the defendants, he continued, "[Your
conduct] is particularly reprehensible because each of you has
benefited significantly from the First Amendment to the Constitution." In fact, members of the Amish religion, he told them,
"are excused from some very important rights and obligations
of citizenship that the rest of us have to bear. You don't have to
perform combat service in the army. You're excused from jury
duty. . . . And while parents in almost every state, including Ohio,
must send their children to school at least through age sixteen,
the Supreme Court determined in the *Wisconsin versus Yoder* case"
that because of their religious faith Amish parents may end the
formal schooling of their children at age fourteen.[26]

"So each of you has received the benefits of that First Amendment, and yet you deprived those benefits from other Amish
citizens. And through force and violence you tried to ram your

religious beliefs down their throats." Judge Polster then observed that it's certainly not unusual for parents and children to
have different religious views and practices. "It happens all the
time. But it's totally wrong and illegal for parents or children to
try and force their religious beliefs down the throats" of other
family members "by violence or by threats."[27]

He acknowledged that the defendants said they were motivated by love and compassion because they thought their parents
and other Amish people "had strayed from the true path and
needed to be chastened or corrected" to return to it. "Sadly," he
continued, "this is the same logic . . . that the Inquisitors in Spain
used five hundred years ago when they tortured and burned their
victims at the stake—many of them were members of my
religion—supposedly to save their souls."[28]

"So my sentences," he concluded, "must be significant enough
to punish you for what you've done and to deter others who
might be tempted to let religious passion or zealotry become a
rationale to inflict physical and psychological pain."[29]

"I Struggled Long and Hard"

At the outset, the judge confessed that he had "struggled long
and hard to figure out" appropriate sentences and understood
that, even so, it was likely that "half the people will say my sentences are too long and half will say they're too short." He said
he agreed with the prosecutors that, for the purposes of sentencing, the defendants should be clustered into five tiers related to the length of their sentences.[30]

He looked directly at Bishop Mullet as he spoke: "Sam Mullet,
Sr., I've concluded that you deserve the harshest, the longest
sentence. I'm convinced [from listening to all the trial testimony]
that these attacks would not have occurred but for you. The jury
clearly rejected the argument that because you did not directly
participate in the attacks, you were not responsible for them. You
ran the Bergholz community with an iron fist. Your law was the
law."[31]

Based on the evidence that he had heard, Judge Polster concluded, "Nothing of consequence occurred in that community

without your direction and your approval." As an example, the defendants brought "the victims' hair and pictures of them disfigured to your house, to make sure you approved and you saw what was done."[32]

Moreover, the judge said, "I don't believe you expressed any remorse for the harm you caused to the victims and to our Constitution, and you didn't [express remorse] during those jailhouse calls, and you didn't in the interviews to the media, and I don't think you did today. And sadly, I consider that you are a danger to the community because of the control you possess over others. They listen to you. They respect you. And they follow what you say or what they think you want them to do, and I think they would do it today. Some of the things, some of the comments from the defendants today, suggest to me that while they're sorry for what they did and they wouldn't do that again, that they still consider you their leader."[33]

After a ten-month federal investigation, dozens of legal motions and countermotions, thousands of hours of prosecution and defense time, a three-week trial, and a hefty price tag for taxpayers, the result for Sam was this: "I think a sentence of life in prison is longer than necessary and is disproportionate for what you did, so I'm going to impose a sentence of fifteen years."[34]

Judge Polster then assigned seven-year sentences to the four men in the second tier: the ministers (Johnny Mullet and Levi F. Miller), Eli Miller, and Lester Mullet. Moving to the third group, he gave Emanuel Shrock, Daniel Mullet, and Lester Miller five-year sentences. Two people, Linda Shrock and Raymond Miller, received two-year sentences. And, finally, the five women and one man (Lovina Miller, Anna Miller, Emma Miller, Elizabeth Miller, Kathryn Miller, and Freeman Burkholder) in tier five received one-year sentences.[35]

The judge empathized with the plight of the six women, who had forty-two children (most under sixteen years of age) among them. In addition, both Anna Miller and Nancy Miller Burkholder, wife of defendant Freeman Burkholder, were pregnant. Although all the women were required to serve their time, they were permitted to do it before or after their husbands so that one of the parents could be at home to care for their children. No one was required to pay a fine, and, as required by federal sentencing law, none of the defendants would be eligible for parole. However, Judge Polster agreed that the length of the sentences for Sam Mullet, Levi F. Miller, and Johnny Mullet, who had been in prison since November 2011, could be reduced by the number of months they had already served.[36]

Along with many of Sam Mullet's siblings, Barb Miller and her husband, Marty, attended the sentencing. Three of her sons, her son-in-law (Freeman Burkholder), and her five daughters-in-law were sentenced. Writing in an Amish newspaper a few days later, she described the scene this way: "Oh, a day we will never forget! To see so many loved ones in orange prison suits and ankle chains, one's mind could hardly grasp it. But no matter what, they are ours and we love them. We trust that God will bring good out of this somehow. He is just and merciful and his mercies are new every morning. He sees the future, we don't. While we were mourning the loss of one brother, another one was on his way home. So, yes, I still believe in miracles!"[37]

The brother "on his way home" was a reference to Sam's sixty-nine-year-old brother who had left his wife for many years and disappeared into the wilderness of the world but had recently returned to care for her because she was ill. Having confessed his sins, he was "on his way home," meaning that he was being restored to membership in the Amish church. The restoration of Barb's brother underscores the standing offer of pardon from Amish congregations for any wayward soul that repents and wants to return to the flock.[38]

A father and son walk along Township Road 280 in Bergholz, Oct. 15, 2012.
(Marvin Fong / *The Plain Dealer* / Landov)

EIGHT

THE AFTERMATH

Behind Bars

After the sentencing in February 2013, Judge Polster asked prison officials to assign the defendants to federal prisons as close as possible to their homes for ease of visitation because the Amish do not drive or fly. The Federal Bureau of Prisons rejected that request and scattered the defendants, placing Sam Mullet in Texarkana, Texas, more than one thousand miles away from his family, and the other men in federal prisons in Minnesota, Massachusetts, Louisiana, Mississippi, Texas, and Illinois. The women served their time in Connecticut, Minnesota, West Virginia, and Ohio.[1] In attorney Ed Bryan's view, the long-distance prison assignments were "deliberate and designed to inflict the maximum hardship possible on the defendants and their families."[2]

It is hard to imagine the culture shock when Amish people abruptly find themselves behind bars in a strange and harsh place. In a letter from prison, Bishop Mullet described it this way: "God knows where I'm at and why . . . [here you] face the real power of Satan! . . . you face Satan all alone, with no one around who wants to help you, no humans, that is. . . . IF you have never been Face-To-Face with Satan all alone!!! There are no words to explain!"[3]

Sam acknowledged that the attacks looked a bit different from prison. He had never denied, he said, that his people had cut hair. "I'm not saying it was right or wrong, but being here in jail—well it looks wrong. Let's suppose that God has done this for a reason."[4]

Sitting behind bars has been a bittersweet time, but Sam has found ways to fold some meaning into his suffering. "We're here because of those two little girls," he said to a reporter. "I told Wilma that I'll suffer whatever I need to, to get her children back. If I sit in jail for the rest of my life just to get her children back, I'll do it."[5] It's difficult to grasp the logic of these words for two reasons. First, Bishop Mullet's conviction and sentence had nothing to do with the two little girls. He was in prison because of his involvement in hate crimes that were not linked to the children. None of the victims of the beard-cutting attacks were directly or indirectly tied to them. The Jefferson County officials who handled the child custody case were not targets of the hate crimes. Second, even if he sat in jail for the rest of his life, it would not bring the children back to the Bergholz community. This twisted narrative links the attacks to the two girls, implies that Sam's incarceration will bring them back to Bergholz, and portrays him as the heroic suffering servant.

In the same jailhouse interview, Bishop Mullet held his flock, rather than himself, responsible for the attacks, noting, "I never ordered anybody . . . to do beard cuts. These haircuts, they told me these things, but [they] didn't want me to get involved." First, the little girls and then his loyal followers are responsible for the crimes, but the bishop himself, the shepherd of the flock, accepts no blame. Instead of taking responsibility for the offense, he is an innocent victim. Heroically, he offers to take on the penalty, to lay down his life, to suffer for the others. He spoke of jail time as a sacrifice for his followers, as a kind of martyrdom, as he evoked a Christian image: "Christ did it for me, so why shouldn't I do it for them?"[6] This myth of martyrdom may be the most effective way to generate ongoing sympathy from his followers and to provide a sustaining purpose for the future of the clan.

May 2013 brought some good news to the Bergholz barbers. When they were incarcerated, the Federal Bureau of Prisons had required them to attend high school equivalency classes in prison. Learning of this, attorney Ed Bryan asked prison officials to exempt the defendants because the US Supreme Court in 1972 (*Wisconsin v. Yoder*) had ruled that Amish children could end their formal education at eighth grade. He noted that the Bergholz inmates were doing well, and besides, he said, they "know the basics of reading, writing, and arithmetic better than most people."[7] Within days, the Federal Bureau of Prisons relented and granted the prisoners an exemption.[8] But are the Bergholz people really Amish? Should they receive exemptions extended to all Amish people?

Are the Bergholz Barbers Amish?

This intriguing question lurked in the shadows of the federal trial but was never clarified in the legal proceedings. Throughout the case, various media called the Bergholz clan such names as Non-Amish, Rogue Amish, Cast-Off Amish, Spinoff Amish, Breakaway Amish, Lone Ranger Amish, and Renegade Amish.

In its indictment of the defendants, the government described them as part of a community "that purported to practice the Amish religion," thus raising questions about their Amish authenticity.[9] Through his attorney, Bishop Mullet filed a motion to strike the word "purported," arguing that if the government stripped him of his Amish identity the jurors would be biased against him.

In response, the prosecutors contended that the word "purported" merely acknowledged that the government lacked "sufficient theological expertise or authority to declare whether the members of the Bergholz community [or anyone] are bona fide practitioners of the Amish faith." The prosecutors also noted that while some of the Bergholz members considered themselves Old Order Amish, other members, in fact, did not.[10] Indeed, as early as 2010, a member of Bergholz had told a visitor, "We're not Amish anymore."[11] After reviewing the arguments, Judge Polster ruled that "purported" would remain in the indictment.[12]

If the government was uncertain about Bergholz's Amish fidelity, their coreligionists were not. In a chorus of nays across Amish country, individuals declared that Bergholz had left the Amish fold. One Amish man who lived near Sam Mullet's birthplace, said simply, "He's not one of us." An Amish preacher in Holmes County declared, "They're not Amish anymore, they just dress Amish," implying that Amish garb was not enough to claim the Amish name.[13]

Writing to the staff of an Amish newspaper, an Amish woman urged them not to print letters from Bergholz because "they are not horse-and-buggy Amish or Mennonites as they don't go to church anymore." For her, the lack of church services at Bergholz was an automatic self-expulsion from the Amish world. An Amish scholar agreed, saying, "They removed themselves from the Amish world when they stopped having church services."[14]

In a more sweeping rejection of the clan's Amish bona fides, an Amish man said emphatically, "These people are *totally* not Amish. We are so embarrassed. It makes such a poor light to the world. And the world just lumps us all together." Focusing on doctrinal heresy, a well-respected bishop in Holmes County, Ohio, said, "Sam Mullet's behavior violates the core of Amish faith: the Sermon on the Mount. He violates all of it. His behavior is so contrary to Amish faith." If any doubts remained about Bergholz's standing in the Amish world, they vanished in 2013 when the names of its ministers were removed from the nationwide listing of ordained Amish leaders.[15]

The pie of Amish identity can be cut into three slices: (1) ethnicity (language, genealogy, common history, cultural background), (2) religious practices, and (3) religious beliefs. The Bergholz community retains certain ethnic practices—Pennsylvania Dutch, Amish foods, German cultural values, and a shared sense of peoplehood with other Amish groups in northeastern Ohio.[16]

The clan upholds some religious-based customs widely practiced in Amish communities of North America—a separatist lifestyle, distinctive clothing, an eighth-grade education, selective use of technology, and horse-drawn transportation for local travel. However, as shown in table 3, Bergholz has dropped many normative Amish practices, such as religious worship services, morning and evening devotional prayers, a nonviolent lifestyle, and the taboo on litigation. They also devised new practices,

Table 3. Twenty-Five Irregular Practices in the Bergholz Community

1. Rejecting a Christian identity
2. Terminating Sunday worship services
3. Discontinuing prayers (morning, evening, and before and after meals)
4. Holding multiple meetings each week at the bishop's home
5. Rejecting core Amish values: humility, nonviolence, forgiveness
6. Ordaining a bishop with only one outside bishop supervisor
7. Using the Old Testament as a primary source of authority
8. Having a bishop portray himself as a prophet like Elijah
9. Condoning physical punishment to discipline adults (paddling)
10. Creating rituals of purification (beard cutting) and isolation (Amish jails)
11. Rejecting ecclesial fellowship with other Amish affiliations
12. Spurning a unanimous vote of a ministers' meeting
13. Using intimidation to prevent members from leaving
14. Asking members to make a list of their sins for the bishop
15. Excommunicating members without just cause or process
16. Censoring some incoming and outgoing mail
17. Permitting ordained officials to meet privately with women
18. Allowing adult women to live in the home of a bishop
19. Accepting sexual misconduct
20. Imposing discipline practices on other Amish groups
21. Attacking members of other Amish groups
22. Making death threats to law enforcement officers
23. Litigating ($35 million suit) against the government
24. Providing media access for photos and video of people
25. Permitting ordained officials to speak on television

such as paddling adults, heretofore unknown in the Amish realm. Their most egregious departure from the heart and soul of Amish faith is their rejection—articulated by Preacher Johnny Mullet—of a Christian identity and, by implication, of Jesus's admonitions to love enemies and forgive wrongdoers, virtues that have been the cornerstone of Amish faith since their Anabaptist origins in 1525.[17]

The lack of state or federal church-naming regulations in the United States means that any group can call itself Amish. Moreover, because *Amish* is not a registered trademark of any denomination, it is impossible to prevent a group from using the label no matter what it believes or practices. In short, no legal or ecclesiastical statutes protect the Amish brand. So who holds the authority, who is privileged to say who is Amish and who is not? One Amish man said that privilege "should be left to the Amish, not to the professors and lawyers."[18]

Although Amish individuals may adamantly want to disown a group like Bergholz, Amish tradition grants considerable authority to the local body. When conflicts cannot be resolved within a Gmay, leaders of affiliated churches typically assist through mediation. Without any nationwide church agencies or written constitutions, the Amish rely on tradition, fraternal relationships, and a package of New Testament values—self-denial, humility, forgiveness, obedience, and yielding to the wisdom of leaders—to govern church life. It is rare for anyone who wants to remain within the Amish fold to rebuke the unanimous counsel of ordained peers.

Explaining why he rejected the advice of three hundred elders at Ulysses, Sam said, "They're telling me . . . what kind of laws I can use. They're not allowed to do that, not according to our Confession of Faith. . . . If they don't follow the Confession of Faith articles the way they are printed up, the way we went for hundreds of years, I do not have to listen to it. There's nothing in the Bible, there's nothing in our Confession of Faith, that tells me I have to. . . . As long as I don't interfere with what they are doing. . . . They can do whatever they want. I don't care. That's up to them. That's their problem if they want to do that. We as a group here will not tolerate that. We will not go along with that."[19]

As noted in chapter 3, Bishop Mullet was an ardent advocate for obedience within his own flock. Yet he refused to obey the highest court of Amish authority by not giving himself up (uffgevva) to the counsel of the church—a firm and long-standing expectation for ordained officials in the Amish world. Bishop Mullet was correct in noting that Amish polity grants some autonomy to the local Gmay; however, it never gives license to *one* bishop to exercise discipline over the leaders or members of another Gmay—certainly not to ambush and attack them, as the beard cuttings did.

Despite the intriguing question of Bergholz's Amish identity, the issue was mostly moot to the hate crime charges. As the jury foreman noted, the key issue was the religion of the *victims*, not the religion or ethnic label of the assailants. Ironically, however, the case is typically described as the first application of the Shepard-Byrd Act within the *same* religion, which assumes that the Bergholz barbers were Amish.

Crazy Cultlike Zombies?

Those who were eager to strip the *Amish* label off of Bergholz had a ready replacement: the word *cult*. As noted in chapter 4, certain outsiders—Amish people, law enforcement officers, and others—had called Bergholz a cult for some time. Sheriff Abdalla, who interacted with the clan for a few years before the attacks, was one of the first to use that label. In his words, "Sam Mullet was always a smooth talker, but very dangerous. I wouldn't have been a bit surprised if someday I received a call saying everyone had drunk the poison Kool-Aid just like they did for Jim Jones" in Jonestown in 1978. An out-of-state Amish man lamented, "It's definitely a cult. I never dreamed something like that would ever come from the Amish."[20]

Bergholz and its defenders eschewed the cult label. Before the sentencing, Defense Attorney Bryan accused the prosecutors of portraying Bergholz as a "crazy cult-like environment where zombies are doing the bidding of Samuel Mullet and his vengeance." Sam's son Christ complained, "They tell us that we're a cult, and it upsets all of us. They can't see what we're trying to do. We're trying to straighten up our lives and live closer to God." At his sentencing, Preacher Levi F. Miller refuted the idea that Sam ran the clan with an iron fist, saying, "We're called . . . a cult, and I just honestly say that's a lie. . . . All the church members, they got the say so, too. Actually they got more say so, too, than what he [Sam] does."[21]

Sam explained that he was dubbed a cult leader because he was one of the few Amish bishops who maintained strict standards for his community's youth—forbidding rollerblades and keeping boom boxes out of their buggies. "As far as I know we're the only group of Amish . . . that don't have a problem with their young folks, and that's why I'm called a cult leader—because we don't allow all that," he said.[22] As a matter of fact, numerous conservative congregations do not have serious problems with their youth, and their bishops are not called cult leaders.[23]

The cult label evokes strong reactions. Social scientists have applied the term to various types of groups.[24] For some people, the word *cult* calls to mind doomsday groups, such as the People's Temple at Jonestown (1978), the Branch Davidians at Waco (1993), and Heaven's Gate (1997), a California UFO group whose members eventually committed suicide. Groups like these are tagged *cults* because they recruit new members into a tightly controlled environment where the leader "brainwashes," or indoctrinates, them into an alternate set of beliefs. They use various forms of coercion and physical punishment to enforce obedience, often resulting in some sort of violence.[25]

One thing that most cults have in common is an extraordinary leader—someone with unique charismatic powers of persuasion, spiritual insights, and mysterious connections to the divine. Certain cultlike groups also exhibit characteristics such as excessive control by a single leader, social isolation, coercion, deceit, deprivation, sexual abuse, conspiracy theories, brainwashing, new beliefs, novel rituals, intimidation, punishment for defection or criticism, a polarized worldview of good/evil and we/they, vilification of other groups, an emphasis on purity, and a doomsday end-of-world ideology.[26] A particular group may develop its own blend of these features as well as other traits. However, numerous groups that would never be labeled a cult also incorporate some of these attributes. Sports teams, for example, may have unique rituals, tight control, intimidation, and a polarized we/they view of opponents.

While some of these trappings were evident in Bergholz, others were not. The Gmay did not aggressively recruit outsiders from various religious backgrounds and brainwash them, for example, nor did it have a fervent doomsday ideology. Rather,

Bergholz was a clan with some cultlike features but not a full-blown cult.

Upsetting the Moral Order

Cult or not, Bergholz did flip the Amish moral order upside down. All human societies have a moral order—a set of understandings about what is right and wrong, good and bad, virtue and vice. This moral compass includes not only values but also rules, laws, and expectations for individual and corporate behavior. Those who comply with the norms of their group receive awards and those who violate them face sanctions ranging from scorn to prison.

Many aspects of the Amish moral order were inverted at Bergholz. Revenge replaced nonresistance. Social gatherings supplanted worship services, the authority of the Old Testament rose above the teachings of Jesus, and forgiveness fell from virtue to vice. A single leader's opinion outranked the counsel of a throng of ministers, coercion replaced free will, intimidation dwarfed persuasion, fear uprooted love, and so on.

As one defector noted in chapter 4, black became white and white became black. This doublespeak blurred and transformed the boundaries of reality as exploitation became "helping," false-hoods were transformed into truth, sin was converted into goodness, and impurity mutated into righteousness. Conversely, facts became rumors, the truth turned into gossip, and integrity was equated with hypocrisy. Offenders were refashioned into victims, and the innocent were blamed when things went awry.[27]

The Bergholz trajectory poses an important question: How did this moral inversion occur? Several psychosocial theories may shed some light on the radical makeover of conventional Amish standards. Although these perspectives apply to groups and social interactions in general, they also provide portals for understanding what happened at Bergholz.

Stanley Milgram's classic experiment, reported in his book *Obedience to Authority*, demonstrates how people willingly obey legitimate and respected authority figures. Milgram found that some of his subjects were even willing to administer "fatal" electric shocks to innocent victims (actors) when a scientist wearing a white lab coat asked them to pull a shock lever.[28] Of course, people are even more likely to obey authorities when obedience does not directly harm others.

René Girard's theory of scapegoating offers another vantage point for understanding Bergholz. He describes how a distressed group may release some of its anxiety by finding scapegoats to send into the wilderness, sacrifice, attack, or otherwise blame for its troubles.[29] The victims of the beard-cutting attacks as well as other Amish "hypocrites" outside of Bergholz may have served as scapegoats for some of the clan's frustrations.

The psychological concept of identification with the aggressor (also known as the Stockholm syndrome) explains the paradoxical way an abused person may closely identify with and even empathize with his or her aggressor.[30] One Bergholz defector, reflecting on his observations, noted, "Sometimes the victim supported the abuser."[31] And in convoluted relationships, predators at times may blame their victims and leaders may point the finger of fault at their followers.

The clan along the Yellow Creek was not just any troubled group. It had sprouted in Amish soil with all of its unique resources. Did such soil encourage the difficulties at Bergholz? Are other Amish congregations similarly susceptible?

Most Amish settlements have several congregations, and some of the larger ones have upward of two hundred Gmays in their geographical area. The clan was the only Gmay in the Bergholz settlement, making it tempting to pin all the group's problems on its isolation from other Amish communities. The facts, however, do not support that conclusion. Of the 469 Amish settlements in 31 states, one-third of them (153) are one-district settlements like Bergholz. Nonetheless, several unique factors did shape the clan's story line. Sam Mullet, the founder who later became the bishop, purchased a vast amount of acreage in an isolated area and never developed strong fraternal ties with other Amish congregations.

The familial character of Bergholz decidedly shaped its destiny. The community had devolved into a clan—everyone was related except Preacher Levi F. Miller's family—by the time of the attacks. Most of the defectors were not relatives. Rarely do all members of an Amish congregation hail from the same family. At Bergholz, three threads of authority—familial, patriarchal, ecclesiastical—were tightly woven into an inseparable cord. A membership of people from more diverse backgrounds would have preempted the Mullet monopoly of power and most likely have prevented Bergholz from veering so far from the Amish way. Some Amish Gmays do morph into related Anabaptist groups, such as the car-driving Beachy Amish. Others disband and the members join various other religious groups, but rarely, if ever, has a settlement exhibited so many irregular behaviors like those at Bergholz.[32]

A host of Amish cultural values make any Amish Gmay susceptible to temptations similar to those that lured the Bergholz leaders. Reflecting on the clan, an Amish entrepreneur in Holmes County observed, "Our strengths of obedience and respect for authority were turned into weaknesses."[33] Amish values of self-denial, yielding to authority, obedience, forgiveness, forbearance, and humility—while important for the smooth functioning of a collective society—can also be exploited by leaders in harmful and abusive ways.

The accent on submission in the role expectations for women and the fact that they are prohibited from holding church leadership positions adds to their vulnerability. Yet, ironically, some of Sam and Martha's daughters exercised considerable influence in the affairs of Bergholz, at least certainly more than their daughters-in-law, pointing again to the familial factor.

The Amish have a sharp sense of the separation of church and state based on their religious origins and persecution in sixteenth-century Europe. That history, alongside America's respect for religious freedom, may give some Amish leaders a false sense of immunity from government scrutiny. For example, after the second round of attacks, Bishop Mullet criticized Sheriff Abdalla for sticking "his nose in our business. . . . I didn't know the courts could stick their nose in religion."[34]

When federal, state, and local governments have "stuck their nose" into Amish religion—to use Bishop Mullet's metaphor—they have in fact generally accommodated Amish religious beliefs and practices by providing exemptions from jury duty, military service, education requirements, Social Security, and some workplace regulations. These waivers have created a tolerant, even favorable, political climate, which has aided the stability and growth of Amish communities in the United States. This history of respect may tempt some Amish leaders to assume that the canopy of religion will shield them from government intrusion and compliance with the law.

In addition, their theological belief in separation from the world creates sharp cultural differences related to language and lifestyle. Amish leaders prefer to resolve their conflicts and problems within their own "court of justice" in each local Gmay. This preference may also lead to a misplaced sense that they are above or outside the law. These same cultural fences sometimes create hurdles for members, especially for women who experience abuse but are reluctant or unsure how to reach outside the community for help. Barriers to reporting may include limited English vocabulary, unfamiliarity with social and legal services, separation from family and community, unwillingness to incriminate relatives, and a fear of being scorned inside the community. Moreover, these same obstacles can embolden predators who have access to a sizable pool of potential victims in large extended families.

Forgiveness at Bergholz?

Imprisonment provides time for a serious reckoning of one's life journey. In a court hearing in 2008, Bishop Mullet explained that if "[you] live a decent life," but in old age "maybe go English and get a car or start drinking or start dope, start fornication or whatever you call it, the good you've done [earlier]" does not matter. "So it's the last part of our life . . . it's where we stop when we die" that matters. Summing up, he said, "Where the tree falls, that's where it's going to stay and it doesn't matter how much good we did before that." Nonetheless, there's always a glimmer of hope, according to Sam, because, as he told the magistrate, if people "change their life from there on, the Bible teaches us that it [their sin] will never be held against them."[35] In a word, forgiveness from God is always possible upon repentance.

Yet Bergholz was not known for promoting interpersonal forgiveness. When one of the men at Bergholz complained to an outside Amish leader that the Troyers had "lied and twisted everything about the two girls," the leader asked, "Well, why don't you forgive them?" The Bergholz member, speaking loudly, said, "We forgive them not!"[36]

For most of the victims—members and defectors—entwined in the troubles at Bergholz, forgiveness does not come easily. The pain and anger lingers. One of Sam's children said, "I try hard to leave it [the trauma] all behind and go on. It is my family. We were close. I still have anger and sometimes I could tear him [Sam] to pieces. He tore our family all to pieces."[37] The journey to forgiveness for victims with such deep hurts may be a long one, if they are ever able to take that road. Forgiveness is an especially difficult journey when offenders show no remorse.

The world learned in October 2006 that forgiveness is a highly lauded virtue in Amish culture when Charles Roberts IV, a non-Amish neighbor in Nickel Mines, Pennsylvania, took twenty-six children hostage in a one-room Amish school. A short while later he shot ten young girls, killing five of them, and then took his own life. Within hours, several Amish men spontaneously visited Roberts' widow and his parents and conveyed words of empathy, grace, and forgiveness. This almost instant forgiveness startled people worldwide, who were accustomed to forgiveness coming slowly, if ever, from victims of violence.[38]

The Amish believe their Christian faith carries a moral obligation to forgive those who wrong them. They cite a line in the prayer that Jesus taught his disciples: "Forgive us our transgressions *as* we forgive those who transgress against us" (Matt 6:12, 14–15). They also note the verse at the end of the prayer—if you forgive, you will be forgiven; if you do not forgive, you will not be forgiven—as well as other injunctions to forgive in the New Testament. For Amish people, forgiveness is a high Christian duty linked to their own salvation because they believe that Jesus taught they must forgive if they want to be forgiven.

Forgiveness involves letting go of bitterness and purging the impulse to retaliate against an offender. Moreover, there are two types of forgiveness, which are distinguished by apology. *Unqualified* forgiveness, a no-strings-attached forgiveness, occurs when a victim lets go of resentment and anger without an apology from the offender. Unqualified forgiveness, in other words, is the hard work of the victim independent of the offender's response.

Qualified forgiveness, however, requires the transgressor to apologize and express remorse. If that occurs, the victim then decides whether to forgive. Both types of forgiveness hold the offender accountable and subject to justice and punishment. The notion of *pardon*, however, goes beyond forgiveness and wipes the offender's moral slate clean by eliminating any penalties. At Nickel Mines, the Amish extended a no-strings-attached forgiveness to the deceased Roberts and his family. Had he survived, they said they would have forgiven but not pardoned him, leaving justice in the hands of the state.

With so many victims and offenders at Bergholz, forgiveness was much more complicated and murky than it was at Nickel Mines, where the tragedy was an unprovoked, once-and-done offense by an outsider who took his own life. At Bergholz, some people were both victim and offender. An Amish leader said, "Sam always said everybody's against him, there's no way he can get justice, no one understands him."[39] In the eyes of some of his followers, Bishop Mullet was a victim of the sanctions of the three hundred elders and of an unfair government prosecution. At the same time, other people—the victims of the attacks, members he expelled, certain women, and some relatives—viewed him as the chief offender. Who exactly carried a moral obligation to forgive?

Should the thousands of Amish people who were shamed by the attacks offer a no-strings-attached forgiveness to the bishop and the clan or wait to forgive until they hear words of apology? Should Bishop Mullet forgive the elders and the government if he was offended by them? Should the attack victims forgive the beard cutters, the abused women forgive their abusers, the Bergholz defectors forgive Bishop Mullet, and family members forgive the relatives who assaulted them? Besides, who should be apologizing to whom. Who should shoulder the hard work of saying "I'm sorry"? Clearly, a throng of offenses were awaiting apology and forgiveness in the wake of the moral morass at Bergholz.

Some people did voice forgiveness. On the witness stand, Bishop Raymond Hershberger said he forgave the attackers. Two years after the attack, Bishop Myron Miller and his wife had let go of any resentment, saying, "We don't even think about the attack anymore; it dropped out of our lives."[40] Within days of being attacked, Barb Miller expressed forgiveness to the children and in-laws who assaulted her. And on the apology side of the equation, all but two of the convicted defendants, including the Miller children, said they were sorry at their sentencing. Bishop Mullet and his son Johnny, however, showed no remorse and made no public expressions of apology.

Despite Bishop Mullet's lack of contrition and the multiple ways that the beard-cutting attacks embarrassed other Amish communities, one ex-member declared that some Amish congregations would welcome him back quickly: "Even today the Fredericktown people and related congregations, even today, they would forgive Sam and accept him back if he was contrite, and confessed, and returned to them." A minister at Fredericktown fully agreed, saying, "Yes, we'd gladly take him back into the church if he repented and confessed."[41]

Despite these offers of qualified forgiveness contingent upon confession, Amish people were not willing to pardon Sam. As noted in chapter 7, the fourteen people who wrote letters to the court prior to the sentencing all recommended imprisonment for Bishop Mullet because they deemed him a danger to their communities.

Any Lessons?

There were no winners, "no happy endings to this," said the wife of one of the bishops who was sheared.[42] Perhaps so, but that conclusion depends on one's perspective on the whole ordeal—the clan, the Amish world, and religious freedom issues.

The lives of the folks at Bergholz have surely been infused with pain, uncertainty, and family disruption, with relatives and leaders incarcerated without the possibility of parole. Outsiders, Amish and non-Amish, worry about the future of the children of the clan. How will they deal with the stigma of this tragedy that will mark their lives forever? Without meaningful ties to other Amish communities, where will they turn for marital partners, and will they be accepted into other Amish groups? Several years before the attacks, a grandfather who was estranged from his grandchildren at Bergholz asked Preacher Johnny Mullet about such issues. Johnny replied, "We'll cross that bridge later."[43] The grandchildren are now crossing that bridge, and their future is uncertain.

It may seem ironic to say that Amish people beyond Bergholz—those who were so embarrassed by what they considered bizarre happenings, those who worried that the eighteen months of relentless publicity had dimmed the light of their witness to the world—had benefited from the episode. But they did. They learned some lessons from this sad saga. A classic sociological adage posits that social deviance is not entirely bad. In fact, it does some good by defining and reinforcing virtue and vice in a group's moral order. Within the Amish world, the Bergholz story drew a sharp line, a stark reminder of what is acceptable and what is not within the Amish faith.

While the sad tale provided graphic examples of Amish virtues run amok, it also held high the Christian virtue of nonviolence preached by Amish ministers over the generations and highlighted by Bishop Hershberger when he pointed to Jesus's rejection of revenge in the face of torture and terror. "These disturbing events," said one Amish man, "remind us that strong communities are good for living together in harmony, but they are not sufficient to bring about the change of heart that is necessary to become a child of God. Even if we have a plain lifestyle, it is still possible to have wicked hearts."[44]

The perplexing events along the Yellow Creek encouraged Amish people to consider how they might preempt similar developments in other congregations. One defector from Bergholz stressed the importance of members speaking up and acting when things go askew. He lamented in retrospect, "I wish the whole Gmay would have stood its ground and blocked and stopped things." Reflecting on the Bergholz story, an Ohio bishop opined, "We forbear and forbear too long. Sometimes things need to be done earlier. We need to step in quicker if we see a problem emerging." Another Amish leader agreed, saying, "Sometimes we tolerate and give people the benefit of doubt too long. This is especially true if someone like Sam takes a conservative stance." He added, "Our community by nature is conservative so we are far more sympathetic to conservative leaders than progressive ones. Taking a conservative attitude gives you much more credence than a liberal one."[45] Claiming a mantle of conservatism, in other words, provided Sam cover for some of the peculiar practices in his Gmay.

It may be mere coincidence that the *Gemeinde Register*, the eastern Ohio Amish newsletter, carried a front-page essay on the role of ordained leaders titled "A Shepherd's Authority" in 2013. The writer described some of those in authority as "moral watchdogs, trained to tear the sinner to pieces," and goes on to say that "all true authority is founded on sympathy." The writer then described two duties of those in authority. The first is "to try to understand" the person who made a mistake. The second is "to seek to reclaim the wrongdoer." The short essay concludes with this statement: "The man set in authority must be like a wise physician, *his one desire must be to heal.*"[46]

The happenings at Bergholz helped to clarify and remind Amish ministers everywhere of their role expectations. The attacks also alerted Amish communities across North America that as citizens of the United States the nation's legal statutes apply to them. And when their informal church-based systems of justice are not adequate to cope with issues such as violence, addiction, or sexual abuse, they have an obligation not only to the victims but also to their own convictions about truth telling and the God-ordained functions of government that should compel them to reach outside their communities and seek help.[47]

What's the Big Deal?

A few days before the sentencing, Sam's nineteen-year-old grandson, Edward Mast, who was not a defendant, spoke with an Associated Press reporter visiting Bergholz. Speaking about the victims, Edward said, "They got their beard back again, so what's the big deal about it?" Sam's wife, Martha, commenting on what she considered an unfair prosecution, offered a similar view of the victims: "They can go on with their lives, their hair and beards will grow back."[48] Despite the long ordeal, Edward and Martha had missed the point.

In the words of US attorney Steve Dettelbach, the "big deal" was this: "We have to be vigilant at protecting the freedom of each person in our society to pray and worship as they wish." Furthermore, he noted, "The idea of people being dragged out of their beds in the middle of the night because of their religious belief and subjected to . . . violence is something that as a Jew causes you to shudder. The fact that it could happen here in our country makes you remember how vigilant we need to be in protecting these freedoms."[49]

The big beneficiaries in this story are the adherents of any religious faith. They can now be assured that their First Amendment right to believe and practice their religion without fear of being attacked by those who oppose it will be protected. Indeed, the government will prosecute those who violate anyone's right of free religious expression. Moreover, religious devotees should be on alert that they cannot use the First Amendment to justify any religiously motivated violence against others in the name of God. These simple, straightforward understandings are significant protections in a world overflowing with interreligious strife and violence.

Moreover, the Bergholz case demonstrates that violence in the name of religion even within religious communities will not be tolerated in the United States. And beyond the realm of religion, the larger circle of winners are those who might suffer hate crime attacks based on their perceived or actual ethnicity, disability, race, sex, or sexual orientation, even if such assaults only disfigure the body in temporary ways.

"From day one, this case has been about the rule of law and defending the right of people to worship in peace," said Dettelbach after the trial. "Our nation was founded on the bedrock principle that everyone is free to worship how they see fit. Violent attempts to attack this most basic freedom have no place in our country."[50]

Thus, ironically, no matter how strange the religious beliefs and rituals might be in the Yellow Creek Valley, the government will protect clan members from anyone who seeks to assault them because of their religion.[51] That is the "big deal," the good news for Edward Mast and the folks at Bergholz, as well as for all people of all religious persuasions in the United States of America.

EPILOGUE

Back at the Ranch

Among other reasons, Sam and Martha had established the Bergholz settlement to curb the drift toward cultural assimilation that was infiltrating some Amish settlements.[1] After the defendants arrived in prison, the worrisome drift arrived in Bergholz. Community telephones, which were previously housed in several outdoor shanties, were now installed in some homes. There were other changes as well. Ferdinand and Lizzie Miller had a baby, and, with the help of others, they were giving leadership to the community, according to one knowledgeable person.

In early December 2013, Daniel Shrock was riding in a horse-drawn buggy on County Road 53 near Bergholz when a drunk driver rear-ended his buggy and injured him. After some time in the hospital, Daniel recovered and returned to Bergholz. His brother Melvin Shrock Jr. (son of Emanuel and grandson of Melvin Sr.) had left the clan, as noted in chapter 8. Trying to find his way in the outside world, Melvin turned to Sheriff Abdalla for help getting his GED and driver's license. The two formed a friendship and the sheriff on one occasion took Melvin for a ride in his police cruiser. Melvin was awed by the ride, and, on an open stretch of road, the sheriff offered him the wheel and he drove for a mile or so. Steering the cruiser offered him an entirely new perspective on life beyond the Yellow River Valley.

Melvin's brother Eli and two of his cousins, Johnny Mast and Edward Mast—all grandsons of Sam and Martha—also left the community. The two sets of brothers moved into a home provided by a non-Amish friend about fourteen miles away from Bergholz. The four young men have driver's licenses and work in construction. As they turn eighteen years old, they receive a one-time payment from the custodial account set up after the $35 million suit that the clan filed against Jefferson County in 2008 (described in chapter 2). Once when visiting the Mount Hope Auction in Holmes County dressed in their mainstream clothing, the boys were "shocked and surprised" by the warm welcome they received from other Amish people. Several of these young men, according to one ex-member, are considering joining Amish churches in other parts of Ohio.

By April 2014, the defendants with one-year sentences—Freeman Burkholder and all but one of the women—had returned to the Bergholz community. For undisclosed reasons, one defendant was excommunicated while serving his five-year sentence in a federal prison in Yazoo City, Mississippi. This abrupt change of status stifled virtually all contact with his family. Such a breach of fellowship, occurring when the offender and all of the clergy of a congregation were in prison, was certainly another first-time oddity in the Amish world. And, in yet another surprise, one of the women inmates serving time in Waseca, Minnesota, was said to be contemplating divorcing her husband so she could marry God.

With its bishop serving a fifteen-year sentence and both of its preachers seven-year sentences, the future of Bergholz is uncertain and unpredictable. The myth of Sam's suffering as a "martyr" in prison may provide emotional energy to sustain the community for some time. If so, the clan may continue to grow and develop its own distinctive lifestyle and identity. However, the martyr myth may fade, and some sheep in the flock may abandon it to affiliate with other Amish or Amish-related groups or with none at all. And, of course, the clan will shrivel if a rapid exodus occurs. The intense bonding produced by the community's travails over the past ten years likely means that a remnant of loyalists will at least maintain the clan for a time.

Meanwhile, beyond Bergholz one of the bishops whose beard was sheared on the evening of October 4, 2011, was still pondering the possible connection between two sets of numbers. In II Samuel 10:4, the Old Book records the time when Hanun, an opponent of King David, shaved off the beards of King David's ambassadors. They were so ashamed by the shearing that they refused to return to Jerusalem. Was there a possible connection between 10/4 of 2011 and chapter 10 verse 4 in II Samuel? he wondered. Were these identical sets of numbers just a coincidence, part of a divine message, or the work of clever strategists at Bergholz?

The Appeal

In late February 2013, the defendants filed a notice of appeal seeking appellate review of their convictions by the United States Court of Appeals for the Sixth Circuit, which has appellate jurisdiction over judgments entered by federal trial courts in Kentucky, Michigan, Ohio, and Tennessee.[2] Likewise, the government filed an extensive brief in February 2014 rebutting the defendants' appeal.[3] The outcome of the appeal process will likely not be known until late 2014.

In March 2013, Judge Polster denied a petition from some of the defendants to be released from custody while their case was being reviewed by the appellate court. The judge also rejected a request in April from Sam Mullet to be released on bond pending the appeal of his case.[4] Mullet then petitioned the appellate court to be released from cruel and unusual punishment in prison while his case was under appeal.[5] The sixth circuit court of appeals turned down the request, noting that the particular issues cited in the petition "are not likely to result in a reversal, a new trial, a sentence that does not include a term of imprisonment, or a reduced sentence."[6]

There are four possible outcomes from the pending appellate court decision. The court may (1) uphold the convictions of the jury, (2) require a new trial because of prejudice or procedural errors in the original one, (3) determine that the hate crimes statute is unconstitutional for all hate crimes or unconstitutional as it was applied to the beard-cutting case, or (4) acquit the defendants on one or more of the charges because of lack of sufficient evidence. The third or fourth option would lead to a dismissal of some of the charges against certain defendants.

The significant legal questions include the following: (1) Did federal prosecutors wield unconstitutional powers in their application of the 2009 hate crimes statute to obtain the convictions? In other words, is the Shepard-Byrd Act itself unconstitutional? (2) Was the evidence of interstate commerce (use of vehicles and travel on interstate highways; out-of-state manufacturing of the shears, clippers, and camera; and use of the US Postal Service) adequate to merit federal jurisdiction of the case?[7] (3) Did Congress intend for the hate crimes statute to cover religiously motivated violence *within* a religious group? (4) Were the victims kidnapped or just restrained? (5) Does beard cutting, as temporary disfigurement, qualify as a form of bodily injury for a hate crime victim? And, finally, (6) does the 2009 Shepard-Byrd hate crimes law infringe on the First Amendment rights of the defendants to freely practice their religion?

A panel of three judges will make the appellate court decision. Attorneys from each side of the case will be given the opportunity to make oral arguments, and then the court will announce its decision, likely by the end of 2014. If the sixth circuit court of appeals upholds the convictions of the jury trial, the defendants may petition to the US Supreme Court. Likewise, if the appellate court reverses any of the convictions, the prosecutors may petition the Supreme Court.[8] Two constitutional law professors as well as Judge Polster consider the issues significant enough that they suspect the case might eventually end up in the Supreme Court.[9] Although the Supreme Court hears very few petitions (only 1 in 111),[10] this case may be of interest if constitutional issues are at stake or if federal circuit courts have inconsistently interpreted and applied the Shepard-Byrd Act.

Legal scholar Christopher DiPompeo, in an analysis of the 2009 Shepard-Byrd Hate Crimes Prevention Act, concludes that "challenges to its constitutionality will accompany any attempted prosecutions." In particular, DiPompeo thinks the federal hate

crimes law enacted by Congress is "on a collision course" with
the Supreme Court's interpretation of the commerce clause in
the US Constitution.[11] The constitutionality question hinges on
whether the US Congress violated the Constitution when it tied
some elements of the 2009 hate crimes law to interstate commerce to grant federal jurisdiction over a crime.[12]

■ ■ ■

The Hate Crimes Debate

Law enforcement agencies at all levels reported 7,164 hate crimes
in 2012. The religion of the victim accounted for one in five (19
percent) of the crimes.[13] The bulk of these criminal acts were
prosecuted by local and state agencies; however, federal officials
prosecuted some religious hate crimes under the federal hate
crimes laws enacted in the Civil Rights Act of 1968.[14] The Bergholz case was the first prosecution of hate crimes motivated by
religion in the country under the Shepard-Byrd Act of 2009 and
the first one where the assailants and victims were from the
same religious tradition.[15]

As noted in the preface, the Anti-Defamation League led a
coalition of forty prominent civil rights, religious, law enforcement, LGBT, educational, and professional organizations in
filing a friend-of-the-court brief urging the United States
Court of Appeals for the Sixth Circuit to uphold the constitutionality of the Shepard-Byrd Act and to affirm that the statute
applies to religiously motivated violence within the same faith
community.[16]

Apart from the general argument for the importance and
constitutionality of Shepard-Byrd, the coalition's brief makes
three specific arguments: (1) Shepard-Byrd does not create ex-
ceptions for crimes committed against people within the same
religion of the perpetrator. That the Bergholz appellants claim
to identify as Amish, as do the victims, cannot shield them from
culpability under Shepard-Byrd.[17] (2) Moreover, Shepard-Byrd
does not infringe on the First Amendment. It criminalizes in-
tentional conduct (i.e., violence); it does not criminalize beliefs

or thoughts. The First Amendment does not protect violence, but it does safeguard beliefs and speech, however obnoxious they may be.[18] (3) Shepard-Byrd "does not interfere with religious free-exercise rights, but rather safeguards such rights."[19]

Opponents of federal hate crime legislation insist that local and state hate crime laws are sufficient to prosecute offenders. Federal laws that privilege special groups of people because of their gender, sexual orientation, religion, race, or disability are unnecessary. Political commentator Michael Savage, an outspoken critic of federal overreach, asked, "Why is [President] Obama persecuting the Amish people?" Savage contends that because of a bizarre internal feud Amish people were "imprisoned out-of-state so their families can't visit them, because the Amish can't fly or drive." Meanwhile, he notes, former New Jersey governor Jon Corzine "gets no jail time for $1.5 billion in missing funds . . . and drug dealers and gang members get less jail time" than the Amish.[20] Savage was so outraged by the convictions that he established a legal defense fund for the convicted Amish, saying "if we do not come to the aid of the Amish, they [federal government] can trump up a case against anyone for any reason."[21]

Harvard law professor Noah Feldman, in an essay titled "Is Cutting Off a Beard a Hate Crime?," contends that charging the beard cutters with federal hate crimes is a misconceived and "potentially harmful extension" of the 2009 Shepard-Byrd hate crimes statute.[22] Feldman thinks the Bergholz prosecution was an overly broad interpretation of the federal statute. He told the Associated Press, "If you accept the interpretation that this is a hate crime, then any dispute within a religious group could be called a hate crime. If I think my wife should obey me and my religion teaches me so and I take a swing at her, then I've committed a hate crime."[23] In reality, Feldman's *own* religious beliefs do not matter for his hypothetical case. What matters for the Shepard-Byrd statute is if he attacks his wife because of *her* religious beliefs.

Nationally syndicated columnist Jacob Sullum worries that the Bergholz case might mean that a "religious leader who uses corporal punishment to discipline wayward followers" will be guilty of a federal hate crime. He suggests these examples: "a Hassid who slugs another Hassid after getting into an argument about who the next rebbe should be, two Catholics who come to blows over the merits of the Latin Mass, or two Mormons who tussle after one condemns the other for drinking caffeinated soft drinks." In short, Sullum thinks that the defendants in the Mullet case were "effectively being punished for their religious beliefs, since they would not have been prosecuted under federal law if their motivation had been nonreligious."[24] Again, Sullum's concerns are tangential to the Bergholz case. The beard cutters were prosecuted because their attacks were motivated by their perceptions of the *victims'* religious practices, and the free exercise clause of the First Amendment does not protect religiously motivated violence.

In a somewhat related vein, a professor of Anabaptist history fears that the guilty verdict might have a "chilling effect" on religious freedom in the United States. Could such a verdict set a precedent for ending any form of church discipline, even making it possible for a shunned Amish person to take the Amish church to court for shunning?[25] Perhaps so, if the shunning involved bodily injury; however, physical force is never espoused by Amish leaders for any type of adult discipline. The 2009 hate crimes statute explicitly states that "solely emotional or psychological harm to the victim" does not constitute bodily injury.[26] Thus, a church member who experiences emotional or psychological harm from excommunication and shunning would have no recourse to Shepard-Byrd.

Finally, Professor Feldman argues that if the convictions of the Amish beard cutters are upheld "it will mark a defeat for religious and civil liberty, not a victory for equality." The professor is wary of turning "everything immoral into a federal case" and especially leery of turning intrareligious group conflict into federal crimes. He contends that "over time, a hate crimes law designed as a shield to protect religious groups against bias could easily become a sword with which to prosecute them."[27]

Postscript

With such a brew of conflicting ideas simmering in the pot of jurisprudence, many minds were awaiting the decision of the United States Court of Appeals for the Sixth Circuit in Cincinnati, Ohio.

On August 27, 2014, the appellate court, in a 2–1 decision, overturned the hate crime convictions while leaving the other convictions—conspiracy, perjury, and obstructing justice—intact. Surprisingly, the majority opinion did not address the constitutionality issues of Shepard-Byrd, but instead focused on the instructions to the jury.

The federal district judge had told the jury that a conviction required that a victim's "actual or perceived religion was a *significant* motivating factor for a defendant's action . . . even if he or she had *other* reasons" for attacking the victim. The appellate court opinion made a distinction between religion as the *primary* motive and religion as a *significant* motive among other motives. Was religion the *primary* reason the assailants attacked the victims or was it only *one* significant reason among others such as familial strife? The district court used a more *expansive* definition of motive(s) driving the Amish hate crimes. The more *restrictive* appellate court interpretation required that religion must be *the* predominant motive for a religious hate crime. The dissenting judge strongly disagreed, saying, "The overwhelming and unrefuted evidence adduced at trial demonstrates that Mullet participated in the assaults because of the victims' religious beliefs."

On October 10, 2014, the prosecution petitioned the appellate court for a full court (en banc) review of the case. With the case going into extra innings, the ensuing legal decisions will establish a judicial standard for how the Shepard-Byrd Hate Crimes Prevention Act is interpreted in the future for all hate crimes sparked by a victim's gender, sexual orientation, disability, race, ethnicity, or religion. If the appellate court's restrictive interpretation remains unchallenged, future hate crime prosecutions will require evidence of a *predominant* motive for attacks that cause bodily injury.

November 1, 2014

Postscript II

The appeals court declined the prosecution's request that all of its judges (en banc) review the case. This upheld the appellate court's decision (2–1) of August 27, 2014, that overturned the hate crime convictions. Consequently, the restrictive interpretation that religion must be the predominant motive for religious hate crime convictions prevailed.

On March 2, 2015, federal judge Polster in the US District court in Cleveland resentenced Bishop Mullet and seven other defendants on charges relating to conspiracy to obstruct justice, making false statements, and kidnapping. Eight other defendants, six of whom were women, had already served their time. The judge shrank the bishop's sentence from fifteen years to ten years and nine months. The seven-year sentences of four men were reduced to five years. Three other defendants saw their sentences decline from five years to three years and seven months.

In December 2016, Sam Mullet's attorney petitioned the US Supreme Court to reduce the length of the new sentences based on the constitutionality of the federal statutes that were used to convict Mullet and two other defendants and the interpretation of the federal sentencing guidelines for kidnapping. In February 2017, the Supreme Court refused to hear the case, thus ending the long legal phase of the Bergholz saga.

In other Bergholz matters, Mullet's wife, Martha, died in November 2014. Some young people and several adults left the Bergholz community, but most of the members remained. Johnny Mast, one of the bishop's grandsons who left, wrote a poignant account of his experiences—*Breakaway Amish: Growing up with the Bergholz Beard Cutters*. Meanwhile, Bishop Mullet, who remained incarcerated, had his seventy-second birthday in September 2017.

November 30, 2017

Appendix I
Mullet Family Tree

Only the relatives of Sam Mullet who are mentioned
in the book appear here.

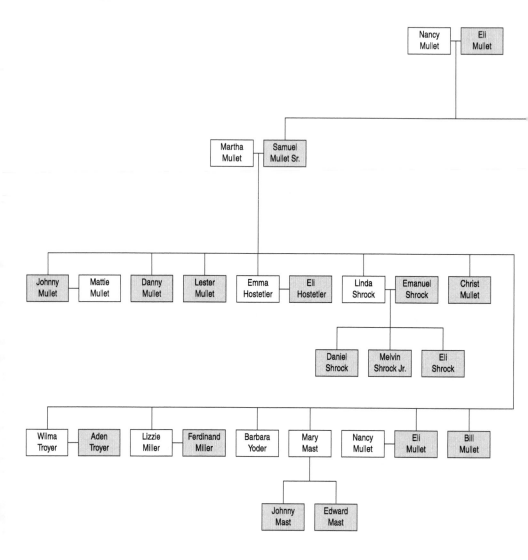

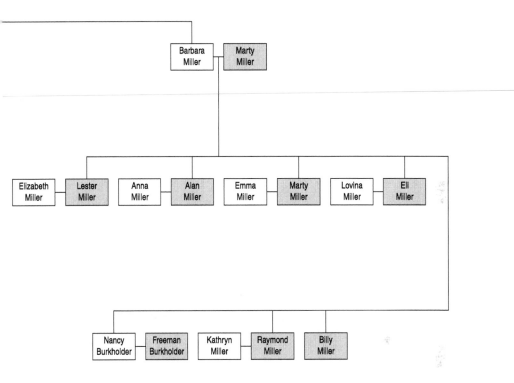

Appendix II
Who Are the Amish?

Roots

The Amish descend from the Anabaptist movement, which emerged in Europe at the time of the sixteenth-century Protestant Reformation.[1] The Anabaptists (rebaptizers) rejected the common practice of infant baptism because they believed that only adults who voluntarily decide to follow the teachings of Jesus should be baptized. Because adult baptism was a capital offense, civic and religious authorities alike condemned Anabaptists as religious heretics and political revolutionaries and sentenced them to the medieval equivalent of the electric chair: burning at the stake. Some twenty-five hundred Anabaptists died a martyr's death between 1527 and 1614. As obedient disciples of Jesus, they renounced violence (even in self-defense) and forgave those who assailed them. Even today, Amish people recount stories from their martyr heritage recorded in the massive twelve-hundred-page *Martyrs Mirror* found in many Amish homes.

The radical reformers established small church communities—sometimes meeting in secret to avoid arrest—that held members accountable to one another for their faith and daily practice. Anabaptists believed that the church should be an alternative community whose values and practices set it apart from mainstream society. To them, the New Testament was a higher source of authority than government edicts, citing the Apostle Peter: "We must obey God rather than men" (Acts 5:29).

In 1693, nearly 170 years after the birth of Anabaptism, the Amish church carved out its own identity when it branched off from the mainline Anabaptists in Switzerland and the Alsace area of present-day France. Their leader and namesake was Jakob Ammann, a recent convert. Ammann called for a sharp distinction between the church and society. He also advocated reforms in church discipline based on the 1632 Dordrecht Confession of Faith written by Mennonites in the Netherlands. Article 17 of that confession explicitly advocates social avoidance on biblical grounds. Ammann expected church members to avoid (shun) expelled members in symbolic ways such as not eating with them.

Within two generations of the beginning of the Amish church, some families began arriving in North America. Amish immigrants from Switzerland, Germany, and France came to North America in several waves between the 1730s and 1850s. About five hundred Amish arrived through the port of Philadelphia before the American Revolution and settled in southeastern Pennsylvania. Some of these households eventually moved into central and western Pennsylvania, and their descendants planted new communities from eastern Ohio to southeastern Iowa by 1840. The last European congregation dissolved in 1937, and by the twenty-first century, all Amish people were living in the United States and Canada.

The first Amish settlers in the state of Ohio came from Somerset County, Pennsylvania. They arrived in Holmes County in 1809, and by 1835, nearly 250 Amish families had settled there. About fifty years later, families from Holmes County moved north about one hundred miles to settle near Middlefield, Ohio, in 1885. They were joined by Amish pioneers from western Pennsylvania who formed what has become the Geauga County settlement, which stretches into Trumbull and Ashtabula Counties.[2]

View of the State

The religious convictions of the Anabaptists, combined with the harsh persecution they experienced in sixteenth-century Europe, honed a sharp separation of church and state, which the Amish also embraced.[3] They make a distinction between two kingdoms: the kingdom of Jesus anchored on peace, forgiveness, and nonresistance to evil, and the political kingdom of this world, which rests on the use of force—or at least the threat of it—to maintain order. Moreover, a political kingdom has the power to conscript citizens to fight and die to protect it. In his Sermon on the Mount, Jesus advocates not resisting enemies but instead loving them, not exacting revenge on evildoers but forgiving them. In the Amish view, the foundational values of these two kingdoms are difficult to reconcile.

The Amish view of the state is perplexing. On the one hand, the Amish affirm that God has ordained government. On the other hand, they assert that people must obey God rather than man. They believe that God has ordained secular government to protect the good and punish the evil; yet they insist that if the government asks them to do something the Bible forbids their first loyalty must always be to God. Since the Amish were founded, their leaders have exhorted the members to respect and pray for civil authorities. The Amish appreciate civic order, legal property ownership, and other benefits of a functional state, and they cooperate with law enforcement as long as doing so does not violate their religious conscience.

Yet they will not fight to defend the state or even participate in noncombatant military activities. To the extent that they can, the Amish also avoid entanglements with the courts and the criminal justice system. The prohibition against using force includes a taboo on holding public office and government employment, because such activities may require litigation. The Amish are permitted to vote, but their turnout is typically low and sometimes nil in the most traditional affiliations. All Amish groups forbid political campaigning.

The Amish are loath to file lawsuits for any reason because they see such action as an expression of force. And they are reticent about testifying in court or serving on juries out of obedience to the teaching of Jesus: "Judge not, that ye be not judged." Despite some reluctance, Amish people do report major criminal acts by other Amish and by outsiders. Yet even when they cooperate with the police, they are very reluctant to press charges against their own people or outsiders because, in their minds, doing so would violate Jesus's admonition to not use force.

Amish leaders prefer to resolve conflicts within their community using established church routines of discipline, confession, repentance, and sanctions determined by the local congregation or—when those fail—excommunication.

The Amish pay state and federal taxes (income, sales, and real estate) and do not object to having a lawyer draw up a will or prepare legal agreements for a business. They believe that they should pay their taxes, express gratitude, live in quiet obedience, and pray for their rulers. For its part, government at all levels in the United States has generally accommodated Amish religious beliefs and practices by providing exemptions from jury duty, military service, education requirements, Social Security, the Affordable Care Act, and some workplace regulations governing child labor.

Tough Love

Excommunication terminates church membership, and shunning pertains to the treatment of ex-members. Only members who refuse to confess a major transgression of church teachings are excommunicated and shunned. Amish congregations do not excommunicate or shun Amish teenagers who decide not to be baptized and eventually leave the church.

Amish churches follow an established process of discipline for those who transgress church teachings and practices. Offenders are given the opportunity to confess their sins, and if contrite, are pardoned and restored into the full fellowship of the Gmay. Transgressors who show no remorse and refuse to heed the counsel of ministers will eventually face a slow, patient process of excommunication, which requires a vote of the membership upon recommendation of the bishop. Excommunicated members are placed "in the ban," meaning that they are banned from participating in Holy Communion, members' meetings, and some other church rites and gatherings.

They are also shunned. Amish leaders did not invent the practice of shunning, which is based on some half-dozen New Testament passages that describe social avoidance.[4] In 1 Corinthians 5, the Apostle Paul urges church members to clean out the "old leaven" of "malice and wickedness" before they eat the Lord's Supper (1 Cor. 5:8). In a pointed admonition, Paul tells the Corinthian church to remove a wicked person from its midst and "deliver such an one unto Satan" so that his or her spirit will eventually be saved (1 Cor. 5:5). Shunning is part of the early Christian tradition and continues to be practiced by some Anabaptist groups (the Hutterites, Old Colony Mennonites, and Holdeman Mennonites) as well as other groups, such as the Jehovah's Witnesses.

Social avoidance reminds offenders of the seriousness of defaulting on their baptismal vows with the hope that they will confess their errors and return to the church. Ex-members are not enemies of the church, leaders are quick to note, but brothers and sisters who must be treated with love. The shunning is not designed to punish wayward members but to remind them of the seriousness of their offense against God and the church, in the hope that they will repent and return to the fold.

Shunning does not mean severing all social ties. Members may, for example, converse with ex-members, but social avoidance does restrict certain types of interaction. Members are permitted to help and visit ex-members, but offenders are not granted the dignity of aiding a member. Church members generally do not accept anything—gifts or payments, for example—directly from the hands of an offender, or accept rides in an offender's car, or eat at the same table. Sometimes, for public meals within the community, a different tablecloth or several inches of separation between tables mark the boundary between present and former members. Because these are *group* rites of shaming—not acts of personal animosity—their importance swells in social settings. A more liberal family, in the privacy of their home, might welcome an ex-member to their table, but they would not be comfortable eating with the same person at a wedding, funeral, or similar public gathering.

Since the early twentieth century, Amish communities have distinguished between those that practice *strict* shunning, which is lifelong (unless the offender repents), and those that practice a more *lenient* form of shunning in which lifting the ban is easier. The stricter style requires transgressors to confess their error to the congregation that excommunicated them. More lenient Amish affiliations will stop shunning a wayward person if he or she joins a plain-dressing Amish Mennonite or Mennonite church. Regardless of how shunning is terminated, its practical application varies from family to family and from affiliation to affiliation. Traditional churches are harsher than liberal ones.

The Amish believe they have a divine responsibility to hold accountable those who break their baptismal vows, to remind them of the eternal consequences of this breach, and to preserve the purity of the church. In the Amish view, shunning is a form of tough love for backsliders. Some ex-members become bitter toward the church and denounce shunning as an abusive, unloving practice. Some of them remain embittered for life. Many others make a more or less smooth transition to the outside world and leave any anger behind. Ex-members can, however, return to the fold anytime and receive pardon—after confessing their transgression.

Growth and Diversity

The state of Ohio has fifty-five different Amish settlements and nearly five hundred church districts (congregations) with more than sixty thousand people. Ohio and Pennsylvania each claim about 23 percent of North America's Amish population. The remaining 54 percent reside in twenty-nine other states and the Canadian province of Ontario. The Holmes County settlement, which sprawls into several other counties, is home to about thirty-two thousand Amish, while the Geauga County area has fifteen thousand.

The Amish population in North America doubles about every twenty years. From a scant six thousand people in 1900, the Amish population now exceeds two hundred eighty-five thousand.[5] Because few outsiders convert and because the Amish do not evangelize or proselytize, their robust growth is fueled almost entirely by their large family size and strong retention. The children of Amish parents are not members of the church unless they choose to join, which typically happens in their late teens or early twenties. Beginning at age sixteen and continuing until baptism, youth engage in Rumspringa. This is a time when they are free to socialize with their friends and interact more freely with outsiders because they are not baptized and restricted by church regulations. Some 85 percent of Amish youth, on average, opt for baptism.

There are some forty different affiliations—clusters of church districts linked by social and spiritual bonds—in the Amish world. Ohio has at least twenty different affiliations. Although all of them subscribe to basic Amish teachings and values, they each have distinct symbols of identity and practices that set them apart, such as the color of their buggies, their dress styles, and their technology. Affiliations fall along a continuum from traditional to progressive. Progressive affiliations are more assimilated into mainstream culture. Members of the most traditional affiliations still use outhouses, milk their cows by hand, and use kerosene lanterns for lights on their buggies at night. Members of the more progressive affiliations, however, install LED lights on their carriages, use automatic milkers, carry cell phones, and advertise their business wares on the Internet.

In many settlements, shop owners, mechanics, carpenters, and factory workers are fast replacing farmers. Homemaking remains the occupation of most Amish women but increasing numbers own and manage small businesses. In some groups, construction crews travel to suburban areas for work. In others, this is prohibited. A growing diversity marks the Amish world. Since each Gmay determines its own regulations, and with more than twenty-one hundred congregations, there are dozens of different ways to be Amish in America.

To fortify their way of life, most Amish groups have constructed certain cultural fences of *resistance*—plain dress, horse-drawn transportation, religious rituals, and a distinctive dialect. They have rejected high school education, public-grid electricity, and television. Some Amish parents paid the high price of imprisonment for their resistance to consolidated public schools and required high school attendance in mid-twentieth-century America.

The more progressive Amish tribes have reached across their cultural fences and *accepted* certain practices of modern life—the use of detergents in homes, insecticides on farms, high-precision milling machines in shops, inline skates, and, in some communities, cell phones, to name but a few. By accepting these innovations from the outside world, they have enhanced their lifestyle and increased the productivity of their farms and shops.

Most interestingly, the Amish have *negotiated* with modernity, re-jecting some aspects of a particular practice while accepting other parts of it. They selectively participate in modern life: riding in cars but not owning them, tapping electricity from batteries but not from the public grid, working in retail sales and light manufacturing but not in the professions, installing gas refrigerators instead of electric ones, using tractors for stationary power at the barn but not for pulling equipment in the fields, and so on. This process of bargaining with modernity—striking cultural compromises that blend aspects of tradition and modernity—has enabled the Amish to maintain their ethnic identity and, at the same time, flourish economically.

Notes

Chapter 1. The Attacks

1. Sources for this section, unless otherwise cited: Trial Transcript, vol. 3, 529–633, United States v. Samuel Mullet, Sr., et al., No. 5:11CR594 (US Dist. Ct., Northern Dist. of Ohio, Aug. 29, 2012); Mullet trial transcript, vol. 4, 641–95 (Aug. 30, 2012).

2. Interview with Amish man, Oct. 3, 2013.

3. *Die Botschaft*, Sept. 19, 2001, 46.

4. Sources for this section, unless otherwise cited: Mullet trial transcript, vol. 6, 1282–347 (Sept. 6, 2012).

5. *Ohio Amish Directory: Fredericktown Settlement 1973–2001*; *Ohio Amish Directory: Fredericktown Settlement 1973–2011*; *Directory of Ashland and Richland County Amish Settlement 2000*.

6. Sources for the first part of this section, unless otherwise cited: Mullet trial transcript, vol. 5, 1073–91 (Sept. 5, 2012).

7. Ibid., 1105.

8. For a history and description of this Amish affiliation, see Hurst and McConnell, *An Amish Paradox*, 43–48.

9. Sources for the second part of this section, unless otherwise cited: Mullet trial transcript, vol. 3, 358–528 (Aug. 29, 2012), vol. 5, 907–1000 (Sept. 5, 2012), and vol. 9, 2176–254 (Sept. 11, 2012).

10. Interview with Amish minister, Nov. 15, 2012.

11. Interview with Amish bishop, Nov. 15, 2012.

12. Interview with Amish woman, Nov. 15, 2012.

13. Interview with Amish minister, Nov. 15, 2012.

14. Interview with Amish man, Nov. 15, 2012.

15. Interview with Amish woman, Nov. 15, 2012; written correspondence from jury foreman, Jan. 15, 2014.

16. Interview with Amish minister, Nov. 15, 2012.

17. Interview with law enforcement officer, Oct. 4, 2013.

18. Interview with Amish minister, Nov. 15, 2012.

19. Sources for this section: Mullet trial transcript, vol. 6, 1175–264 (Sept. 6, 2012), and vol. 5, 1073–91 (Sept. 5, 2012); interview with Amish man, Nov. 16, 2012; and interview with Amish woman, Nov. 16, 2012.

20. Sources for this section, unless otherwise cited: Mullet trial transcript, vol. 5, 1092–150 (Sept. 5, 2012), and vol. 7, 1640–86 (Sept. 7, 2012).

21. The text of the October 17 letter appears in Mullet trial transcript, vol. 7, 1654–56 (Sept. 7, 2012).

22. The text of the October 24 letter appears in Mullet trial transcript, vol. 7, 1657–59 (Sept. 7, 2012). Emphasis added.

23. The text of the November 5 letter appears in Mullet trial transcript, vol. 7, 1661–62 (Sept. 7, 2012).

24. Interview with law enforcement officer, Jan. 15, 2014.

25. Interview with Amish man, Feb. 24, 2014.

26. Interview with law enforcement officer, Jan. 15, 2014.

27. See Byers, Crider, and Biggers, "Bias Crime Motivation"; Byers and Crider, "Hate Crimes against the Amish"; Byers, "Amish Victimization and Offending."

28. For background on Amish views of the state, see Kraybill, *The Amish and the State*; Kraybill, Johnson-Weiner, and Nolt, *The Amish*, chapters 2 and 19; and Hurst and McConnell, *An Amish Paradox*, 177–79, 276–77.

29. Kraybill, Nolt, and Weaver-Zercher, *Amish Grace*, 23–24.

30. For an overview of the Amish affiliations in North America, see Kraybill, Johnson-Weiner, and Nolt, *The Amish*, chapter 8. For a description of the different affiliations in Holmes County, Ohio, see Hurst and McConnell, *An Amish Paradox*, chapters 2 and 3, and Beachy, *Unser Leit*, vol. 2.

31. Ammann, "Summary and Defense (November 22, 1693)," 43.

32. These four documents are reprinted in Byler, *Alte Schreibens*: Apr. 29, 1752, Steinseltz, Alsace Diener Versammlung, Article 7, 43; Oct. 21 and 22, 1779, Essingen, Germany, Diener Versammlung, Article 13, 50; Oct. 17, 1809, Pennsylvania Diener Versammlung, Article 7, 54; July 1, 1865, Holmes County, Ohio, Diener Versammlung, 67.

33. Stoll, "War of the Whiskers," 8–10.

34. *1001 Questions*, 137.

35. Mullet trial transcript, vol. 3, 531–32 (Aug. 29, 2012).

36. Interview with Amish bishop, Aug. 8, 2012; interview with Amish man, Aug. 20, 2012.

37. Interview with Amish bishop, Nov. 15, 2012.

38. An incident with only faint similarity, which did not involve beard cutting, occurred in the Holmes County settlement in the early 1990s when some vindictive Amish youth cut the hair of a minister they did not like. Hurst and McConnell, *An Amish Paradox*, 41–43; Stevick, *Growing Up Amish*, 112.

Chapter 2. The Clan

1. Trial Transcript, vol. 3, 535–37, United States v. Samuel Mullet, Sr., et al., No. 5:11CR594 (US Dist. Ct., Northern Dist. of Ohio, Aug. 29, 2012); *Ohio Amish Directory: Geauga County, 1973 Edition*, 85; interview with Amish man, Oct. 3, 2013.

2. Hearing Transcript, vol. 1, 5–7, 22–23, 100–101, Aden L. Troyer v. Wilma S. Troyer, Nos. 2007-CU-74 and 2007-CU-75 (Ct. of Common Pleas Juvenile Div., Jefferson Co., Ohio, Jan. 11, 2008).

3. See Hurst and McConnell, *An Amish Paradox*, 99–100, for a discussion of Amish birthrates in Ohio. Birthrates vary considerably among Amish groups. More progressive groups average five children per family, and more traditional groups average ten children. An overview of birthrates by group appears in Kraybill, Johnson-Weiner, and Nolt, *The Amish*, 156–58.

4. *Ohio Amish Directory: Fredericktown Settlement 1973–2001*, 23; *Hazen Amish Directory 2011*, 22.

5. Interview with Amish man, Feb. 24, 2014.

6. Letter from Sam and Martha Mullet to Amish leader (unpublished correspondence), Dec. 28, 2006.

7. Interview with Amish man, Mar. 4, 2014; Hearing Transcript, 185–86, 220–21, Aden Troyer v. Wilma S. Troyer, Nos. 2007-CU-74 and 2007-CU-75 (Ct. of Common Pleas Juvenile Div., Jefferson Co., Ohio, Oct. 5, 2007).

8. Troyer hearing transcript, 219 (Oct. 5, 2007).

9. Interview with Amish man, Aug. 20, 2012.

10. Letter from Sam and Martha Mullet to Amish leader (unpublished correspondence), Dec. 28, 2006. Emphasis in the original.

11. Stoll, "War of the Whiskers," 9–10.

12. *Who Is Who in the* Budget, 267.

13. Letter from Sam and Martha Mullet to Amish leader (unpublished correspondence), Dec. 28, 2006. Emphasis in the original.

14. Sources for the early years of Bergholz: "Fredericktown, OH," *Budget*, May 3, 1995; "Bergholz, OH," *Budget*, Jan. 26, 2000, 23; "Bergholz, OH," *Budget*, Feb. 2, 2000, 17; "Bergholz, OH," *Budget*, Feb. 7, 2001, 29.

15. M. L. Nestel and Jebediah Reed, "A Bishop behind Bars," *Daily*, Dec. 3, 2012.

16. The meeting included seventeen bishops, some of whom were from the Ashland settlement where the leaders met. Interview with Amish man, Mar. 4, 2014.

17. Kraybill, Johnson-Weiner, and Nolt, *The Amish*, 90–92; Kraybill, Nolt, and Weaver-Zercher, *The Amish Way*, 51–53.

18. Sources for the ordinations: "Bergholz, OH," *Budget*, Apr. 26, 2000, 17; "Bergholz, OH," *Budget*, Oct. 25, 2000, 2; "Bergholz, OH," *Budget*, May 16, 2001, 5; "Bergholz, OH," *Budget*, Oct. 17, 2001, 4; Raber's *New American Almanac*, 2001, 2002, 2003.

19. Interview with Amish man, Aug. 20, 2012. However, another member did not recall anything unusual prior to the ordination. Interview with Amish man, Feb. 28, 2014.

20. Interview with Amish bishop, Aug. 8, 2012.

21. Interview with Amish man, Aug. 15, 2012. The Paraguay settlement lasted only from 1967 to 1978.

22. Interview with Amish man, Mar. 4, 2014; interview with Amish man, Feb. 24, 2014; and interview with Amish man, Aug. 20, 2012.

23. Interview with Amish man, Aug. 20, 2012. One bishop disagreed that the first ordination at Bergholz was rushed: "We go by the disciples. We look at how short a time it was after Judas's death when a replacement was selected." Interview with Amish bishop, Nov. 17, 2012.

24. The quotations and the eyewitness descriptions of the psychotic break are found in Troyer hearing transcript, 22–79 (Oct. 5, 2007), and in Mullet trial testimony, vol. 4, 813–26 (Aug. 30, 2012).

25. Interview with ex-member of Bergholz, Aug. 20, 2012.

26. "Bergholz, OH," *Budget*, Apr. 12, 2006, 36; "Bergholz, OH," *Budget*, May 3, 2006, 5.

27. Interview with Amish leader, Aug. 30, 2012.

28. For numerous testimonies about intimidation, see Troyer hearing transcript, 58–209 (Oct. 5, 2007).

29. "Bergholz, OH," *Budget*, Sept. 20, 2006, 28.

30. Interview with Amish bishop, Nov. 17, 2012.

31. Kraybill, Johnson-Weiner, and Nolt, *The Amish*, 164–68.

32. Some other Anabaptist churches, as well as the Jehovah's Witnesses, also practice shunning. For an Amish explanation of the practice,

see *Biblical Guidelines in Shunning*. Bible verses typically cited to support shunning include I Corinthians 5:2–8; Matthew 18:15–18; Romans 6:17; II Thessalonians 3:6, 14–15; II Timothy 3:2–5; and Titus 3:10.

33. The text of the eighteen articles of the Dordrecht Confession of Faith appears in *In Meiner Jugend*, an Amish publication.

34. Interview with Amish bishop, Aug. 20, 2012.

35. Interview with Amish bishop, Nov. 17, 2012.

36. Ibid.

37. Ibid.

38. Interview with ex-member of Bergholz, Aug. 20, 2012.

39. In Amish documents and parlance, the two committees are called "the Five-Bishop Committee" and "the Seven-Bishop Committee." In this narrative, they are labeled the investigation committee and the listening committee, respectively.

40. Interview with Amish bishop, Nov. 17, 2012.

41. The bishops in some Amish communities might act more decisively to prohibit a wayward bishop from preaching, performing religious ceremonies, and disciplining than the Amish leaders did at Ulysses. Despite such a firm, official action, a "silenced" bishop could continue to serve as an independent bishop for any members willing to follow him.

42. Troyer hearing transcript, vol. 1, 101–15 (Jan. 11, 2008).

43. Troyer hearing transcript, 232–33 (Oct. 5, 2007); Troyer hearing transcript, vol. 1, 102–13 (Jan. 11, 2008).

44. Interview with ex-member of Bergholz, Oct. 25, 2012. A different defector expressed a very similar view. Interview with Amish man, Feb. 24, 2014.

45. Letter from Sam and Martha Mullet to Amish leader (unpublished correspondence), Dec. 28, 2006.

46. The history of this case is summarized in Opinion, 1–17, Troyer v. Troyer, No. 09 JE 5 (Ct. of Appeals of Ohio, Seventh Appellate Dist., Jefferson Co., June 28, 2010), http://www.supreme courtofohio.gov/rod/docs/pdf/7/2010/2010-ohio-3276.pdf. The hearing transcripts provide extensive testimony from Bishop Mullet and other witnesses about some unorthodox practices in the Bergholz community.

47. Amish people typically do not file lawsuits or involve the courts in church or family matters, even custody disputes, unless they need to respond to legal actions against them.

48. Interview with law enforcement officer, Jan. 15, 2014.

49. Troyer opinion (June 28, 2010).

50. Complaint for Violation of Civil Rights, 15–18, 23, Samuel Mullet, et al. v. Jefferson County Sheriff's Department/Office, et al., No. 2:08-CV-00857 (US Dist. Ct., Southern Dist. of Ohio, Sept. 12, 2008).

51. Order, Samuel Mullet, et al. v. Jefferson County Sheriff's Department/Office, et al., No. 2:08-CV-00857 (US Dist. Ct., Southern Dist. of Ohio, July 9, 2009); interview with law enforcement officer, Jan. 15, 2014.

52. *Hazen Amish Directory 2011*, 22.

53. *Die Botschaft*, Mar. 7, 2011, 30.

Chapter 3. The Bishop

1. Letter dated Aug. 7, 2006 (unpublished correspondence). Emphasis in the original; names of the writer and the recipient are pseudonyms.

2. Interview with Amish man, Oct. 5, 2013; Hearing Transcript, 186, Aden Troyer v. Wilma S. Troyer, Nos. 2007-CU-74 and 2007-CU-75 (Ct. of Common Pleas Juvenile Div., Jefferson Co., Ohio, Oct. 5, 2007).

3. Interview with Amish man, Mar. 4, 2014; Troyer hearing transcript, 190–95, 207, 215–21 (Oct. 5, 2007).

4. Trial Transcript, vol. 3, 546–47, United States v. Samuel Mullet, Sr., et al., No. 5:11CR594 (US Dist. Ct., Northern Dist. of Ohio, Aug. 29, 2012); Troyer hearing transcript, 217–18 (Oct. 5, 2007); Mullet trial transcript, vol. 7, 1645 (Sept. 7, 2012).

5. Troyer hearing transcript, 207, 211–13, 225 (Oct. 5, 2007).

6. Interview with ex-member, Oct. 5, 2013.

7. Interview with Amish man, Feb. 28, 2014. See also Troyer hearing transcript, 188, 204, 251 (Oct. 5, 2007).

8. Interview with Amish bishop, Aug. 8, 2012.

9. Hearing Transcript, vol. 1, 9, Aden L. Troyer v. Wilma S. Troyer, Nos. 2007-CU-74 and 2007-CU-75 (Ct. of Common Pleas Juvenile Div., Jefferson Co., Ohio, Jan. 11, 2008).

10. Ibid., 211.

11. This description of the role of the bishop draws on Kraybill, Johnson-Weiner, and Nolt, *The Amish*, 79–80, 175–77.

12. Troyer hearing transcript, vol. 1, 8 (Jan. 11, 2008); interview with Amish man, Aug. 20, 2012; interview with Amish woman, Feb. 24, 2014; and interview with Amish man, Feb. 24, 2014.

13. Interview with Amish man, Sept. 4, 2012.

14. Interview with Amish bishop, Aug. 20, 2012.

15. The illustration was drawn by Bishop Mullet's daughter Lizzie Mullet Miller.

16. Bishop Mullet's interpretation of this illustration, which was presented as Plaintiff's Exhibit E, appears in Troyer hearing transcript, vol. 1, 190–98 (Jan. 11, 2008).

17. Troyer hearing transcript, vol. 1, 192–99 (Jan. 11, 2008). On various occasions, Sam Mullet refers to "Articles of Faith" and "Confession of Faith," by which he means the 1632 Dordrecht Confession of Faith written by Mennonites in the Netherlands.

18. Interview with Amish bishop, Nov. 15, 2012.

19. Interview with Amish man, Aug. 24, 1012.

20. Discussion of the Amish lectionary and a list of the scriptures appear in Kraybill, Nolt, and Weaver-Zercher, *The Amish Way*, 65–66, 205–7.

21. Interview with Amish man, Aug. 20, 2012. These same themes parallel some of the beliefs of Joseph Smith, founder of the Mormons.

22. Interview with Amish man, Aug. 24, 1012; interview with Amish bishop, Aug. 30, 2012; Mullet trial transcript, vol. 3, 545 (Aug. 29, 2012); and interview with Amish bishop, Nov. 17, 2012.

23. Interview with Amish man, Aug. 24, 2012; interview with Amish bishop, Nov. 15, 2012; and Mullet trial transcript, vol. 9, 2176–254 (Sept. 11, 2012). Despite Sam's emphasis on the Old Testament, he still used Christian imagery; for example, when he spoke with journalists in December 2012 (M. L. Nestel and Jebediah Reed, "A Bishop behind Bars," *Daily*, Dec. 3, 2012) and in a letter written from prison on Aug. 30, 2013.

24. Interview with Amish man, Aug. 24, 2012; interview with Amish man, Aug. 20, 2012; and Erik Eckholm, "Community Says Punitive Cutting of Hair Began as a Reminder to Repent," *New York Times*, Dec. 29, 2012.

25. Interview with Amish man, Aug. 20, 2012; interview with Amish bishop, Nov. 16, 2012; interview with Amish man, Feb. 24, 2014; and Mullet trial transcript, vol. 8, 1747 (Sept. 10, 2012).

26. Interview with Amish woman, Nov. 16, 2012; interview with Amish preacher, Aug. 17, 2012; interview with Amish woman, Feb. 24, 2014; and interview with Amish man, Mar. 4, 2014.

27. Paul Kline, "Gelassenheit" (sermon, Holmes County, OH, n.d.). The sermon later appeared, with minor changes, as "Gelassenheit" in Mary Schlabach, comp., *Message Mem'ries* (Millersburg, OH: Emanuel and Mary Schlabach, 2007), 147–53.

28. Kline, "Gelassenheit"; *1001 Questions*, 76–77; and Stoll, "Cheap Shirts and Shallow Reasoning," 10.

29. Interview with Amish man, Jan. 28, 2014; Kraybill, Johnson-Weiner, and Nolt, *The Amish*, 37.

30. Interview with Amish man, Oct. 10, 2010; *Guidelines in Regards to Parochial Schools*, 47, 50; and interview with Amish man, Oct. 10, 2010.

31. For more on obedience, see Kraybill, Nolt, and Weaver-Zercher, *The Amish Way*, 34–37, and Kraybill, Johnson-Weiner, and Nolt, *The Amish*, 98–103.

32. Interview with Amish man, Aug. 24, 2012. Emphasis added.

33. Troyer hearing transcript, 156 (Oct. 5, 2007). Emphasis added.

34. Bishop Mullet's statements in this and the next two paragraphs are from Troyer hearing transcript, vol. 1, 26–34 (Jan. 11, 2008). Emphasis added.

35. Bishop Mullet's statements in this and the next paragraph are from Troyer hearing transcript, vol. 1, 44–46, 50–53 (Jan. 11, 2008).

36. Interview with Amish bishop, Nov. 17, 2012.

37. Interview with former member, Oct. 5, 2013.

38. Mullet trial transcript, vol. 4, 799 (Aug. 30, 2012). See also Troyer hearing transcript, 224 (Oct. 5, 2007).

39. Interview with Amish woman, Feb. 28, 2014.

40. Interview with Amish woman, Oct. 5, 2013; Troyer hearing transcript, 226 (Oct. 5, 2007).

41. Interview with Amish man, Mar. 4, 2014.

42. "A Copy Concerning Baptism," 189.

43. "Rules of a Godly Life," 89.

44. Troyer hearing transcript, 183 (Oct. 5, 2007).

45. Troyer hearing transcript, vol. 1, 57 (Jan. 11, 2008).

46. Troyer hearing transcript, 197 (Oct. 5, 2007).

47. Troyer hearing transcript, 27–58, 122–24 (Oct. 5, 2007); interview with Amish bishop, Aug. 30, 2012; and interview with Amish man, Oct. 25, 2012.

48. Troyer hearing transcript, vol. 1, 182–86 (Jan. 11, 2008).

49. Interview with Amish woman, Nov. 16, 2012; interview with Amish man, Oct. 5, 2013.

50. Troyer hearing transcript, 88–89 (Oct. 5, 2007); interview with Amish man, Aug. 20, 2012.

51. Interview with Amish man, Feb. 24, 2014.

52. Mullet trial transcript, vol. 4, 809 (Aug. 30, 2012).

53. Nestel and Reed, "A Bishop behind Bars."

54. Interview with Amish man, Feb. 24, 2014.

55. Correspondence from Amish woman, Feb. 28, 2014.

56. Interview with Amish man, Aug. 20, 2012.

57. Interview with Amish man, Feb. 24, 2014.

58. Interview with Amish man, Aug. 20, 2012, Troyer hearing transcript, 87–92, 100 (Oct. 5, 2007).

59. Interview with Amish man, Aug. 20, 2012.

60. Troyer hearing transcript, 107–14 (Oct. 5, 2007).

61. Interview with Amish woman, Nov. 16, 2012; Troyer hearing transcript, 117–18 (Oct. 5, 2007).

62. Troyer hearing transcript, 129–31 (Oct. 5, 2007). Emphasis added.

63. Mullet trial transcript, vol. 3, 544–45 (Aug. 29, 2012). See also Troyer hearing transcript, 204, 251 (Oct. 5, 2007).

64. Troyer hearing transcript, vol. 1, 115 (Jan. 11, 2008).

65. Troyer hearing transcript, 58–67, 86–97, 115–19, 180–93 (Oct. 5, 2007); Mullet trial transcript, vol. 4, 797–98 (Aug. 30, 2012).

66. Troyer hearing transcript, 88–90 (Oct. 5, 2007).

67. Ibid., 30–31.

68. Ibid., 49, 58–69.

69. Interview with Amish man, Mar. 4, 2014.

70. Interview with law enforcement officer, Jan. 15, 2014; interview with Amish woman, Nov. 16, 2012; and interview with Amish man, Feb. 24, 2014.

71. Interview with Amish man, Aug. 20, 2012.

Chapter 4. The Cult?

1. Interview with Amish bishop, July 26, 2012; interview with Amish woman, Nov. 15, 2012; interview with Amish bishop, Nov. 16, 2012; interview with Amish bishop, Nov. 17, 2012; and interview with Amish deacon, Mar. 4, 2014.

2. John Caniglia, "Amish Community Remains Close, Yet Fearful after Samuel Mullet and Others Were Convicted of Hate Crimes," *Cleveland Plain Dealer*, Oct. 22, 2012; Opinion, 10, Aden L. Troyer v. Wilma S. Troyer, No. 09-JE-5 (Ct. of Appeals, Seventh Dist., Jefferson Co., Ohio, June 28, 2010).

3. Non-Amish man, e-mail message to author, Oct. 9, 2011.

4. Interview with Amish man, Aug. 24, 2012.

5. Interview with Amish man, Nov. 17, 2012; interview with Amish man, Oct. 5, 2013; interview with Amish woman, Feb. 24, 2014; interview with Amish man, Feb. 24, 2014; Hearing Transcript, 47, Aden Troyer v. Wilma S. Troyer, Nos. 2007-CU-74 and 2007-CU-75 (Ct. of

Common Pleas Juvenile Div., Jefferson Co., Ohio, Oct. 5, 2007); Trial Transcript, vol. 3, 547–48, United States v. Samuel Mullet, Sr., et al., No. 5:11CR594 (US Dist. Ct., Northern Dist. of Ohio, Aug. 29, 2012); Mullet trial transcript, vol. 4, 808 (Aug. 30, 2012); interview with Amish woman, Feb. 24, 2014; and interview with Amish man, Mar. 4, 2014.

6. These general allegations were not part of the criminal charges. Superseding Indictment, 2–3, United States v. Samuel Mullet, Sr., et al., No. 5:11CR594 (US Dist. Ct., Northern Dist. of Ohio, Mar. 28, 2012).

7. Mullet trial transcript, vol. 4, 802 (Aug. 30, 2012).

8. Erik Eckholm, "Braced for Hardship, an Amish Clan Awaits Sentences in Shearing Attacks," *New York Times*, Dec. 29, 2012; M. L. Nestel and Jebediah Reed, "A Bishop behind Bars," *Daily*, Dec. 3, 2012.

9. Mullet trial transcript, vol. 3, 548 (Aug. 29, 2012); interview with Amish woman, Feb. 24, 2014.

10. Interview with Amish man, Aug. 20, 2012.

11. Troyer hearing transcript, 83–92 (Oct. 5, 2007).

12. Interview with Amish man, Aug. 16, 2012; interview with Amish man, Feb. 24, 2014.

13. Interview with Amish woman, Feb. 24, 2014.

14. Interview with Amish woman, Nov. 16, 2012; interview with Amish woman, Feb. 24, 2014.

15. Interview with Amish bishop, July 26, 2012.

16. Source for this section, unless otherwise cited: Mullet trial transcript, vol. 4, 801–24 (Aug. 30, 2012).

17. Emphasis added in this paragraph.

18. Emphasis added in this paragraph.

19. Nestel and Reed, "A Bishop behind Bars."

20. Interview with Amish bishop, Nov. 16, 2012.

21. This is the author's term to describe this time period in the life of Bergholz. It was not used by the clan nor does it originate from the Bible.

22. Mullet trial transcript, vol. 8, 1764–66 (Sept. 10, 2012).

23. Mullet trial transcript, vol. 8, 1765 (Sept. 10, 2012); Sentencing Transcript, 38, United States v. Samuel Mullet, Sr., et al., No. 5:11CR594 (US Dist. Ct., Northern Dist. of Ohio, Feb. 8, 2013).

24. Mullet trial transcript, vol. 8, 1769 (Sept. 10, 2012).

25. Mullet trial transcript, vol. 8, 1766 (Sept. 10, 2012).

26. Nestel and Reed, "A Bishop behind Bars."

27. Mullet trial transcript, vol. 5, 1121, 1146 (Sept. 5, 2012), vol. 7, 1523, 1580–81 (Sept. 7, 2012), and vol. 8, 1715–17, 1739, 1752 (Sept. 10, 2012); interview with Amish woman, Feb. 24, 2014.

28. Interview with Amish man, Feb. 24, 2014.

29. Interview with Amish man, Mar. 4, 2014.

30. Correspondence from Amish woman, Feb. 28, 2014.

31. Ibid.

32. Mullet trial transcript, vol. 7, 1580–81 (Sept. 7, 2012).

33. Interview with Amish man, Feb. 24, 2014; correspondence from Amish woman, Feb. 28, 2014.

34. Mullet trial transcript, vol. 8, 1717 (Sept. 10, 2012).

35. Nestel and Reed, "A Bishop behind Bars."

36. Correspondence from Amish woman, Feb. 28, 2014 (emphasis in the original).

37. Mullet trial transcript, vol. 7, 1582–83 (Sept. 7, 2012); interview with Amish bishop, Aug. 8, 2012.

38. Interview with Amish woman, Feb. 24, 2014.

39. Interview with Amish bishop, Nov. 17, 2012.

40. Mullet trial transcript, vol. 8; 1715–16 (Sept. 10, 2012).

41. Ibid., 1715.

42. Mullet trial transcript, vol. 5, 1120–21 (Sept. 5, 2012), vol. 7, 1582–83 (Sept. 7, 2012); and vol. 8, 1715, 1766 (Sept. 10, 2012).

43. Interview with Amish man, Mar. 4, 2014; correspondence from Amish woman, Feb. 28, 2014.

44. Nestel and Reed, "A Bishop behind Bars."

45. Correspondence from Amish man, Feb. 21, 2014.

46. This pattern of paddling, which was determined by those who had grudges, subverted all the authority and hierarchical relationships in customary Amish social roles. Besides, it was completely contrary to the customary use of forgiveness in Amish life.

47. Interview with Amish man, Feb. 24, 2014.

48. Interview with Amish woman, Nov. 16, 2012; interview with Amish woman, Feb. 20, 2013; and interview with law enforcement officer, Jan. 15, 2014.

49. Interview with Amish bishop, Aug. 8, 2012.

50. Correspondence from Amish woman, Feb. 28, 2014.

51. J. Howard Powell, "The Historical and Biblical Significance of the Beard," Philadelphia Baptist Church, Decatur, Alabama, http://www.pbcofdecaturalabama.org/JHPowell/GodlyBeards.html.

52. Samson, whose superhuman strength is described in the book of Judges (chapters 14–16), had taken the Nazarite vow and never cut his hair. An enemy cut it while Samson slept, and he lost all his strength.

53. Mullet trial transcript, vol. 7, 1476–78, 1575–80 (Sept. 7, 2012).

54. Nestel and Reed, "A Bishop behind Bars"; Mullet trial transcript, vol. 8, 1718 (Sept. 10, 2012).

55. Mullet trial transcript, vol. 8, 1751–52 (Sept. 10, 2012), and vol. 4, 792 (Aug. 30, 2012). See also vol. 4, 775–76 (Aug. 30, 2012), and vol. 8, 1718, 1739, 1764 (Sept. 10, 2012).

56. Mullet trial transcript, vol. 8, 1767 (Sept. 10, 2012). One ex-member contends that it was Sam Mullet's idea to cut beards and that he asked two women to propose the idea to some of the men. Interview with Amish man, Mar. 4, 2014.

57. Mullet trial transcript, vol. 7, 1578–80 (Sept. 7, 2012).

58. Mullet trial transcript, vol. 6, 1356–58, 1434 (Sept. 6, 2012), and vol. 5, 1120, 1138, 1145–47 (Sept. 5, 2012).

59. Mullet trial transcript, vol. 6, 1418–22 (Sept. 6, 2012); Mullet sentencing transcript, 37–38 (Feb. 8, 2013).

60. Mullet trial transcript, vol. 8, 1765–66 (Sept. 10, 2012).

61. Erik Eckholm, "Community Says Punitive Cutting of Hair Began as a Reminder to Repent," *New York Times*, Dec. 29, 2012.

62. Interview with Amish man, Feb. 24, 2014.

63. Interview with Amish man, Aug. 20, 2012.

64. Interview with Amish man, Aug. 24, 2012.

65. Interview with Amish woman, Nov. 15, 2012; interview with bishop's wife, Nov. 16, 2012.

66. Interview with Amish man, October 4, 2013.

67. Interview with Amish man, Feb. 19, 2013; interview with Amish bishop, Nov. 16, 2012.

68. Hearing Transcript, vol. 1, 198, Aden L. Troyer v. Wilma S. Troyer, Nos. 2007-CU-74 and 2007-CU-75 (Ct. of Common Pleas Juvenile Div., Jefferson Co., Ohio, Jan. 11, 2008).

69. Unpublished correspondence (emphasis in the original).

70. Interview with Amish man, Mar. 4, 2014.

71. Interview with ex-member of Bergholz, Aug. 20, 2012.

72. Unpublished correspondence sent to *Die Botschaft* in early Feb. 2011 (emphasis in the original).

73. Another Amish cult story is the three-part account of Patricia Hochstetler, *Growing Up in an Amish-Jewish Cult*, which details the Lael colony in Mississippi, where members were kept isolated for years by controlling leader Mack Sharky. Also, at certain stages, the Amish Christian Church in Adams County, Indiana, was a renegade group, with leader David Schwartz claiming to have a direct telephone line to God.

74. Interview with Amish preacher, Nov. 15, 2012; interview with Amish woman, Nov. 15, 2012.

75. Interview with Amish man, Mar. 20, 2014.

76. Interview with Amish woman, Nov. 16, 2012.

77. Isaiah 50:6, Jeremiah 48:37–38, Isaiah 15:2, Isaiah 7:17, 20.

78. Mullet trial transcript, vol. 4, 709, 738–43 (Aug. 30, 2012).

79. Mullet trial transcript, vol. 6, 1422, 1359–60 (Sept. 6, 2012), vol. 7, 1478–79 (Sept. 7, 2012), vol. 8, 1740 (Sept. 10, 2012).

80. Mullet trial transcript, vol. 4, 784 (Aug. 30, 2012), and vol. 7, 1588 (Sept. 7, 2012).

81. Mullet trial transcript, vol. 8, 1718–19 (Sept. 10, 2012).

82. Mullet trial transcript, vol. 6, 1359–73 (Sept. 6, 2012) (emphasis added).

83. This narrative reflects the thoughts and perspectives of Bergholz members that emerged in hundreds of pages of testimony in Troyer v. Troyer and US v. Mullet.

Chapter 5. The FBI

1. Sources for this section and the next, unless otherwise cited: Detail Incident Report, Incident No. 11HC04195, Holmes County Sheriff's Office; Trial Transcript, vol. 5, 873–91, 907–1001, United States v. Samuel Mullet, Sr., et al., No. 5:11CR594 (US Dist. Ct., Northern Dist. of Ohio, Sept. 5, 2012); and interview with law enforcement officer, Oct. 4, 2013.

2. Interview with Amish minister, Aug. 16, 2012; interview with Amish bishop, Nov. 15, 2012.

3. Interview with law enforcement officer, Oct. 4, 2013.

4. Ibid.

5. Detail Incident Report, Holmes County Sheriff's Office.

6. Ibid.

7. Transcripts of phone conversations from prison are found in Detail Incident Report, Holmes County Sheriff's Office. Excerpts of the conversations were used as evidence by the prosecutors in the federal trial.

8. Eli Miller and Daniel Mullet did not serve jail time until later in November 2011.

9. Interview with law enforcement officer, Jan. 15, 2014.

10. Interview with law enforcement officer, Oct. 4, 2013.

11. The sequence of the FBI's involvement, the US Department of Justice's involvement, and the arrests at Bergholz are based on the testimony of FBI Agent Michael S. Sirohman at the hearing and at the trial. Preliminary Examination/Detention Hearing Transcript, 8–96, United States v. Samuel Mullet, Sr., No. 4:11mjo6134; United States v. Johnny S. Mullet, No. 4:11mjo6135; United States v. Daniel S. Mullet,

No. 4:11mj06135. United States v. Emanuel Shrock, No. 4:11mj06139 (US Dist. Ct., Northern Dist. of Ohio, Nov. 30, 2011); Mullet trial transcript, vol. 8, 1792–962 (Sept. 10, 2012).

12. Interview with law enforcement officer, Oct. 4, 2013.

13. Mullet trial transcript, vol. 5, 881–82 (Sept. 5, 2012); Government's Consolidated Opposition to Defendants' Motions to Dismiss, 8, United States v. Samuel Mullet, Sr., et al., No. 5:11CR594 (US Dist. Ct., Northern Dist. of Ohio, Apr. 16, 2012).

14. Holmes County Detective Joseph Mullet clarified the reasons that prompted the US Department of Justice to undertake the case.

15. Interview with law enforcement officer, Oct. 4, 2013.

16. Mullet trial transcript, vol. 8, 1809–10 (Sept. 10, 2012).

17. Ibid., 1812–13.

18. Ibid., 1814–21.

19. Ibid., 1821–22.

20. Investigators never tried to link the marijuana and cocaine directly to the defendants. Interview with law enforcement officer, Jan. 16, 2014. One ex-member had suspected that Bishop Mullet was raising marijuana. Correspondence from Amish man, Feb. 28, 2014.

21. Mullet preliminary examination/detention hearing transcript, 12–15 (Nov. 30, 2011); interview with law enforcement officer, Jan. 15, 2014.

22. Mullet trial transcript, vol. 6, 1395–98, 1425–28 (Sept. 6, 2012), and vol. 7, 1505 (Sept. 7, 2012).

23. Mullet trial transcript, vol. 7, 1504–6 (Sept. 7, 2012).

24. Mullet trial transcript, vol. 6, 1397 (Sept. 6, 2012).

25. Interview with law enforcement officer, Apr. 13, 2012.

26. Interview with Amish man, Oct. 3, 2013; interview with FBI agent, Jan. 16, 2014.

27. Matthew Shepard and James Byrd, Jr., Hate Crimes Prevention Act of 2009, 18 U.S.C. § 249 (2009). The government's legal arguments are described in Superseding Indictment, United States v. Samuel Mullet, Sr., et al., No. 5:11CR594 (US Dist. Ct., Northern Dist. of Ohio, March 28, 2012), and Government's Consolidated Opposition to Defendants' Motions to Dismiss, 8, United States v. Samuel Mullet, Sr., et al., No. 5:11CR594 (US Dist. Ct., Northern Dist. of Ohio, Apr. 16, 2012).

28. Government's opposition to motions to dismiss, 10, 18–28 (Apr. 16, 2012).

29. Order, United States v. Samuel Mullet, Sr., et al., No. 5:11CR594 (US Dist. Ct., Northern Dist. of Ohio, May 29, 2012).

30. Interview with Amish man, Oct. 5, 2012.

31. The $250,000 bond paid by Bishop Mullet was possibly money derived from oil or gas rights. Mullet preliminary examination/detention hearing transcript, 21 (Nov. 30, 2011); Erich Schwartzel, "Will Shale Boom Change Lifestyle of the Amish?," *Pittsburgh Post-Gazette*, Feb. 3, 2013; and Erik Eckholm, "Braced for Hardship, an Amish Clan Awaits Sentences in Shearing Attacks," *New York Times*, Dec. 29, 2012.

32. The names of the defendants and their respective charges are listed in chapter 6.

33. Interview with prosecutor, Jan. 10, 2014; Associated Press, "Sixteen Amish in Ohio Reject Beard-Cutting Plea Deals," fortwayne .com, July 30, 2012, http://www.fortwayne.com/apps/pbcs.dll/article ?AID=/20120730/APO1/307309923/0/TOPNEWS.

34. At the sentencing, Judge Polster reminded a defense attorney of what he told the defendants as they considered plea bargains. Sentencing Transcript, 111, United States v. Samuel Mullet, Sr., et al., No. 5:11CR594 (US Dist. Ct., Northern Dist. of Ohio, Feb. 8, 2013).

35. Interview with Amish man, Mar. 4, 2014.

36. M. L. Nestel and Jebediah Reed, "A Bishop behind Bars," *Daily*, Dec. 3, 2012.

37. Johnny Mullet, unpublished correspondence from prison, Aug. 16, 2012.

38. Interview with prosecutor, Aug. 22, 2012.

39. Johnny Mullet, unpublished correspondence from prison, Aug. 16, 2012.

Chapter 6. The Trial

1. Trial transcripts (excluding the jury selection) are available in vols. 2–11, 180–2586, United States v. Samuel Mullet, Sr., et al., No. 5:11CR594 (US Dist. Ct., Northern Dist. of Ohio, Aug. 28–Sept. 20, 2012).

2. Because I did not witness any of the attacks nor had any knowledge about the immediate circumstances surrounding them, I was not permitted in the courtroom until I was called to testify. I am grateful for the assistance of my colleague Prof. David Weaver-Zercher of Messiah College, who accompanied me to the trial and provided helpful counsel and support as I prepared to testify.

3. Source for this paragraph: Mullet trial transcript, vol. 10, 2341–82, 2534–53 (Sept. 12, 2012).

4. Carlo Wolff, "Amish Case Strikes Close to Home," *Cleveland Jewish News*, Feb. 14, 2013, http://www.clevelandjewishnews.com/news /local/article_fe5d8546-76c3-11e2-a188-001a4bcf887a.html.

5. In the early days of the trial, one of the jurors frequently fell asleep and was dismissed. She was replaced by one of the alternates.

6. Weiner, "Professor J. Dean Carro Discusses the Amish Hair-Cutting Trial," 14.

7. Mullet trial transcript, vol. 2, 226–30 (Aug. 28, 2012).

8. Matthew Shepard and James Byrd, Jr., Hate Crimes Prevention Act of 2009, 18 U.S.C. § 249 (2009). For a description of the act, see "Matthew Shepard and James Byrd, Jr., Hate Crimes Prevention Act of 2009," US Department of Justice, http://www.justice.gov/crt/about /crm/matthewshepard.php.

9. The opening statements of the prosecution and defense are found in Mullet trial transcript, vol. 2, 199–344 (Aug. 28, 2012).

10. "Four Arrests Made in Beard-Cutting Raids, More to Come," WKYC, Oct. 8, 2011, http://archive.wkyc.com/news/story.aspx?storyid =210063.

11. Bryan was aided by Wendi L. Overmyer, an assistant federal public defender.

12. Mullet trial transcript, vol. 4, 682 (Aug. 30, 2012).

13. Ibid., 700–92.

14. United States v. Samuel Mullet, Sr., et al., No. 5:11CR594, 2012 US Dist. LEXIS 173118 (Dec. 6, 2012). Immediately after Nancy Mullet's testimony, Judge Polster reminded the jury that the defendants were not charged with any sexual offenses. Mullet trial transcript, vol. 4, 810–11 (Aug. 30, 2012). He repeated these instructions in his charge to the jury before their deliberations began. Mullet trial transcript, vol. 10, 2312–13 (Sept. 12, 2012).

15. Mullet trial transcript, vol. 7, 1640–86 (Sept. 7, 2012).

16. Sentencing Transcript, 144–45, United States v. Samuel Mullet, Sr., et al., No. 5:11CR594 (US Dist. Ct., Northern Dist. of Ohio, Feb. 8, 2013).

17. Mullet trial transcript, vol. 5, 1093–150 (Sept. 5, 2012).

18. Mullet trial transcript, vol. 4, 826–50 (Aug. 30, 2012), and vol. 8, 1712–91 (Sept. 10, 2012).

19. Mullet trial transcript, vol. 6, 1353–456 (Sept. 6, 2012).

20. Mullet trial transcript, vol. 7, 1473–626 (Sept. 7, 2012).

21. For my testimony, see Mullet trial transcript, vol. 8, 1962–2021 (Sept. 10, 2012), and vol. 9, 2041–174 (Sept. 11, 2012).

22. Mullet trial transcript, vol. 8, 2012 (Sept. 10, 2012).

23. Mullet trial transcript, vol. 9, 2055–57 (Sept. 11, 2012).

24. Ibid., 2061–175.

25. Ibid., 2250.

26. The closing arguments of the prosecution and defense are found in Mullet trial transcript, vol. 10, 2341–533 (Sept. 12, 2012).

27. Quotations in the prosecution summary are excerpted from Mullet trial transcript, vol. 10, 2341–82 (Sept. 12, 2012).

28. Quotations in the defense summary are excerpted from Mullet trial transcript, vol. 10, 2383–533 (Sept. 12, 2012).

29. Mullet trial transcript, vol. 10, 2534–53 (Sept. 12, 2012).

30. Ibid., 2554–65 (Sept. 12, 2012).

31. I am grateful for the kind assistance of Steve King, the foreman of the jury, who explained the jury's process of sorting through the evidence to arrive at a verdict. Although the jurors were not aware of his background, they had elected a foreman with a degree in engineering, an MBA, and work experience leading problem-solving team activities for a manufacturer. These skills enabled him to facilitate jury deliberation and an open process for speaking and voting.

32. Interview with jury foreman, Nov. 17, 2012.

33. Jury Instructions, 2–62, United States v. Samuel Mullet, Sr., et al., No. 5:11CR594 (US Dist. Ct., Northern Dist. of Ohio, no date). Emphasis added. The website of Cornell University Law School's Legal Information Institute provides the specifics of the law at www.law.cornell.edu/uscode/text/18/249 except for the definition of bodily injury, which is described in a different section of Title 18: Section 1365 (h)(4) and can be found at www.law.cornell.edu/uscode/text/18/1365.

34. Interview with jury foreman, Nov. 17, 2012.

35. Ibid.

36. Mullet trial transcript, vol. 11, 2583 (Sept. 20, 2012).

Chapter 7. The Sentencing

1. Erik Eckholm, "Braced for Hardship, an Amish Clan Awaits Sentences in Shearing Attacks," *New York Times*, Dec. 29, 2012.

2. Ibid.

3. Robert Barnett, "Judge May Not Cut Amish Hair-Shearing Culprits a Break," *All Things Considered*, NPR, Feb. 6, 2013, http://www.npr.org/2013/02/06/171281873/judge-may-not-cut-amish-hair-shearing-culprits-a-break.

4. John Caniglia, "Amish Community Remains Close, Yet Fearful after Samuel Mullet and Others Were Convicted of Hate Crimes,"

Cleveland Plain Dealer, Oct. 22, 2012; ibid.; and Eckholm, "Braced for Hardship."

5. M. L. Nestel and Jebediah Reed, "A Bishop behind Bars," *Daily*, Dec. 3, 2012.

6. Associated Press, "Ohio Amish Guilty of Hair Attacks Lose Appeal for New Trial; Judge Won't Overturn Convictions," *Washington Post*, Dec. 6, 2012; United States v. Samuel Mullet, Sr., et al., No. 5: 11CR594, 2012 US Dist. LEXIS 173118 (Dec. 6, 2012).

7. Caniglia, "Amish Community Remains Close"; Eckholm, "Braced for Hardship"; and Erik Eckholm, "Community Says Punitive Cutting of Hair Began as a Reminder to Repent," *New York Times*, Dec. 29, 2012.

8. Amish people cite the second of the Ten Commandments, Jesus's admonishment not to practice religion in public, and communal restrictions that frown on individuals seeking the spotlight and placing themselves on a pedestal as the reasons for their aversion to publicity. For in-depth discussions, see Umble and Weaver-Zercher, *The Amish and the Media*.

9. Barnett, "Judge May Not Cut Amish Culprits a Break."

10. Sentencing Transcript, 41, 34, United States v. Samuel Mullet, Sr., et al., No. 5:11CR594 (US Dist. Ct., Northern Dist. of Ohio, Feb. 8, 2013).

11. Sources for this and the next two paragraphs: Mullet sentencing transcript, 14–15 (Feb. 8, 2013).

12. Mullet sentencing transcript, 38–39, 46–47 (Feb. 8, 2013).

13. Ibid., 54.

14. Ibid., 62, 59.

15. Ibid., 82–83, 90 (emphasis added), 93.

16. Ibid., 115, 122.

17. Ibid., 79.

18. Ibid., 69.

19. Ibid., 65–66 (emphasis added).

20. Ibid. (emphasis added).

21. Ibid., 142.

22. Ibid.

23. This letter is dated Aug. 23, 2012. The fourteen letters were written over a period of eighteen months. "Fellow Amish Want Life in Prison for Sam Mullet," WKYC-TV, Feb. 5, 2013, http://origin.wkyc .com/(S(5gc40445twtwgj453gk2liai))/news/article/281942/6/Fellow -Amish-want-life-in-prison-for-Sam-Mullet.

24. Mullet sentencing transcript, 144–45 (Feb. 8, 2013).

25. Ibid., 146–47.

26. Ibid., 147–48.

27. Ibid., 148–49.

28. Ibid., 149.

29. Ibid.

30. Ibid., 141–42, 150.

31. Ibid., 150.

32. Ibid., 151.

33. Ibid.

34. Ibid., 151–52.

35. Ibid., 152–54.

36. Ibid., 154–60.

37. *Die Botschaft*, Feb. 18, 2013, 30.

38. *Ohio Amish Directory: Geauga County, 1973 Edition*, 85; *Ohio Amish Directory: Geauga County and Vicinity, 2009 Edition*, 23; and interview with Amish man, Oct. 3, 2013.

Chapter 8. The Aftermath

1. James F. McCarty, "Mullet and Amish Followers Claim Cruel and Unusual Punishment, Request Release," *Plain Dealer*, Apr. 5, 2013; Kantele Franko, Associated Press, "Amish Gather before Start of Prison Terms," Apr. 26, 2013.

2. James F. McCarty, "Amish Bishop Samuel Mullet Renews Quest for Release with Federal Appeals Court," *Plain Dealer*, Apr. 23, 2013.

3. Unpublished correspondence, Aug. 30, 2013.

4. M. L. Nestel and Jebediah Reed, "A Bishop behind Bars," *Daily*, Dec. 3, 2012.

5. Ibid.

6. Ibid.

7. James F. McCarty, "Amish Bishop Sam Mullet Opposes Federal Prison Rule Requiring Him to Attend School Classes," *Plain Dealer*, May 17, 2013.

8. James F. McCarty, "Sam Mullet, Thirteen Amish Followers Exempted from Compulsory Prison School Classes," *Plain Dealer*, May 22, 2013.

9. Superseding Indictment, 2, United States v. Samuel Mullet, Sr., et al., No. 5:11CR594 (US Dist. Ct., Northern Dist. of Ohio, Mar. 28, 2012).

10. Government's Response in Opposition to Defendant's "Motion to Strike Surplusage from Superseding Indictment," 7, United States v.

Samuel Mullet, Sr., et al., No. 5:11CR594 (US Dist. Ct., Northern Dist. of Ohio, May 15, 2012).

11. Interview with Amish deacon, Mar. 4, 2014.

12. Order, United States v. Samuel Mullet, Sr., et al., No. 5:11CR594 (US Dist. Ct., Northern Dist. of Ohio, May 29, 2012).

13. Interview with Amish man, Oct. 3, 2013; interview with Amish preacher, Aug. 17, 2012.

14. Unpublished letter to *Die Botschaft* staff, Feb. 2011; correspondence from Amish scholar, Mar. 10, 2014.

15. Interview with Amish man, May 16, 2013 (emphasis added); interview with Amish bishop, July 26, 2012; and Raber's *New American Almanac*, 2013.

16. For a discussion of Amish ethnicity, see Nolt and Myers, *Plain Diversity*, 54–70.

17. In 1693, the Amish become a distinctive branch of the Anabaptist movement, which began in 1525.

18. Interview with Amish man, Jan. 28, 2014.

19. Hearing Transcript, vol. 1, 197–98, Aden L. Troyer v. Wilma S. Troyer, Nos. 2007-CU-74 and 2007-CU-75 (Ct. of Common Pleas Juvenile Div., Jefferson Co., Ohio, Jan. 11, 2008).

20. Interview with law enforcement officer, Jan. 15, 2014; interview with Amish man, May 16, 2013.

21. Sentencing Transcript, 34, United States v. Samuel Mullet, Sr., et al., No. 5:11CR594 (US Dist. Ct., Northern Dist. of Ohio, Feb. 8, 2013); John Caniglia, "Amish Community Remains Close, Yet Fearful after Samuel Mullet and Others Were Convicted of Hate Crimes," *Cleveland Plain Dealer*, Oct. 22, 2012; and Mullet sentencing transcript, 79 (Feb. 8, 2013).

22. Nestel and Reed, "A Bishop behind Bars."

23. Correspondence from Amish scholar, Mar. 10, 2014.

24. One example is an audience cult composed of the followers of an adored leader, often a celebrity. The term *cult* also applies to a small religious group that may evolve into a more stable group called a sect, and it is also used to describe New Religious Movements that start within or outside of established religious groups. For literature on New Religious Movements, see Dawson, *Cults and New Religious Movements*; Lewis, *New Religious Movements*; and Lucas and Robbins, *New Religious Movements in the Twenty-First Century*.

25. Aldridge, *Religion in the Contemporary World*, 175–79. See also Coates, "Cult Commitment," and Goldman, "Cults, New Religions, and the Spiritual Landscape."

26. Hunt, *Alternative Religions*, 24–25.

27. See Ambre Biehl's research, "Amish Beard Cutting," for an extended study of the inverted Amish moral order at Bergholz.

28. Milgram, *Obedience to Authority*.

29. Girard, *The Scapegoat*.

30. Parker, "Identification with the Aggressor"; Joseph M. Carver, "Love and Stockholm Syndrome: The Mystery of Loving an Abuser," Counselling Resource.com, http://counsellingresource.com/lib /therapy/self-help/stockholm/.

31. Interview with Amish man, Feb. 24, 2014.

32. David Luthy, in *The Amish in America: Settlements That Failed,* discovered that about 145 Amish settlements failed in the twentieth century for a variety of reasons, including economic, climate, conflict with government, and internal squabbles. Of course, the final destiny of Bergholz is not known.

33. Interview with Amish man, Oct. 5, 2013.

34. "Four Arrests Made in Beard-Cutting Raids, More to Come," WKYC, Oct. 8, 2011, http://archive.wkyc.com/news/story.aspx?storyid =210063.

35. Troyer hearing transcript, vol. 1, 38 (Jan. 11, 2008).

36. Interview with Amish man, Oct. 4, 2013.

37. Interview with Amish man, Oct. 25, 2012.

38. Kraybill, Nolt, and Weaver-Zercher, *Amish Grace*, 17–52.

39. Interview with Amish man, Oct. 4, 2013.

40. Interview with Amish woman, Mar. 21, 2014.

41. Interview with former member, Aug. 20, 2012; interview with Amish minister, Mar. 4, 2014.

42. Thomas J. Sheeran, Associated Press, "Amish Beard Cutters Sentenced Friday," *Huffington Post*, Feb. 8, 2013, http://www.huffing tonpost.com/2013/02/08/amish-beard-cutters-sentenced_n_2644959 .html.

43. Interview with Amish minister, Mar. 4, 2014.

44. Correspondence from Amish man, Feb. 21, 2014.

45. Interview with Amish man, Feb. 24, 2014; interview with Amish man, Jan. 27, 2014; and interview with Amish man, Jan. 28, 2014.

46. "A Shepherd's Authority," *Gemeinde Register*, June 26, 2013, 1 (emphasis in the original).

47. Yoder, "The Amish View of the State."

48. Sheeran, "Amish Beard Cutters Sentenced Friday"; Erik Eckholm, "Braced for Hardship, an Amish Clan Awaits Sentences in Shearing Attacks," *New York Times*, Dec. 29, 2012.

49. Carlo Wolff, "Amish Case Strikes Close to Home," *Cleveland Jewish News*, Feb. 14, 2013, http://www.clevelandjewishnews.com/news /local/article_fe5d8546-76c3-11e2-a188-0014bcf887a.html.

50. Kevin Koeninger, "Amish Beard-Cutters Face Life for Hate Crimes," *Courthouse News Service*, Sept. 21, 2012, http://www.court housenews.com/2012/09/21/50539.htm.

51. The government would intervene, of course, if the clan's religious practices involved any abuse or physical harm to their own members or outsiders.

Epilogue

1. Sources for this section: Interview with Amish man, Mar. 4, 2014; interview with law enforcement officer, Apr. 7, 2014; interview with Amish man, Feb. 24, 2014; interview with Amish woman, Feb. 24, 2014; and interview with Amish woman, Mar. 21, 2014.

2. Criminal Docket for Case No. 5:11CR594-DAP All Defendants Docs. 397, 398, 399, 400, 402, 403, 414, 415, 417, 418, 419, 425, 427, 430, 431, 444, Feb. 15–25, 2013 (US Dist. Ct., Northern Dist. of Ohio).

3. Brief for the United States, United States v. Lovina Miller, et al., Nos. 13–3177, 3181, 3182, 3183, 3193, 3194, 3195, 3196, 3201, 3202, 3204, 3205, 3206, 3207, 3208, 3214 (US Ct. of Appeals for the 6th Cir., Feb. 28, 2014).

4. Criminal Docket for Case No. 5: 11CR594-DAP All Defendants, Doc. 495, Mar. 6, 2013 (US Dist. Ct., Northern Dist. of Ohio); Opinion and Order, United States v. Samuel Mullet, Sr., et al., No. 5:11CR594 (US Dist. Ct., Northern Dist. of Ohio, Apr. 9, 2013).

5. James F. McCarty, "Amish Bishop Samuel Mullet Renews Quest for Release with Federal Appeals Court," *Plain Dealer*, Apr. 23, 2013.

6. James F. McCarty, "Amish Bishop Samuel Mullet Denied Latest Attempt to Win Release from Prison in Beard-Cutting Case," *Plain Dealer*, July 24, 2013.

7. On March 31, 2014, Sam Mullet challenged his fifteen-year prison sentence in a renewed appeal filed before the US Court of Appeals for the Sixth Circuit. The appeal contended that the federal hate crimes law (Shepard-Byrd) under which he was convicted violates the US Constitution and was improperly applied in his case. Torsten Ove, "Amish Sect Leader Challenges U.S. in New Appeal in Beard-Cutting Case, *Pittsburgh Post-Gazette*, Mar. 31, 2014.

8. Another option before petitioning the United States Supreme Court (but an unlikely one) is the possibility that attorneys from either side could petition for an en banc session, which would involve a

rehearing of the case before *all* the judges of the sixth circuit court of appeals, rather than just a panel of three.

9. Amanda Lee Myers, Associated Press, "Convicted Amish Fight for Release," *New York Times*, Apr. 5, 2013.

10. Thompson and Wachtel, "An Empirical Analysis of Supreme Court Certiorari Petition Procedures," 237, 241.

11. DiPompeo, "Federal Hate Crime Laws," 617–72.

12. The Shepard-Byrd Hate Crimes Prevention Act (18 U.S.C. § 249) has three sections, each of which is based on different constitutional authority. Section 2, related to the authority of the US Congress's Commerce Clause, is the only element in question in this case. A discussion of the sources of constitutional authority is found in Brief for the United States, United States v. Lovina Miller, et al., Nos. 13-3177, 3181, 3182, 3183, 3193, 3194, 3195, 3196, 3201, 3202, 3204, 3205, 3206, 3207, 3208, 3214 (US Ct. of Appeals for the 6th Cir., Feb. 28, 2014).

13. "Latest Hate Crime Statistics," Federal Bureau of Investigation, Nov. 25, 2013, http://www.fbi.gov/news/stories/2013/november /annual-hate-crime-statistics-show-slight-decease/annual-hate-crime -statistics-show-slight-decrease.

14. See DiPompeo, "Federal Hate Crime Laws," 627, for a discussion of these laws. A sample of religious hate crimes committed in 2012 is found in "Hate Crimes and Religious Intolerance," Center for the Study of the Presidency and Congress, accessed Apr. 1, 2014, http://www.thepresidency.org/programs/past-programs/religion-and -public-policy/761-hate-crimes-and-religious-intolerance.

15. Weiner, "Professor J. Dean Carro Discusses the Amish Hair-Cutting Trial," 14.

16. *Amicus* Brief, United States v. Lovina Miller, et al., Nos. 13-3177, 3181, 3182, 3183, 3193, 3194, 3195, 3196, 3201, 3202, 3204, 3205, 3206, 3207, 3208, 3214 (US Ct. of Appeals for the 6th Cir., Mar. 6, 2014).

17. Ibid., 19.

18. Ibid., 29–30.

19. Ibid., 31.

20. "Why Is Obama Persecuting the Amish People?," Michael Savage daily e-mail newsletter, Apr. 12, 2013.

21. "Amish Prosecuted Because Scissors 'Crossed State Lines,'" Michael Savage website, Apr. 12, 2013, http://www.wnd.com/2013/04 /amish-prosecuted-because-scissors-crossed-state-lines/.

22. Noah Feldman, "Is Cutting Off a Beard a Hate Crime?," *Bloomberg View*, Sept. 9, 2012, http://www.bloombergview.com/articles /2012-09-09/is-cutting-off-a-beard-a-hate-crime-.

23. Myers, "Convicted Amish Fight for Release."

24. Jacob Sullum, "How the Justice Department Transformed an Amish Feud into a Federal Hate Crime," *Hit & Run Blog*, reason.com, Sept. 21, 2012, http://reason.com/blog/2012/09/21/how-the-justice -department-transformed-a. Jacob Sullum is a senior editor at *Reason* magazine and a nationally syndicated columnist.

25. E-mail message to author, Sept. 20, 2012. The 1990 case of Aaron Glick in Pennsylvania suggests the shunning can be limited by the state if it is construed as religious discrimination in the economic sphere; that is, if excommunication has implications beyond typical religious practices such as worship. Kraybill and Nolt, *Amish Enterprise*, 181–82.

26. "18 U.S. Code § 249—Hate Crime Acts," Cornell University Law School, Legal Information Institute, accessed Apr. 1, 2014, www .law.cornell.edu/uscode/text/18/249.

27. Feldman, "Is Cutting Off a Beard a Hate Crime?"

Appendix II. Who Are the Amish?

1. Parts of this essay are adapted from Kraybill, Johnson-Weiner, and Nolt, *The Amish*. For a general history of the Amish, see Nolt, *A History of the Amish*.

2. *Ohio Amish Directory: Geauga County, 1973 Edition*, 7–10; *Ohio Amish Directory: Holmes County and Vicinity*, 2005, xiv–xvi. See Hurst and McConnell, *An Amish Paradox*, and Beachy, *Unser Leit*, vol. 2, for historical background on Holmes County.

3. The essays in Kraybill, *The Amish and the State*, provide an introduction to Amish views of the state.

4. The primary biblical texts that support shunning include Matthew 18:15–18; Romans 16:17; 1 Corinthians 5; 2 Thessalonians 3:6, 14–15; 2 Timothy 3:2–5; and Titus 3:10. For an articulate Amish explanation of shunning, see *Biblical Guidelines in Shunning*.

5. For Amish population statistics, see www2.etown.edu/amish studies/.

Bibliography

Aldridge, Alan. *Religion in the Contemporary World: A Sociological Introduction.* 2nd ed. Cambridge: Polity Press, 2000.

Ammann, Jakob. "Summary and Defense (November 22, 1693)." In *Letters of the Amish Division: A Sourcebook,* translated and edited by John D. Roth, 29–48. Goshen, IN: Mennonite Historical Society, 1993.

Beachy, Leroy. *Unser Leit: The Story of the Amish.* 2 vols. Millersburg, OH: Goodly Heritage Books, 2011.

Biblical Guidelines in Shunning. Pathway Reprint Series, no. 7. LaGrange, IN: Pathway Publishers, 2008.

Biehl, Ambre. "Amish Beard Cutting: Religious Practice or Hate Crime?" Undergraduate thesis, Elizabethtown College, 2013.

Byers, Bryan D. "Amish Victimization and Offending: A Rural Subculture's Experiences and Responses to Crime and Justice." *Southern Rural Sociology* 23, no. 2 (2008): 226–51.

Byers, Bryan D., and Benjamin W. Crider. "Hate Crimes against the Amish: A Qualitative Analysis of Bias Motivation Using Routine Activities Theory." *Deviant Behavior* 23, no. 2 (Mar. 2002): 115–48.

Byers, Bryan, Benjamin W. Crider, and Gregory K. Biggers. "Bias Crime Motivation: A Study of Hate Crime and Offender Neutralization Techniques Used against the Amish." *Journal of Contemporary Criminal Justice* 15, no. 1 (Feb. 1999): 78–96.

Byler, John M., ed. *Alte Schreibens: Amish Documents and Record Series.* Sugarcreek, OH: Schlabach Printers, 2008.

Coates, Dominiek D. " 'Cult Commitment' from the Perspective of Former Members: Direct Rewards of Membership versus Dependency Inducing Practices." *Deviant Behavior* 33 (2012): 168–84.

"A Copy Concerning Baptism." In *In Meiner Jugend: A Devotional Reader in German and English*, translated by Joseph Stoll, 188–91. Aylmer, ON: Pathway Publishers, 2000.

Dawson, Lorne L., ed. *Cults and New Religious Movements*. Malden, MA: Blackwell Publishing, 2003.

DiPompeo, Christopher. "Federal Hate Crime Laws and United States v. Lopez: On a Collision Course to Clarify Jurisdictional-Element Analysis." *University of Pennsylvania Law Review* 157 (2008): 617–72.

Directory of Ashland and Richland County Amish Settlement 2000. Compiled by Rosa H. Yoder. Ashland, OH, 2000.

Girard, René. *The Scapegoat*. Baltimore: Johns Hopkins University Press, 1986.

Goldman, Marion S. "Cults, New Religions, and the Spiritual Landscape: A Review of Four Collections." *Journal for the Scientific Study of Religion* 45, no. 1 (2006): 87–96.

Guidelines in Regards to the Old Order Amish or Mennonite Parochial Schools. Gordonville, PA: Gordonville Print Shop, 1978. Fourth printing 1981.

Hazen Amish Directory 2011. Compiled by Crist and Sara Miller. Sugarcreek, OH: Carlisle Printing, 2011.

Hochstetler, Patricia. *Growing Up in an Amish-Jewish Cult*. Book 1, *Delusion*. Book 2, *Deception*. Book 3, *Deliverance*. Winona Lake, IN: Baker Trittin Press, 2007–2008.

Hunt, Stephen J. *Alternative Religions: A Sociological Introduction*. Burlington, VT: Ashgate Publishing, 2003.

Hurst, Charles E., and David L. McConnell. *An Amish Paradox: Diversity and Change in the World's Largest Amish Community*. Baltimore: Johns Hopkins University Press, 2010.

In Meiner Jugend: A Devotional Reader in German and English. Translated by Joseph Stoll. Aylmer, ON: Pathway Publishers, 2000.

Kraybill, Donald B., ed. *The Amish and the State*. 2nd ed. Baltimore: Johns Hopkins University Press, 2003.

Kraybill, Donald B., Karen M. Johnson-Weiner, and Steven M. Nolt. *The Amish*. Baltimore: Johns Hopkins University Press, 2013.

Kraybill, Donald B., and Steven M. Nolt. *Amish Enterprise: From Plows to Profits*. 2nd ed. Baltimore: Johns Hopkins University Press, 2004.

Kraybill, Donald B., Steven M. Nolt, and David L. Weaver-Zercher. *Amish Grace: How Forgiveness Transcended Tragedy*. San Francisco: Jossey-Bass, 2007.

———. *The Amish Way: Patient Faith in a Perilous World*. San Francisco: Jossey-Bass, 2010.

Lewis, James R., ed. *New Religious Movements*. New York: Oxford University Press, 2004.

Lucas, Phillip Charles, and Thomas Robbins, eds. *New Religious Movements in the Twenty-First Century: Legal, Political, and Social Challenges in Global Perspective*. New York: Routledge, 2004.

Luthy, David. *The Amish in America: Settlements That Failed, 1840–1960*. Aylmer, ON: Pathway Publishers, 1986.

Milgram, Stanley. *Obedience to Authority: An Experimental View*. New York: Harper and Row, 1974.

Miller, Nathan. *Out of Deception: The True Story of an Amish Youth Entangled in the Web of a Cult*. Medina, NY: Ridgeway Publishing, 2010.

Nolt, Steven M. *A History of the Amish*. Rev. ed. Intercourse, PA: Good Books, 2003.

Nolt, Steven M., and Thomas J. Meyers. *Plain Diversity: Amish Cultures and Identities*. Baltimore: Johns Hopkins University Press, 2007.

Ohio Amish Directory: Fredericktown Settlement 1973–2001. Compiled by Anna Mary Byler. Gordonville, PA: Gordonville Print Shop, 2001.

Ohio Amish Directory: Fredericktown Settlement 1973–2011. Compiled by Neil and Anna Mary Byler. Gordonville, PA: Gordonville Print Shop, 2011.

Ohio Amish Directory: Geauga County and Vicinity, 1973 Edition. Compiled by Ervin Gingerich. Baltimore: Johns Hopkins University School of Medicine, 1973.

Ohio Amish Directory: Geauga County and Vicinity, 2009 Edition. Compiled by John J. Miller. Sugarcreek, OH: Schlabach Printers, 2010.

Ohio Amish Directory: Holmes County and Vicinity, 2005. Compiled by Ervin Gingerich. Sugarcreek, OH: Carlisle Press, 2005.

1001 Questions and Answers on the Christian Life. Aylmer, ON: Pathway Publishers, 1992.

Parker, Martin M. "Identification with the Aggressor: How Crime Victims Often Cope with Trauma." In *The Corsini Encyclopedia of Psychology*, 4th ed., edited by Irving B. Weiner and W. Edward Craighead, 800. Hoboken, NJ: John Wiley and Sons, 2010. Also available at http://www.parkerphd.com/PDFs/Identificiation With the Aggressor.pdf.

"Rules of a Godly Life." In *In Meiner Jugend: A Devotional Reader in German and English*, translated by Joseph Stoll, 65–103. Aylmer, ON: Pathway Publishers, 2000.

Stevick, Richard A. *Growing Up Amish: The Rumspringa Years*. 2nd ed. Baltimore: Johns Hopkins University Press, 2014.

Stoll, Elmo. "Cheap Shirts and Shallow Reasoning." *Family Life*, Jan. 1972, 11–12.

———. "The War of the Whiskers." *Family Life*, Aug./Sept. 1983, 8–10.

Thompson, David C., and Melanie F. Wachtel. "An Empirical Analysis of Supreme Court Certiorari Petition Procedures: The Call for Response and the Call for the Views of the Solicitor General." *George Mason Law Review* 16, no. 2 (2009): 237–302. http://www.georgemasonlawreview.org/doc/16-2_Wachtell.pdf.

Umble, Diane Zimmerman, and David W. Weaver-Zercher, eds. *The Amish and the Media*. Baltimore: Johns Hopkins University Press, 2008.

Weiner, Richard. "Professor J. Dean Carro Discusses the Amish Hair-Cutting Trial." *Akron Law Alumni Magazine*, Fall 2012, 14–15.

Who Is Who in the Budget: Budget *Scribes from the United States and Canada*. Compiled by Joas and Lillian Yoder. N.p., 2000.

Yoder, Paton. "The Amish View of the State." In *The Amish and the State*, 2nd ed., edited by Donald B. Kraybill, 23–40. Baltimore: Johns Hopkins University Press, 2003.

Index

Page numbers in *italics* indicate photographs.

Abdalla, Fred: arrest warrants served by, 87; on cult, 141; custody dispute and, 38, 39; as devil, 57; on fear in Amish community, 15–16; Kanoski and, 84; Shrocks and, 14, 95, 154; Wengards and, 6

affiliations of church districts, 17, *171*

aggressor, identification with, 144

Amish: Anabaptists and, 166–67; aversion to publicity of, 190n8; beliefs of, 52–57, 110–11, 166–70; benefits of First Amendment to, 130–31; birthrates of, 175n3; cultural factors and, 145–46; diversity of, 17, 45–46, 170–72; growth of population of, 170–71; identity as, 137–38; immigration of, to North America, 167; individualism and, 52–54; rejection of Bergholz clan by, 137–38; separation of church and state and, 16–17, 145–46, 167–68; view of state of, 167–68

Amish Christian Church, Indiana, 184n73

Amish jails, 68–70

Ammann, Jakob, 18, 166–67

Anabaptists, 166

Anti-Defamation League, brief of, x, 158–59

appeal, filing of, x, 156–58

assault charges, 103, *103*, 104

authority, obedience to, 143–44, 145

ban. *See* shunning

baptism, 23, 33, 45

beard cutting: in Old Testament, 71–72; as sign of judgment on disobedience, 77; as symbolic act, 114; as warning, 78; during winter of lament, 72–74

beard cutting attacks: animosity leading to, 39–40; fear after, 15–16, 90; on Hershbergers, 9–10; humiliation of, 19, 72; media coverage of, xi; on Miller (Myron), 11–12; on Millers (Marty and Barb), 3–5; moral dilemma after, 16–17; motivation for, 113–16, 119–20, 127; photographs taken during, *2*, *62*, *106*; religion as motivation for, 96–97, 104–5, 130, 140–41; revenge on hypocrites as motivation for, 80, 98, 110; on Shrock, 13–15; theoretical explanations of, 143–44; on Wengerd, 6–7

beards, importance of, 17–19. *See also* beard cutting; beard cutting attacks

Bergholz, Ohio, 25

Bergholz settlement: building of, 26–30; chronology of, xv; church services at, 50–51, 138; as clan, 40, 144–45; as cult, 76–77, 141–43; dress of women in, 75; drift in, 154; future of, 155; grandchildren in, 150; land in, 25–26, 30, 59; legal timeline of, xvi; lessons learned from saga of, 150–52; media coverage of, xi, 125; Miller children and, 3–5; narrative of, 79–80; non-Amish practices of, 137–41, *139*; ordination of ministers of, 28–30; origins of, 25–26; pivotal points in changes at, 43–44; purge at, 30–34; reputation of, 56; school in, 22, 38–39; strict shunning practices and, 33; symbolic boundaries around, 74–75; threat of excommunication at, 36; thwarting of plans to leave, 59; ties cut to relatives outside of, 56–57; Township Road 280 in, *82*, *134*; between trial and sentencing, 123; unique aspects of, 144–45; as upsetting moral order, 143–46; views of devil and magic in, 57–58; winter of lament in, 67–74. *See also* Mullet, Samuel E.

bishops, role of: Hershberger on, 112; S. Mullet on, 55–56, 128; overview of, 44–46. *See also* clergy

Brennan, Bridget, 105, 116

Bryan, Ed: closing summation by, 113, 115–16; on cult, 142; media coverage and, 125; opening summary by, 106; poll of jurors and, 121; on prison assignments, 135; sentencing and, 126–27

Burkholder, Freeman, 4, *104*, 132, 155

Burkholder, Nancy Miller, 3, 4, 78, 107, 132

Carro, J. Dean, 114

Carroll County, Ohio, 11

charges, 103–4

Christianity, denunciation of, 50, 139

chronology: Bergholz timeline, xv; legal timeline, xvi

church districts, 23. *See also* Gmay

church services, 50–51, 138

clergy: bishops, role of, 44–46, 112; as directors and executors of attacks, 20; investigation committee of, 34–36; meeting of, about S. Mullet, 34–37, 48–49, 76, 105, 110; ordination of, 27–30, 45; role of, 151

congregations, 23. *See also* Gmay

conservatism, claiming stance of, 151

conspiracy charges, 103, *103*, 120

criminal acts, reporting of, 17, 146, 168

cult: Bergholz settlement as, 76–77, 141–43; types of, 192n24; use of term in trial, 110

custody dispute over Mullet grandchildren, 37–39, 136

Dawdyhaus, 9

defense: closing arguments of, 113–16; media coverage and, 125; opening statement of, 106; request for new trial from, 124; at sentencing proceedings, 126–27; strategy of, 112. *See also* Bryan, Ed

Dettelbach, Steve, 152, 153

devil, views of, 57

Diener, 44

DiPompeo, Christopher, 157–58

disfigurement, definition of: in Shepard-Byrd Act, 118–19; in trial defense, 115

disobedience, other Amish as drowning in sea of, 79–80

diversity within Amish society, 17, 45–46, 170–72

Dordrecht Confession of Faith, 33, 110, 167

drawing lots, 28, 45

drift, 25, 154

Eash, Wilbur Lee, 77
exclusion, practice of, 68–70
excommunication: S. Mullet on, 54–55; overview of, 32–33, 168–69; response to, by ministers, 34–36; of Shrocks, 13; threats of, 59; treatment after, 32–33
expert witness: author as, xii, 101, 109–11; defense discrediting of, 115–16

FBI: calls between sheriff's offices and, 90–91; charges of lying to, 103, *103*; cooperation with, 93; information gathered by, 93; multi-county attacks and, 91; searches conducted by, 93–94
fear after beard cuttings, 15–16, 90
federal justice officials, 91–92. *See also* FBI
Feldman, Noah, 159, 160
First Amendment issues, 96–97, 130, 152–53
forgiveness: R. Hershberger on, 112; B. Miller and, 5; overview of, 147–49; paddling and, 183n46
fracking, hydraulic, 97
Fredericktown, Ohio, 24–25, 149

gas and oil leases, 97, 123
Geauga County, Ohio, 26, 167
Geauga County Amish settlement, 170
Gentile, James S., 113
Getz, Thomas, 110
Girard, René, 144
giving up. See *uffgevva*
Glick, Aaron, shunning case of, 196n25
Gmay, 23, 44–46
grand jury, 96
grief and beard cutting, 72

hair, cutting of: of Hershbergers, 10; of Millers (Marty and Barb), 4–5;

of minister, 175n38; of Wengerd, 7; during winter of lament, 72–74
hair, uncut, of women, 19
Halloween prank, 90
hate crimes: debate about, 158–61; federal definition of, 118
Hate Crimes Prevention Act. *See* Shepard-Byrd Hate Crimes Prevention Act
"hauling Amish," 8
Hershberger, Andy: attack on, 9–10, 83, 84; pressing of charges by, 84, 86
Hershberger, Levi, 9, 10, 83, 84
Hershberger, Miriam, 83
Hershberger, Raymond: after attack, 105; Andy Weaver churches and, 9; attack on, 2, 9–10, 83–84, *103*; forgiveness by, 149; humiliation of, 19; listening committee statement and, 35; nonresistance and, 85; sheriff's office and, 86; as witness, 101, 111–12
Hershberger, Sara, 9, 10
Hochstetler, Wilbur, 76–77
Holmes County, Ohio, 26, 167
Holmes County Amish settlement, 170
Holmes County Sheriff's Office, 83, 84
Hostetler, Eli, 39, 70, 71
Hostetler, Emma Mullet, 39
humiliation, beard and hair cutting as, 19, 72
hypocrisy: helping other Amish hypocrites, 77–78; narrative of, 79–80; of other Amish, accusations of, 75–77; winter of lament for, 68–74

identification with aggressor, 144
indictment by grand jury, 96
individualism in Amish society, 52–54
interstate commerce, evidence of, 104, 157

jailhouse wedding, 123–24
Jefferson County, Ohio, 25
Jefferson County Sheriff's Office, lawsuit against, 39
jury: deliberations of, 118–21; findings of, 121; instructions to, 117, 188n14

Kanoski, Michael, 7–8, 11, 12–13, 84
King, Steve, 189n31
Knowling, Steve, 87

Lael colony, Mississippi, 184n73
lawsuits: Amish view of, 168; against Jefferson County Sheriff's Office, 39
lying to FBI, charges of, 103, *103*

Mast, Edward, 152, 154–55
Mast, Johnny: as barber, 73; camera hidden by, 95; as leaving clan, 154–55, 162; paddling and, 70–71; on witness stand, 109
Mast, Mary Mullet, 109
Mast, Vernon, 32
media coverage: of beard-cutting saga, xi, 125; of S. Mullet, 91, 105, 112–13, 136, 179n23
Middlefield, Ohio, 23, 167
Middlefield Amish community, 23, 24, 167
Milgram, Stanley, 143–44
Miller, Alan, 4, 78
Miller, Anna, 95, *104*, 132
Miller, Arlene, 11–12
Miller, Atlee, 31, 35, 47, 49
Miller, Barb Mullet: apologies to, 127–28; attack on, 3–5, 40, *103*; forgiveness by, 149; on hair and prayer cap, 19; as hypocrite, 78; on sentencing, 133; threat made to, 96; on witness stand, 107
Miller, Eli: apology of, 127; arraignment of, 89–90; arrest of, 95; arrest warrant for, 87; assault of L.

Troyer by, 37–38; beard cutting attacks and, 7, 94; as defendant, 103; indictments of, *104*; on parents as hypocrites, 78; photo of, *100*; sentencing of, 132
Miller, Elizabeth: apology of, 128; as defendant, 103; hair cutting of, 73; indictments of, *104*; sentencing of, 132
Miller, Emma, *104*, 132
Miller, Ferdinand, 123–24, 154
Miller, Kathryn, 103, *104*, 127–28, 132
Miller, Lester: apology of, 127; arrest of, 87, 95; beard cutting attacks and, 4, 84; as defendant, 103; indictments of, *104*; lack of remorse of, 87–88; on parents as hypocrites, 78; sentencing of, 132
Miller, Levi F.: Amish jail and, 69–70; arraignment of, 89–90; arrest of, 87; beard cutting attacks and, 6–7, 84; on cult, 142; cutting of beard of, 73; indictments of, *104*; lack of remorse of, 87–88, 128; Mount Hope Auction and, 8; not guilty decision of jury on, 121; phone calls of, 88–89; photo of, *100*; as preacher, 28; sentencing of, 132; sister of, 6
Miller, Lizzie Mullet, 123–24, 125, 154, 178n5
Miller, Lovina, 94, 103, *104*, 132
Miller, Marty: apologies to, 127–28; attack on, 3–5, 40, *103*; on beard cutting, 127; as hypocrite, 78; threat made to, 96
Miller, Marty, Jr., 78
Miller, Mary, 6
Miller, Myron: attack on, 11–12, *103*; forgiveness by, 149; as hypocrite, 78; pressing of charges by, 86
Miller, Raymond: Amish jail and, 69; apology of, 127; as defendant, 103; indictments of, *104*; on parents as hypocrites, 78; sentencing of, 132

ministers: meetings of, 27, 34–36, 45;
ordination of, 27–30, 45. *See also*
clergy; Ulysses, Pennsylvania
modernity, negotiations with, 172
moral dilemmas: after beard cuttings,
16–17, 85–86; after excommunication from Bergholz, 33–34
moral order, Bergholz settlement as
upsetting, 143–46
Mount Hope Auction, 7, 8, 155
Mullet, Bill, 11, 58
Mullet, Christ: conviction of, 63; on
cult, 142; custody dispute and, 38;
optimism of, 124; E. Shrock and,
70; on witness stand, 108
Mullet, Daniel (grandson of Sam), 95
Mullet, Danny S. (son of Sam):
arraignment of, 89–90; arrest of,
95; arrest warrant for, 87; indictments of, *104*; nomination for
preacher, 28; photo of, *100*;
sentencing of, 132
Mullet, Eli (father of Sam), 23, 24
Mullet, Eli (son of Sam): assault of
L. Troyer by, 37–38; devil and, 58;
hospitalization of, 65–66; as
leaving for Pennsylvania, 67;
psychotic break of, 30–31
Mullet, Joe, 83–87, 93
Mullet, Johnny S.: Amish jail and, 69;
arraignment of, 89–90; arrest of,
87, 95; beard cutting attacks and,
2, 9–10, 11, 12, 84; denunciation of
Christianity by, 50; devil and, 58;
indictments of, *104*; investigation
committee and, 34; lack of remorse
of, 87–88, 128, 149; Mount Hope
Auction and, 8; phone calls of, 88;
photo of, *100*; on possibilities of
trial, 98–99; as preacher, 28;
psychotic break of brother and,
30–31; sentencing of, 132
Mullet, Lester: arraignment of,
89–90; arrest of, 87; beard cutting
attacks and, 84; indictments of,

104; phone calls of, 89; photo of,
100; remorse of, 88; sentencing of,
132; D. Shrock and, 73
Mullet, Lizzie. *See* Miller, Lizzie
Mullet
Mullet, Martha D. Miller: Amish jail
and, 69; on convictions, 123, 152;
on drift, 25, 26; marriage of, 24;
N. Mullet and, 66; paddlings of,
71; promotion of husband for
ordination by, 29; on psychological
assessment of husband, 36–37; on
winter of lament, 74
Mullet, Mary, 69
Mullet, Mattie, 69
Mullet, Nancy (daughter-in-law of
Sam), 65–67, 107–8
Mullet, Nancy (mother of Sam), 24
Mullet, Samuel E. (Sam): arrest and
search warrants for, 93, 94–95;
"Atlee and his helpers" illustration
and, 47–48, *48*; as bishop, 28–30,
45, 54, 55–56, 128; bishop supervision and, 27; children of, 24, 26, 36;
on cult, 141–42; custody dispute
over grandchildren of, 37–39, 136;
early life of, 23–24; on excommunication, 54–55; family tree of,
164–65; fear of, 58, 59–61; on
hypocrites, 75–76; indictments of,
104; as intolerant of dissent, 44;
investigation committee and,
34–36; in jail, 123–24; lack of
remorse of, 128–29, 136, 149;
letters from prison of, 135–36;
letters to judge about, 129;
marriage of, 24; as martyr, 136,
155; media coverage of, 125, 136;
media quotes of, 91, 105, 112–13,
179n23; Myron Miller and, 11;
ministers meeting and, 48–49,
140–41; not guilty decision of jury
on, 121; offer to cut own beard by,
98; payment on gas and oil leases,
97; phone calls to, 88–89; photo of,

Mullet, Samuel E. (*continued*)
42; as prophet, 47–49, 57–58, 79–80;
on reckoning of life journey, 146–47;
rejection of Amish practices by,
75–76, 138–39, *139*; relationships
with women of, 63–65, 66–67,
107–8; reliance on Old Testament
by, 49–52, 67; run-ins with church
leaders of, 25; sentencing of,
131–32, 162; on sheriff and
religion, 145; sheriff interview
with, 90; Shrocks and, 13; Troyer
and, 31; volatile behavior of, 36–37,
60. *See also* Bergholz settlement

New Religious Movements, 192n24
Nickel Mines shooting, x–xi, 17, 147,
148
nonviolence, 16–17, 85, 110, 112

obedience, 53–54, 143–44, 145
obstruction of justice charges, 103,
103
Ohio, first Amish settlers in, 167
Old Testament, S. Mullet reliance
on, 49–52, 67
ordination. *See* clergy; ministers

paddling of adults, 70–71
pardon, concept of, 148
Parker, Kristy, 113, 125–26
photographs, as evidence at trial, 95,
106, 112
plea bargains, offer of, 97–98
Polster, Daniel Aaron: appeals and,
156; comments at sentencing, 108;
denial of motion by, 96–97; denial
of request for new trial by, 124;
experience of, 102; instructions to
jury by, 117, 188n14; sentencing
decisions of, 129–33, 162; thanking
of jury by, 121; US Supreme Court
and, x
prayer coverings of women, 19
prisons, assignment to, 135

prosecution: author involvement in,
xi–xii, 101, 109–11; closing
arguments of, 112–13; evidence
presented by, 106–9; general counts,
103; opening statement of, 104–5;
"purported to practice the Amish
religion" statement of, 137; response
to defense, 116–17; at sentencing
proceedings, 125–26; in single case,
reasons for, 92–93; summary of, 101;
trial indictments, *104*
purification and beard cutting, 72

relatives, cutting ties to, 56–57
religion: as motivation for attacks,
96–97, 104–5, 130, 140–41;
protection of freedom of, 152–53
resistance, cultural fences of, 171
revenge on and vengeance against
hypocrites, 80, 98, 110
"Rules of a Godly Life," 110
Rumspringa, 171

Savage, Michael, 156
scapegoating, theory of, 144
Schwartz, David, 184n73
sect, 192n24
self-denial, 52–53
sentencing, 108, 125–29
separation of church and state in
Amish communities, 16–17,
145–46, 167–68
settlements: establishment of, 27;
leadership of, 44–46; ordination of
ministers in, 27–30
sexual impropriety: of S. Mullet,
63–65, 66–67, 107–8; questions
about, 59–60
Sharky, Mack, 184n73
Shepard-Byrd Hate Crimes Prevention Act: assault charges and, 104;
case built around, 96; constitutionality of, 157–59; instructions to
jury and, 118–20; legal precedent
and, ix–x; as overreaching, 159–60

Shrock, Anna, 13–15, 44, 108
Shrock, Daniel, 73, 78, 109, 154
Shrock, Eli, 154–55
Shrock, Emanuel: Amish jail and, 69; arrest of, 95; beard cutting attacks and, 7, 13–15; as defendant, 103; indictments of, *104*; C. Mullet and, 70; sentencing of, 132
Shrock, Linda Mullet: attack on Wengard and, 7; as defendant, 103; hiding of camera and, 95; indictments of, *104*; in-laws of, 13; sentencing of, 132
Shrock, Melvin: attack on, 13–15, 93, *103*, 108; as hypocrite, 78; S. Mullet and, 46
Shrock, Melvin, Jr., 74, 108, 154
shunning: differences of opinion over, 24; of excommunicated members, 32–33; as social avoidance, 169–70; types of, 33–34, 170
Sirohman, Mike, 94
social avoidance, shunning as, 169–70
social deviance, benefits of, 150–51
sources for information, xii–xiii
state, Amish view of, 167–68
Stockholm syndrome, 144
Stoll, Elmo, 25
submission of women, 145
Sullum, Jacob, 159–60

transgressors, treatment of, 32–33, 169–70
trial: author as expert witness at, xii, 101, 109–11; closing arguments of defense, 113–16; closing arguments of prosecution, 112–13, 116–17; complexity of case presented at, 102–4, *103*, *104*, 117; courtroom description, 102; dates of, 101;

evidence presented by prosecution at, 106–9; jury deliberations during, 118–21; opening statement of defense in, 106; opening statement of prosecution in, 104–5; sentencing proceedings, 108, 125–29; written instructions to jury in, 117
Troyer, Aden, 37–39
Troyer, Laverne, 28, 31, 38, 49
Troyer, Wilma Mullet, 37–39
Trumbull County, Ohio, 3, 23

uffgevva (giving up) in Amish society, 52–54, 76, 140–41
Ulysses, Pennsylvania: ministers' meeting at, 9, 35–36, 47, 76, 105; Troyer family move to, 31, 37–38
United States Court of Appeals for the Sixth Circuit, x, 156, 158, 161–62
US Department of Justice, 91–92
US Federal Courthouse, Cleveland, *122*

Wengerd, David, 6–7, 62, *103*, 121
Wengerd, Sara, 6–7
winter of lament: Amish jails and, 68–70; hair and beard cuttings during, 71–74; origins of, 67–68; paddling of adults during, 70–71
Wisconsin v. Yoder, 26, 137
women: abuse of, 146; dress of, in Bergholz settlement, 75; hair of, 19; S. Mullet relationships with, 63–65, 66–67, 107–8; submission of, 145

Yoder, Barbara Mullet, 74, 108
Yoder, Eli, 27, 28, 29, 39

Zimmerly, Timothy, 84–85, 86, 87, 91

DONALD B. KRAYBILL is Distinguished College Professor and Senior Fellow *emeritus* at the Young Center for Anabaptist and Pietist Studies at Elizabethtown College.

Internationally recognized for his scholarship on Anabaptist groups, Kraybill is the author, co-author, or editor of some twenty books and dozens of professional articles (see http://www.etown.edu/donkraybill). His books on Amish life include his flagship work, *The Riddle of Amish Culture*, as well as the award-winning *Amish Grace: How Forgiveness Transcended Tragedy* and *The Amish Way: Patient Faith in a Perilous World* (both with Steven Nolt and David Weaver-Zercher). His most recent book, *The Amish* (with Karen Johnson-Weiner and Steven Nolt), describes the diversity of Amish culture in North America.

Kraybill's research and commentary on Amish groups is often featured in magazines, newspapers, radio, television, and online media. He is the editor of Young Center Books in Anabaptist and Pietist Studies, a series published by Johns Hopkins University Press.

Kraybill was born in Lancaster County, Pennsylvania, where he resides with his family.